LAST WALTZ
IN GOODHUE

D1526954

Popcorn Press
Forthcoming *Books*

by Jim Franklin

Folk Dancing out on the High Prairie
Upper Midwest Settlement
Historical fiction
Publication 2006

A Real Slow Drag in Upper Mulberry
A Midwestern Small Town Novel
Publication 2008

Wheeling & Whistling on the Open Road
Living by 12-Volt
Publication 2010

Dancing Along the Upper Mississippi
Historical Novellas
Catalog 1997

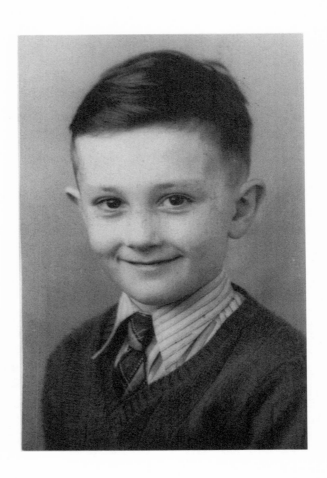

LAST WALTZ

IN GOODHUE

Adventures of a Village Boy

Jim Franklin

Jim Franklin

For Jim,
Merry Christmas
from Mom,

**POPCORN
PRESS**

*Books of the
Upper Midwest*

Popcorn Press
McGregor, Iowa

Frontispiece: Jimmy Franklin, circa 1943
Goodhue area drawing, pages 14 & 15, by Ron Hunt—Artist

Library of Congress Catalog Card Number: 97-91757

ISBN 0-9634689-1-X

Printed in the United States of America

5 4 3 2

Popcorn Press
Main Street
P.O. Box 237
McGregor, Iowa 52157

Contents

Preface

As with many writers, my first attempts in the eighties were autobiographical, writing about what I knew. I knew the village. Those first pages were a way to reflect upon earlier times in a later life. As the pages multiplied they eventually became *Last Waltz in Goodhue* (1997). I later wrote a sequel but delayed its publication. Meanwhile, my thoughts hadn't left the village as I realized there was more to tell. Those recollections have now become T H E G O O D H U E T R I L O G Y with part II, *Slow Waltzing Back To Goodhue* (2002) and part III, *Whistling Down County Rd. No. 9* (2004). The thread is autobiographical. The focus is the village, its people, its values, its idiosyncrasies. Although a tiny village, it has become, for non-native readers, *their* village, a larger, universal village. What occurred in Goodhue is not unique. That's what makes it unique.

Although I have not lived in Goodhue since 1960, I have walked its streets, smelled its aromas, heard its sounds in my dreams. *Slow Waltzing . . .* continues where *Last Waltz . . .* left off, somewhere on a hushed Upper Street. *Whistling . . .* extends that journey.

I entered the village in 1936 and graduated from Goodhue High School in 1954 before attending St. John's University in Collegeville, Minnesota (1954 - 1958). During my college years I would return to Goodhue to spend summers with my mother and to work at Libby's pea viners or Heaney and Gorman or Majerus Appliance, or paint barns and houses in Goodhue and surrounding rural areas.

I was the third child of Thomas B. Franklin of Goodhue Township and Lucille (Haustein) Franklin Ryan of Red Wing. There were six Franklins in our village family: Father Thomas Bernard (1893-1951), mother Lucille (1900-1970), sister Rose Marie, brother Thomas Edward (1934-1987), James Leo, and baby brother Daniel (c. 1940 - 1940).

If our paths crossed sometime around Goodhue, you'll probably recall many of the experiences I have written about. Most are true, and if they aren't, they should have been. (JLF 2002)

POPCORN PRESS' POPULAR HISTORY SERIES OF THE UPPER MISSISSIPPI VALLEY

by Jim Franklin

A multi-volume series telling the story, through historical accounts and photos, of the hearty, courageous people and benchmark events in the Upper Mississippi River Valley.

No. 1____
Pioneering Goodhue County
The villages, burgs, hamlets, whistle-stops, ghost towns, townships and good folks of Goodhue County, Minnesota
Publication 2002

No. 2____
Settling Lake Pepin's Shores
The majestic lake, steamboats, rafting, anchoring towns
Publication 2003

No. 3____
Pike's Peak and the Five Rivers' Valley
The Mississippi, Wisconsin, Kickapoo, Turkey and Yellow Rivers

Publication 2003

No. 4____
Grand Excursion 2004
Paddlewheelers, sidewheelers, captains, pilots, roustabouts, scoundrels again ply the Upper Mississippi River

Publication 2004

Popcorn Press

presents

THE GOODHUE TRILOGY

by Jim Franklin

*One boy finds meaning growing up, later moving beyond a
tiny, dusty village out on the rolling prairie. His adventures
and escapades are those of universal youth. Relive your own
in this heartwarming, whimsical trilogy. Come along.*

Part I

Last Waltz in Goodhue

Adventures of a Village Boy

Publication 1997

Part II

Slow Waltzing Back to Goodhue

Once Upon a Time in a Village

Publication 2002

Part III

Whistling Down County Road No. 9

Remembering a Village

Publication 2004

FRANKLIN HOME PLACE
BELLE CREEK

ST. COLUMBKILLE CHURCH

BAR BAR

GOODHUE

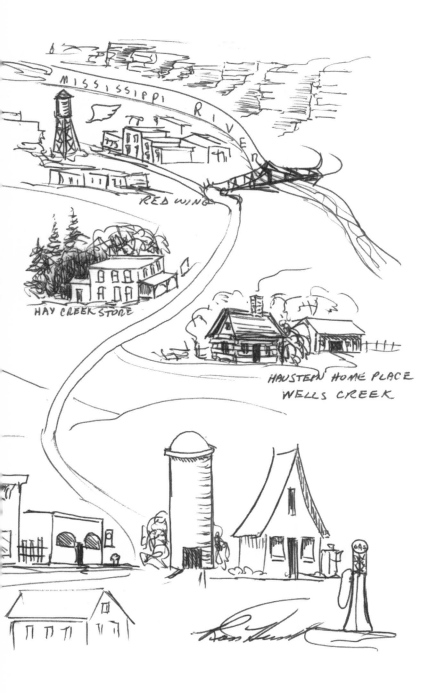

MISSISSIPPI RIVER

RED WING

HAY CREEK STORE

HAUSTEIN HOME PLACE
WELLS CREEK

Schoolboy days are no happier than the days of afterlife, but we look back upon them regretfully because we have forgotten our punishments at school and how we grieved when our marbles were lost and our kites destroyed—because we have forgotten all the sorrows and privations of that canonized epoch and remember only its orchard robberies, its wooden sword pageants, and its fishing holidays.

—Mark Twain, *Innocents Abroad*, 1869.

Chapter 1

Catholic and Democrat

Holy Trinity Confirmation Class, 1948

B LESS ME, FATHER, FOR *I* HAVE SINNED . . . *I* ATE MEAT *twice on Fridays. I disobeyed my mother three times. I disobeyed my father twice. I lied two times. I looked at dirty pictures ten times. I had fifteen impure thoughts. I am sorry for all of my sins.*

_____1

The Confessional

God it was hard growing up Catholic, in Goodhue, in the 1940s. It was about the hardest task one could expect of a boy, but undoubtedly the hardest part was going to confession. You had to go to confession; you couldn't be Catholic without going to confession. You couldn't receive communion at Sunday Mass without confession, because everyone at Holy Trinity knew you _must_ have sinned since you last received communion. Confession was an automatic. Hard? I don't know if there was anything harder. It was terribly difficult to tell the priest you had fifteen impure thoughts last week. You just knew the moment you confessed, the church bells would begin clanging and the village fire siren would shriek its piercing wail all over town. At that moment, everyone in town would know. After confession you would walk downtown, people pointing knowing fingers saying, "You're the kid who had all those impure thoughts, aren't you? We know your type. Straighten up, kid, or you're going straight to hell!"

It was embarrassing enough that the priest and God knew, but now all the folks in town would know, particularly those guys hanging around the Corner Bar, and you had to pass there to get to Heaney and Gorman's Market—there was no avoiding it. My goodness, impure thoughts were potent; they had the power of lasers. They were so powerful they could cut right through the confessional curtain, through the wooden clapboard walls of Holy Trinity and out into the hot, humid air of Goodhue on a blistering summer day. "Have you heard the latest? They say that little Franklin boy had lots of impure thoughts last week."

"You don't say?"

"Yes, I've heard tell that he had as many as fifteen of them."

"Oh my! Think of his poor mother."

Oh, it was hard growing up Catholic in Goodhue.

Confession was only part of the difficulty. Other activities were also trying for a boy, such as serving Mass for thirty hours during Holy Week—more about that later.

Being Catholic was not merely being part of a religious faith. It was genetic. It was in your bones. You were Catholic from the moment of conception. In the thirties, you were Catholic beginning with the twinkle in your father's eye.

Catholics were white, Lutherans were black. No one was gray. You were either Catholic or you weren't. You were either going to heaven or hell. Thank the Lord we were Catholic. We knew where we were going and we knew where the Lutherans were going. Every night our mothers had us on our knees thanking God we weren't Lutheran. That was probably the best part of being Catholic. I used to feel sorry for those Lutheran boys. They looked so nice dressed in dark blue suits and ties, even on a ninety-degree blistering, steamy July Sunday, yet they were going to hell. Poor fellows. Too bad they weren't born Catholic . . . like me.

Growing up Catholic meant attending Mass every Sunday. During Lent, it meant Stations of the Cross every Friday evening, giving up everything you liked to eat for six weeks, attending the state basketball tournament in Minneapolis and not being able to eat a hot dog or popcorn, because eating between meals wasn't permitted. It meant memorizing the *Baltimore Catechism* and sit–ting in the front pew of Holy Trinity on Friday afternoons at catechism class praying that Father Smith wouldn't call on you because you hadn't memorized the entire lesson . . . "Mary, who made you?"

"God made me."

"Very good, Mary."

"Jimmy, why did God make you?"

"I don't know, Father, why He made me."

"That's not the right answer, Jimmy. Now, try again. Why did God make you?"

"God made me to serve him, to love him, and to pray for him."

"God doesn't want you to pray for him; only for you."

"Did you memorize your lesson this week?"

"No, Father, I'm sorry. I was too busy bouncing my basket-ball."

"I'll expect to hear that in this week's confession!"

If you grew up Catholic in the thirties and forties you weren't permitted to think. No thinking allowed when it came to theology, just recite the words in that catechism from Baltimore, wherever Baltimore was. Where was Baltimore? Is that where God lived? Is that where the Archbishop lived? Is that where sins were forgiven? What's the big deal with Baltimore? But I knew that if I didn't recite those exact words to every question in the *Baltimore Cate-chism*, I was running the risk of being a non-Catholic. I was running the risk of being a Lutheran, and you know where they were going, so study that lesson, memorize every word—no thinking allowed.

But I wish I would have been permitted to think for myself, just a little. I wish I wouldn't have had to accept everything on faith alone. I knew faith was good, because Father Smith said we were lucky to have it. The English Methodists and the German Luther-ans didn't have it. "Don't question it, kid, just answer the ques-tions."

But *I* had questions, questions for which I didn't get answers, because they weren't in the *Catechism*: "*Why* are Catholics going to heaven and Lutherans to hell? *Why* did God make me just to have impure thoughts? If He doesn't want me to have them, why do I? *Why* fifteen in one week?"

God can control things. Why did he let me have them and then make me confess to the priest—in the confessional, in front of the altar, in front of the entire congregation where everyone knew how long I had been in there because they had watches and the confessional line was long and Mass began at nine o'clock and, "That Franklin boy sure has been in the confessional a long time." Those impure thoughts caused me problems, not to speak of everyone else at Holy Trinity who worried about me. "How come, God? How come, pope? How come, Father Smith?"

I had questions. The *Baltimore Catechism* didn't answer them. Oh! it was hard growing up Catholic.

Hubert Humphrey was the most important Democrat to ever come out of Minnesota—Norwegian bachelor farmers notwithstanding—but he was Presbyterian. Even so, he would have made a fine Catholic, because Presbyterian is about as close to Catholic as one can get. At least that's what we thought. If you're not going to be Catholic, Presbyterian wouldn't be so bad. Hubert would have made a good pope in that he never became president anyway. He was kind, warm, sensitive and loving, but most importantly, a talker. He was loquacious. I can imagine Hubert standing on the Vatican's veranda speaking to the multitudes below. It didn't make any difference what he spoke about, because folks didn't actually listen to what he said, only how he said it. He was an orator. He could deliver the spoken word. He should have been pope. Pope Hubert.

At a nine o'clock Sunday Mass, an August day so stifling that my shorts stuck to my crotch (I was forever pulling them down, Mother forever clipping me on the ear), I suddenly realized, somewhere between the *Credo* and the *Agnus Dei*, that most of the good parishioners at Holy Trinity were also Democrats. It was an amazing revelation. For the first time in my life, I realized that being a Catholic also meant being a Democrat. To be non-Catholic meant being a Republican. That meant my Lutheran friends were Republicans, and Father Smith hadn't discussed it in class. The *Baltimore Catechism* hadn't addressed Democrats and Republicans, but I, a little pulling-your-shorts-away-from-your-crotch kid realized Catholics and Democrats were as interrelated as brothers and sisters. What a heavenly revelation.

From that moment on I became more aware of the religious, political and social activities around the village and the nation. I realized Lloyd Cook, editor of the *Goodhue County Tribune*, was non-Catholic and Republican. General Eisenhower was non-Catholic and Republican. Harry Truman was non-Catholic and a Democrat. Humphrey was Presbyterian and Democrat, but that was close enough. I wondered how God was able to work that out. How was he able to have Congressional Catholic-Democrats attend Mass together on Sunday? Thomas Jefferson and our founding fathers wrote about separation of church and state. They certainly didn't anticipate Father Smith and the rest of the Goodhue Catholics.

Chapter 2

The Village

Upper Street in the Village

GOODHUE OFFICIALLY BECAME A VILLAGE IN 1897, a railroad hamlet in the gentle, rolling prairie of southeastern Minnesota, but even then it was simply, ". . . a little one-eyed, blinking sort o' place." (Thomas Hardy) The village grew slowly over the years, but the railroad didn't make it boom like St. Paul and Minneapolis. It did help area farmers market their crops and livestock to the rest of Minnesota, though.

1

The Dinky: The Little Train That Could

It certainly was a peculiar railroad that day I took my first ride with Mother in 1946, fifty-seven years after its inception. Freight and passenger trains traveled over bumpy, bent rails to carry grain and cattle to St. Paul, or passengers to an out of town destination. The passenger unit was a slow-moving, quaint, tiny train—The Dinky.

It had a small engine, one passenger car and a red caboose which puffed into town two days per week from Red Wing—up the rocky, white sandstone bluffs of Hay Creek, then down the western slope through the meadows of Claybank and across the rolling grain fields into Goodhue. Another day it chugged from Rochester through the wooded hills of the Zumbro Valley. You might wonder what effect such a toddling train had on the image of a town, on the spirit of Goodhueites. Could we explain the Dinky to friends and relatives living in St. Paul where trains had three and four engines pulling a hundred or more freight cars, or passenger trains with twenty coach cars? I don't know what lasting effect the Dinky had on our psyches, but at least we had a train. Bellechester didn't have one. White Rock didn't have one. Belle Creek township wanted it to come their way in 1888, but they didn't get it. Goodhue did. We were happy to have it even if it was tiny and only chugged along twenty-five miles an hour.

Village children received courage from the Dinky; it was an inspiration, a symbol of fortitude. If the Dinky could chug up Hay Creek bluff, then we could also succeed. After all, we had innumerable barriers to overcome. The village was a tiny, dusty, lonesome, one-stop-sign village in the middle of southern Minnesota cornfields, a long way from the rest of the world, or so it seemed in the forties. Villagers were truckers, farmers and merchants, hard-working, church-going people. We didn't know about doctors, lawyers, and corporate presidents, because we didn't have those professions in town. Frank O'Gorman lawyered above the hardware store for years—started practicing law in 1907—but no new attorneys hung out a shingle when he died. The town never kept a doctor for more than a year or two, because it was simply too difficult to make a living, not enough sick people to keep a doctor busy, and if folks came down with the consumption they simply drank a few swigs of Bohn's Cure-All from the traveling Watkins salesman. Yes, we needed the Dinky to inspire us, to help us get out of bed in the morning and get our work done.

We sat on warped wooden benches at the railroad station craning our necks toward Claybank. The rails were uneven and crooked causing the Dinky to move slowly as it chugged toward the station. It took forever for it to waddle to a stop.

Mother purchased tickets from Mr. Overby, the stationmaster, then we climbed the steps of the coach car to enter a strange new world. To get on a passenger train for the first time was a special occasion for me.

Slowly, we pulled out of the station, crept past the village's towering landmark white grain silo, then slithered through corn, soybean, and wheatfields on our way north. I looked through the back window and saw Goodhue getting smaller as we chugged out of town. I saw water tank hill where we sledded in the winter, the grain silo where we played rubber gun wars, the baseball field where my heroes played, the downtown streets where the Westside Catholics finally defeated the Eastside Lutherans in the great Rubber Gun Battle; Heaney and Gorman's Locker Plant where Dennis Heaney was butchering because today was Monday—butchering day; I saw steers and hogs waiting patiently in their pens before going to their final resting place in that great Hog Heaven. I saw the steeples of the English Methodist and German Lutheran churches, and the tiny, bare cross sitting catawampus on top of Holy Trinity; I saw the school and . . . all of that through the window.

Soon, everything became smaller until I couldn't see the village anymore and for a moment, I felt sad. Mother reassured me, however, that everything would be all right. We would see it all again upon our return.

The Dinky was small, cozy and red. It swayed vigorously from side to side as we trekked toward Claybank, Hay Creek, and Red Wing. I had had short rides on a twenty-four wheel, highballer steam locomotive from the station to the grain elevator before, but never a long passenger ride. We sat on warped, tobacco-stained, whiskey-spotted benches in the coach car which emitted a pot-pourri of stale aromas—cigars, cigarettes, chewing tobacco, beer, whiskey, perfume. Tangy smells were tucked into every nook and cranny of the car. Mother said it smelled of Pat Rowles' cigars, Erv Richter's beer, O.T. Parker's cigarettes, Henry Prolow's whiskey. The Dinky had transported early settlers for fifty-seven years, and had remembered the signature of every man, women and child who rode it. Those pungent aromas attacked my nostrils that day and have never left.

Crimson, braided ropes swung gently in the windows as we swayed down the tracks. Above them were filthy, gray-pleated drapes creating the ambiance of a turn-of-the-century funeral parlor, or at least Ole Haga's Funeral Parlor on upper street. Each rope and drape had accumulated the odors and memories of generations of villagers.

I sat by a window watching fields of corn, oats and swaying wheat for as far as I could see. Barns and silos periodically poked through the sea of crops like German U Boat periscopes in the North Atlantic I had seen on Movietone News. And there was color everywhere: green fields, red barns, white houses. Guernseys and Holsteins grazed leisurely in the pastures filling their tummies with emerald green grass to make milk for Wheaties' bowls. The countryside looked pleasant and peaceful as we approached Claybank Crossing.

Claybank wasn't much of a place in 1946; in fact, it was only a general store and a Standard Oil gas pump located at the base of a hill at the intersection of the tracks and a county road. But it was a cozy store, one I visited many times as I grew older. Several years later, scout leader Jimmy Ryan, Jack, Bob and Larry O'Reilly and I hiked those same tracks on Boy Scout outings in the dead of winter, hiking three miles from town to camp in the hills above the store. We learned how to survive the winter elements by building fires without using matches, sleeping in tents and tying square knots.

There weren't any passengers waiting at the store, so the fireman shoveled more coal into the fire box for the pull up Claybank hill. By the time we reached Hay Creek the Dinky was working hard to navigate the steep bluffs. I could tell the engine was exerting extra effort when I saw thick, black smoke curling out of the smokestack as we approached the Mississippi River bluffs guarding Red Wing.

We reached the crest of the bluff having left the tranquil valley with its picturesque farms and creek after which Hay Creek was named. The creek meanders slowly, gently around rock formations through the bottom land of the valley around the Mississippi, the great river that begins as a brook in the forests of northern Minnesota and ends as a mighty waterway in the Gulf of Mexico. The Mississippi is so tiny at its fountainhead that one need only take a giant Captain May I step to cross it. It meanders through Grand Rapids, St. Cloud, Lake Wobegon, Minneapolis, St. Paul and Hastings until in brushes Goodhue County at Red Wing. Along the way it flows into backwaters creating thousands of islands and lakes. For centuries it has cut its way through the bluffs of southern Minnesota and Wisconsin. It displays its power and majesty by the way it has transformed the countryside.

But the Hay Creek is only a stream that trickles toward the Mississippi, a river so expansive and full of majesty it doesn't even know the creek joins it. The creek is one of a thousand little tributaries joining the mighty Mississippi as it persistently surges toward the Gulf. But like the Dinky, Hay Creek is also doing its job. It's not the most important stream in Goodhue County, but it is making a contribution.

As I gazed beyond the braided ropes, I could see for several miles along the Mississippi Valley. High bluffs cradled the river on both sides keeping it in its bounds. I could see the river flowing toward Lake City, and the high bridge arching to the backwaters of Wisconsin. It was a view I never saw back on the rolling prairie. We descended cautiously into Red Wing from the crest of the bluff.

The return trip wasn't as exciting, but I was curious to see if the Dinky could climb back up the steep bluff from the levee. I had acquired some knowledge of how Dad's Model A worked—more pulling power in lower gears than higher ones—but I didn't know about trains. The Dinky had no problem traversing the Mississippi bluffs.

Although I enjoyed seeing the river I anticipated our familiar countryside. We reached the crest, then descended into the wooded, green valley past the Hay Creek General Store, up the far side of the valley and down into Claybank once again. As we rounded a curve south of Claybank, I saw our village in the distance through the summer haze. It was only a fly speck on the horizon, not much larger even when standing in the middle of upper street.

The Dinky didn't look like much of a train; in fact, some people wouldn't even call it one, but it was important to us. Our whistle-stop town had no soda fountain, Dairy Queen, pay telephone nor indoor movie theater. We needed that train.

Most GHS graduates would eventually leave the village to make their mark in the world. Maybe the courageous Dinky would provide us with inspiration during troubled times. Maybe, somewhere in the future, when we were far away, when we were struggling to make it on our own, we might think back to our childhood and remember the courage of The Little Train That Could.

2

Frieda's General Store

We stepped from the train to walk uptown where Mother wanted to purchase fabric and thread for a dress she was sewing. We entered Frieda Vieths' General Store on upper street. I hadn't been there before, but I was familiar with Heaney's Market which we passed—people buying groceries, Dennis cutting a quarter of beef, Dody doing bookwork, George trimming meat for hamburger, Davie Franklin stocking shelves, folks sitting and talking around the potbellied stove—but Frieda's lacked any sign of activity, no one in sight as we walked through the squeaking screen door. The store was crammed with more paraphernalia—dry goods, antiques, whatnots—than I had ever seen in one store. The shelves were sagging from the weight of canning jars, hats, kerosene lanterns, fabric, spools of thread, boxes, hammers, axes and soap. Work shirts, caps, rakes and shovels dangled from ceiling hooks. I had difficulty walking through the maze of boxes, bottles and shovels. No wonder we couldn't find Frieda. We snaked through the merchandise toward the back—dark, musty, spooky. I was filled with trepidation.

Frieda and Fred had opened the store in 1917, and I don't believe they had discarded a single item in all those years. If it didn't sell it was simply shoved aside to make room for newer merchandise. Harnesses and bridles hung on those walls long after the Model T had replaced horses for transportation to town. Frieda used every inch of floor space. Searching the maze, I stubbed my toe on a kerosene can, bumped into a water pump handle, hit my head on a lawn mower handle, scratched my knee on a scythe and still hadn't seen Frieda.

Mother knew where she was going, though. She had been

here before. She pulled me toward the back without stubbing her toe or bumping her head one time. We found Frieda in a dim dungeon behind cases of Quaker State motor oil and axle grease sitting in a swivel chair with tiger claws on the legs in the yellowish glow of a flickering kerosene lamp. She was a diminutive, bespec-- tacled, gray-haired lady dwarfed by an antique cigarette-stained roll top desk. I wanted to get out of there, the sooner the better. It was spooky and smelly, and those objects hanging from the ceiling were stirring my imagination. I began seeing bears, snakes, tigers and lions ready to pounce from a dark corner. In fact, there *were* mounted deer and bear heads on the walls. The more I looked at them the more alive they became. I grabbed Mother's hand tightly. I wanted out of Frieda's store.

Mother selected thread and three yards of fine blue flannel, paid Frieda and we were gone. It felt good escaping from the bear's menacing eyes, to see the sunlight, to smell fresh air even though there was a putrid aroma floating up the street from Uncle Dave's barn. On this day the scent of horse manure was preferable to the odors in the dank store.

But when I was older I grew to like Frieda's, even venturing there by myself. I realized those animal heads weren't going to leap from the wall to devour me, and I even began enjoying the dark, shadowy store. I found an assortment of items I couldn't find at Heaney's Market or Campbell's Hardware or even Marshall-Wells Hardware. I could rummage through the store shifting a box here and there finding knickknacks nobody else was interested in, items Frieda had long forgotten. I found six heavy-duty washers for my peach box racer under a box of Quaker State Oil. I found two red streamers for my bicycle handle bars in a lady's hat box. I found a long strand of copper wire for a walkie-talkie behind a coal shovel. I found an antique claw hammer behind the Bon Ami soap. There was a gold mine of treasure in the store. It didn't have squirting bow ties and hand buzzers found in my favorite Johnson-Smith Catalog, but it was in town.

3

Talking To Villagers

Mother had two more stops after Frieda's. We walked past Art's Bar to the bank, a stately and imposing building for a boy of ten, the only building in town with marble. Behind the marbled tellers' cage I saw the walk-in safe which I imagined held all the money in the world, or at least the county. It certainly was different from Frieda's store—light, airy, and I didn't stumble over a single box.

After Mother finished her banking we crossed the street to the Goodhue Hotel, one of the village's first permanent major structures. It was a two-story, red-brick building with second floor rooms to rent by the month, week or night, and a sitting parlor on the first floor. A few years later I talked with Pat Rowles and other old-timers by the hour in those oversized, cracked leather chairs, cigar smoke seeping into them, aromas lasting for generations.

I was a precocious boy who liked to talk, but I was only carrying on a heritage I had learned from parents, townsfolk and relatives. One couldn't be Catholic and Irish-German without developing extensive talking skills. I had fifteen aunts and uncles, and forty-five first cousins who we visited frequently. Imagine the talking that transpired when the Franklins and Hausteins assembled. You either talked or you didn't survive.

On many days in the village there wasn't much to do anyway; besides, talking was cheap. Oh, Eddie Fischer at the drugstore wasn't a big talker, but I was more interested in looking at his magazines, anyway. Frieda didn't talk and she kept her store so dark I didn't feel comfortable sitting and talking. Those two stores were good places to go when even I didn't feel like conversing. Heaney's was the biggest *talking* store in town. If you didn't want to talk, that wasn't the place to go. Under the "Heaney & Gorman

Meats and Locker Plant" sign there was a smaller hand-painted sign . . . *If you don't like talking, don't come in!*

At age ten or eleven I began venturing out on my rounds. I talked with Pat Rowles about his early farming years in Belle Creek as he puffed on a cigar, blowing smoke rings gently to the ceiling. Sitting on a new tractor, I chatted with Karl Tomfohr at the International Harvester Shop about farm machinery and the basketball team of 1944 which he coached and they were good and they were my heroes and they lost in the Regional Tournament. I chatted with Dennis Heaney at the Locker Plant as he butchered a pig or made sausage or cut pork chops. I spoke with Luverne Haas as he tuned a '48 Chevy, swearing a blue streak. I talked with Bill Mans at the Shell Station about fox hunting and fishing and the big walleye that got away down by Collischan's Landing. I talked with Cy Benda about electricity, because I liked experimenting with it. I chatted with Sidney Berg about shoes, with Bill Huebner about shoeing horses, with Naurice Husbyn about chicken eggs and chicken feed and chicken houses. I talked with Jesse Campbell about three-quarter-inch bolts and green enamel paint, with Heinie Swenson about chocolate ice cream: "Where does malt come from?"

I talked with Les Banidt about trucks, with Casey Ryan about painting houses: "What is paint made from?"

I spoke with Bert Majerus about sewer pipe and propane gas and plumbing, with Art Lohman about Standard Oil gas. "How do they get gas all the way to Goodhue from the oil fields of Texas?"

I spoke with Vince O'Reilly at the Standard Oil station. Now, Vince was a master talker. He might have been even more long-winded than Uncle Dave or Dennis. Vince knew most people in the county, being one of the few men I knew who actually read a county plat book. If you wanted to know something about the county, ask Vince.

I talked with Clarence Lunde at the grocery store on lower street and thought it funny when he advertised a "Clarence Clearance Sale." I talked with Art Haas outside Art's Bar, because I was too young to go in, although Dad occasionally took me in when he stopped for a cool Grain Belt on the way home from his milk route. Art liked talking with kids even though he wasn't in the kid business.

I spoke with Jim Ryan about the hatchery business, with Francis Moran about talking, with Reinhold Schulz about semi-trailer trucks, with Henry Befort about being a cop and locking up drunks in the jail. I talked with Fred Rusch about pipe cutters and left-handed monkey wrenches, with Lefty O'Reilly at the post office about how my packages from the Johnson-Smith Catalog traveled all the way from Cleveland to Goodhue: "How long does it take and how much does it cost and how do those people in Cleveland know where Goodhue is?"

I talked with Leonard Lodermeier about selling tractors and hay balers and corn pickers and about why he left Wisconsin to live in Goodhue, and did he like having three brothers and did they ever fight when they were kids like I did with Tom and Rose Marie. I talked with Tom O'Reilly about school buses, with Bill O'Reilly about hauling cattle to South St. Paul and what it felt like to take cows, hogs and sheep to their death. I talked to Agnes O'Reilly about flowers and baking pies and making crusts: "How do Angel Cakes get fluffy?"

I talked to Leone Ryan about Father Smith and cleaning the church for Sunday Mass: "Does Father Smith make you say five Hail Marys and four Our Fathers if you don't clean the altar good enough?"

I spoke with Mary Haas about everything in the world. I talked with Julius at his Barber Shop; rather, I listened, because Julius was among the best. Has there ever been a barber that wasn't? It is a requirement for being admitted to barber school. They assume they can teach you to cut hair, but teaching talking to a nontalker is more difficult. Dad once considered barber school, but he couldn't pass the talking test as he was on the quiet side— an oddity for a Franklin. But Julius could rattle on. He talked continuously during thirty-five years of hair cutting. He competed admirably with Vince, Dennis and Dave.

I talked with Ole Haga about being an undertaker: "What does a corpse feel like?" I did most of the talking in this case, because it was difficult retrieving that information from Ole, although it was worth it. I talked with Bill Hennings and Herman Diercks, with John Yungers at his tool shop as he fine-tuned one of his Rube Goldberg contraptions, Lloyd Cook about publishing *The Goodhue County Tribune:* "How do you read type backwards and upside down?"

I conversed with Joyce Shelstad about baseball and the Yankees and the Cleveland Indians and the Goodhue Town Team. I talked to Marldine Richter about making music and playing clarinet: "How do you read music? Does it make you feel good?"

I talked with Art Eppen about the new Frigidaire: "How does it keep milk cold when it doesn't use ice?"

I talked with Florence Taylor at her Eat Shop: "Do you like serving meals to strangers? Does Eddie Fischer ever say anything about Jimmy spending so much time at the Drugstore looking at magazines?"

I talked with Lyle Pritchard at Streater's Lumber about plywood and two-by-fours and tenpenny nails as he cut boards with the circle saw. I talked with Willie Holm about tractors and end loaders and earth movers, with Al and Bob Allers about building houses and kitchen cabinets. They could saw, shave, bevel, set a two-by-four and talk at the same time.

I was talked out.

4

Sidney's Shoe Shop

I don't remember exactly when Mother and Dad let me traipse downtown by myself for the first time, but it must have been about 1942 when I was six. That may seem young but growing up in Goodhue meant growing up faster than children from Rochester or Minneapolis. We had earlier earthy experiences. We were in contact with nature. Certainly, a six-year-old Minneapolis boy wouldn't have been permitted to walk down Hennepin Avenue by himself, but Goodhue didn't have a Hennepin Avenue or anything resembling it. We had rutted, unpaved upper and lower streets where Studebakers and Reo trucks drove five miles per hour lest they lose a muffler or bumper in one of the bigger pot holes. Besides, downtown was only three blocks from my house; what could possibly happen in Goodhue?

I liked visiting Sidney Berg's Shoe Shop on upper street. It might have been the smell of new leather and shoe polish that attracted me, or maybe it was simply the cozy shop, a tiny, yellow, clapboard shop tucked into a small lot between Mans & Benda's Shell Station and Marshall-Wells Hardware. Sidney must have liked kids, because he certainly spent a lot of time talking with me. Dad would toss me a nickel—of course, it burned a hole in my pocket until I spent it on a rich Hershey Bar at Swenson's Cafe— then on the way home I would stop by Sidney's to hear what stories he had that day. As he spun an old chestnut I would watch in awe as he repaired the many pairs of shoes and boots lining the shelves. It was magical to see him transform worn-out work boots into shiny ones. I liked making things myself; I suppose that's why I was fascinated by watching him work. His hands moved so swiftly I could hardly see them. Sidney could tie, cut, shape, polish and spin an epic story at the same time.

Another reason I liked his shop was that I liked shoes myself. Every kid has to like something. I had a favorite pair of high-tops with silver-hook buckles that I wore every day, parental approval or not. They had leather laces I learned to tie in five seconds flat, and holes in both soles from dragging my feet in the street while kicking rocks through the gutter. The heels were worn down to the nails from walking web-footed like a duck. I wore them everyday except Sunday and would have worn them to Mass if I could have, but I didn't get by with that. Every boy and girl had to wear Sunday shoes to church. They couldn't wear everyday shoes or any everyday clothing article to church. Sundays brought out the best clothes in town. If a stranger drove through town on Saturday, then returned Sunday, he wouldn't think he was even in the same town because everyone would look completely different. The entire town would seem transformed. That's because all the Sunday clothes and shoes had been brought out Saturday night in anticipation of Sunday services. Monday-through-Saturday-everyday-shoes were set aside for tight, squeeze-your-toes-and-feet-aching-Sunday-shoes. For a boy, Sunday shoes were a penance. If he could survive wearing them for a couple of hours during Mass and Sunday dinner, he surely would receive overflowing indulgences and graces. Well, Sidney couldn't help me avoid wearing Sunday shoes, but he did keep my high-tops in good repair throughout my early years.

I didn't know anything about Sidney's personal life—if he was born and raised in Goodhue, had a wife, a cocker spaniel, a Model A, an International tractor, or if he was Norwegian, Swedish, German Lutheran-Republican or Irish Catholic-Democratic. But I do know he fixed a good pair of shoes. His tiny shop stood there for many years until razed in the early fifties. It was a good shoe shop with a good shoe-shop man running it. He kept a young boy and his high-tops together.

5

Bill Huebner's Blacksmith Shop

Another merchant I enjoyed visiting was Bill Huebner at his Blacksmith Shop located on the same street as Husbyn's Hatchery, diagonal from the Corner Bar on upper street. It was a fascinating place. Sauntering in, I would see red-hot coals in the forge, smell sizzling iron, hear the clang of hot metal being shaped on the anvil—a new horseshoe, a wagon tongue, a tractor hitch for a John Deere.

Blacksmithing is an old-world art, one developed out of necessity for farmers and our village was surrounded by farms and farmers, hard-working men and women who had emigrated from

Norway, Sweden, Germany, Austria or Ireland. They worked the land as their fathers or grandfathers had done in a foreign country before coming to another foreign land in southeastern Minnesota. To those farmers land was good, everything important. The only thing more important was church on Sunday, and even it may have come in second best. German Lutherans, Swedish Lutherans, English Lutherans, Norwegian Lutherans, Methodists of all sizes and shapes, and Irish Catholics dotted the countryside. Regardless of their ancestry, they worked the land from sunup to sundown, toiling with their hands and with what meager machinery they could purchase. That machinery broke down frequently, needing repair. Some were adept enough to fix it, but when the job became too big or difficult they drove to Huebner's Blacksmith Shop. Bill was the farmers' friend. If a new wagon hitch was needed, Bill was there. If a new hay wagon axle was needed, Bill was there. If that favorite pair of draft horses needed shoeing, Bill was there.

He played songs on his anvil as harmonious as any heard in *Aida*. I don't suppose there was a person in the village during the forties who could have sung or even whistled an aria from the opera, much less explain what an opera was, but we didn't need to. We had Bill.

Beautiful music ascended from his anvil. If he happened to be working late on a Saturday night for a farmer in the throes of bringing in the fall harvest and the boys across the street at the Corner Bar were celebrating excessively while lifting their voices in song, one could imagine Verdi's *Anvil Chorus* emanating from Bill's anvil . . .

Proudly our banner now gleams with golden luster!
Brighter each star shines in the glorious cluster!

Then from across the street . . .
From the tables down at Morey's,
To the place where Louis dwells . . .

From the blacksmith shop . . .
Hail! Hail! banner of the free!

And Peace and Union, And Peace and Union,
Throughout our happy land!

From the bar . . .
Gee, but I'd give the world to see,
That old, gang of mine . . .

Goodhue had its own Saturday-night opera. There was no need to drive to St. Paul or Chicago for a performance. All one needed to do was park the car by the Blacksmith Shop, roll down the windows, close your eyes and listen. Bill would take a piece of raw iron, thrust it into the blazing forge until glowing red, then massage it ever so carefully and gently. With long, black, wooden-handled tongs he would turn the iron slowly and evenly, taping it gently, first on the end, then sides, bending it slowly into the right shape. Finally, he would thrust the red-hot iron into a wooden bucket of water creating a sizzling column of steam that spiraled gently through the leaky roof.

He was a sculptor but didn't know it. If he could have been a blacksmith in the eighties, he would have been an artist iron sculptor receiving thousands of dollars for each creation. He could have created soaring works of iron art instead of horseshoes and wagon tongues. He could have sold his creations to the wealthy arts patrons in Minneapolis and Chicago. His iron sculptures could be gracing the halls of the Hennepin County Court House and the Governor's mansion in St. Paul.

But his *art* was functional, practical. One might have called it Post Industrial Age Minnesota Rural. He didn't create it for wealthy Minneapolis patrons; he created rural iron art for farmers. But he was much more than a smithy; he was a sculptor, Goodhue's first. Today, artists with less talent receive thousands of dollars to sculpt bronze and iron and marble into art objects. He could have been a giant sculptor if he hadn't had so many horses to shoe, so many wagon tongues to repair, so many threshing machines to fix. He could have started the first art colony in southeastern Minnesota. He could have put Goodhue on the map, making it into something other than a farming community, changing the entire face and future of the village. All he needed to do was make something nonfunctional. He might have thrust a piece of iron into the furnace, filled the bellows with air and massaged it into the village's first sculpture. People would have journeyed from throughout the county to view his masterpiece thrusting its head toward the leaden sky, wondering . . . "Now, what would a man want to go and do something like that for?"

"If that don't beat all."

"I think the man has gone off his rocker, don't you think so, Eileen?"

"I don't know, Cecelia, what do you think it is?"

"Don't know, but it sure doesn't look like a horseshoe."

"Do you think Bill's feeling okay?"

"We'd better check on him first thing Monday morning."

Yes, it would have been difficult to be the village's first iron sculptor. Bill would have had to tolerate considerable chiding and disapproving glances to do that.

He was a good man operating a good blacksmith shop. He didn't take that step to be an artist, choosing instead to stay to his task making horseshoes and wagon tongues and hitches. But even today when I return to Goodhue and become restless on a Saturday night, I walk downtown as I did when a boy. If it's late, quiet and the crickets aren't noisy and the moon is shimmering over the grain elevator, I can still hear the faint sounds of Bill's anvil . . .

Hail! Hail! banner of the free!
And Peace and Union, And Peace and Union,
Throughout our happy land!

6

Uncle Dave's Dray Line

I gradually expanded my meanderings around town. Mother let me travel farther until I eventually reached the outskirts, which wasn't far. She didn't need to worry; in fact, Goodhue mothers didn't need to worry as much as they did. Actually, they wouldn't have needed to worry at all. What trouble could we get into? We didn't have marijuana then, weren't old enough to drink beer, Camel cigarettes were hard to acquire, and child molesters were unheard of. What could possibly happen? The only thing they really needed to worry about was whether we wore clean underwear in the event we were in an accident and needed to be taken to the hospital, or whether we were having impure thoughts. Even then they didn't need to worry, because impure thoughts were only between us, Father Smith, God, and maybe some of the guys hanging around the bar. But our moms didn't see it that way. You see, they were taught to worry by their own mothers. They couldn't be a mother without worrying.

My roving frequently brought me to a large, red barn right in the middle of downtown. You might be thinking, "A barn downtown?" It's true. Goodhue didn't have a master plan for the village in the forties, so a barn could have been erected anyplace. The closest thing to a master planner would have been Luverne Haas when he was Police Chief and Master Flipper at the sewage plant. That's what he called it, *flipping*. Luverne would announce, "I need to go to the sewage plant now to flip 'em over," and he would be gone in a cloud of dust. He also had innumerable ideas about town planning, and if he had an idea, everyone would soon know about it. He had a way with words, too, the choicest words. When Mother and I would walk past Mans and Benda's Shell Station where he was an auto mechanic before becoming Police Chief, she would place her hands over my ears so I wouldn't hear those choice words emanating from under the hood of a '47 Plymouth. Luverne used spicy words . . . but back to the barn.

My uncle, Dave Franklin, owned that barn from which he operated a dray line business: Dave's City Dray Line: Don't drag it, Dray it was his motto painted on both sides of the wagons. He boarded his draft horses at the barn along with a couple of rubber-wheel wagons, and also rented stalls for folks who wanted to board their horses in town, not that Goodhue was an equestrian town, you understand. It wasn't that chic. They were functional, wagon-pulling horses, not for pleasure riding or racing.

Every day, except Sunday, Dave hitched his team to a wagon to distribute dry goods to the stores. He was operating long before eighteen-wheelers began delivering merchandise to town. If I rose early enough and Mother permitted me to go downtown to make my talking rounds, I would find Dave delivering to Campbell's Hardware or Diercks' Grocery or Swenson's Cafe or Art's Bar or Majerus' Gas and Appliance. He wasn't persnickety about what he delivered, be it groceries, nails or booze. I could find him by following the trail of road apples.

While Dad collected milk from the farmers on his daily rounds, Uncle Dave would let me ride with him on the wagon, occasionally permitting me to take the reins. Of course, farm boys drove horses all the time, but what a thrill for a town boy. "Giddyup! . . . Whoa there, Mable."

"How 'bout an ice cream cone before you go home, Jimmy?"

"You bet."

Chapter 3

Buddies

Neighborhood Pals

W E SPENT MANY EARLY CHILDHOOD SUMMER evenings playing Captain May I on the Holy Trinity church lawn with the O'Reilly boys—Bob, Larry, Jack—Patricia Ryan, Isabelle Mans, Bettie Lunde, Mary Benda, Janice Cook and Lee Johnson. When we tired of it we changed to roof tag around a freestanding, dilapidated garage behind the parish house, or an adjacent outhouse. It's difficult for children to play games such as that today; there aren't many free-standing garages, and virtually no outhouses.

1

Sandbox Bob's Make-Believe World

Bob O'Reilly's sandbox was a popular pastime for the neighborhood children. Bob and brothers Pat and Mike played in that six-by-eight-foot make-believe world where we each had an area to build our domain, Bob's the biggest. Even in that simple culture, he surpassed the rest of us. The same buddy who talked with me on Dixie Cup-string-walkie-talkies strung between our houses had a vision larger than the sandboxes of Goodhue. He knew he would leave some day, move to California and drive a five-holer Buick down Hollywood's Sunset Strip, movie stars at his side. I don't know where he acquired those ideas, because Bob and I walked to school together every day, sat next to each other in arithmetic class, walked to Mass together and went to catechism class together, but I didn't have Hollywood ideas. My vision was limited to the county—Mazeppa to White Rock, Bellechester to Wanamingo. I hadn't found the girlie magazines at Eddie's Drugstore yet, but Bob had found the Hollywood magazines. He devoured movie star stories like I devoured Swenson's chocolate ice cream.

On Saturdays after receiving his allowance, Bob trekked to Eddie's for his magazines. He immersed himself in them, dreaming of moving out of our lonesome farming village someday—the village with only two 100-watt street lights downtown—to southern California's bright lights, fast cars and fast women. He even knew famous Hollywood street names. The street in front of his sandbox house was Sunset Boulevard while Hollywood and Vine skirted his mansion. He talked of Clark Gable, Myrna Loy, Bette

Davis, Douglas Fairbanks, Jr., and he built his sandbox estate next to those stars.

Bob knew Hollywood, but I only knew our village. Bob was the master of the sandbox, erecting the biggest house, the widest street, the longest driveway curving into his estate like Myrna Loy's. And he drove the biggest car. I drove a Chevy pickup, my house a dilapidated bungalow on the other side of the tracks, not a fancy estate with a curving driveway.

But a child can learn much from sandbox play. It is more than pushing sand around. Sure, some brats threw sand and made a pest of themselves, but the better players didn't accept that behavior. And if you played in Bob's box, you had to behave. He ran a tight sandbox.

I don't believe our parents realized how much we were learning about life in the sandbox. We were just imitating them, after all. Dad was a trucker hauling grain, milk and cattle for area farmers. He picked up milk every day, dumped each eighty-pound can at the Creamery, then hauled a load of cattle to the South Saint Paul Stockyards on Saturdays. That was good enough for me. Not Bob. His dad was a farmer even though he lived in town. Now, some folks said that wasn't farming, but Skeezix drove to the country every day to work the farm, but Bob never took to farming. He was a movie star driving a black convertible down Sunset Strip. Socioeconomic differences arose between Bob and I in that sandbox—Bob drove his convertible and I drove my pickup with a cracked window, one door falling off, and a right rear bald tire. It had one hundred thirty thousand miles and two ring jobs. Heckuva truck.

Keeping up with Sandbox Bob required continual effort. Even if my lot improved, he had a way of keeping ahead of me. If I bought a new pickup, he bought a better one. If I added onto my shack, he built another drawing room. If I built an asphalt driveway, he built a circular, cement driveway.

Bob was nobody's fool.

I couldn't compete with Bob in the sandbox, but by the time we entered fifth grade, I found something I was better at:building model airplanes. Finally, I had gained one-upmanship on him. He didn't do well modeling airplanes. They looked as if they had been run over by a tractor by the time he finished them. Mine were better, because I didn't build them only to hang from my bedroom ceiling; I built them to fly. Maybe I would leave Goodhue someday in a Piper Cub.

Goodhue didn't have an airport; in fact we were lucky to have the Chicago Great Western's Dinky. But we could watch Northwest Orient planes fly over on their way to somewhere else. It could have been worse.

On a Friday afternoon as Bob and I were playing Captain May I with Mary Benda at her home on the edge of town, a Piper Cub circled an adjacent oat field. None of us had seen a Cub up close before, so we became increasingly fascinated as it circled. We rushed to the field as it touched down throwing up a cloud of oat husks. The pilot was a long-lost uncle of Mary's from Wisconsin who had rented the plane for a pleasure ride. It was a small red, one-engine airplane, and I knew from the moment I saw it that it was the plane I wanted when I grew up. I fell in love with it immediately, and knew that on my next trip to Woolworths in Red Wing, I would buy a model kit of the Cub. I did.

At supper I told Mom and Dad about the plane landing in the oat field. I said I needed a ride to Red Wing right away to buy a modeling kit. We didn't get there the next day; in fact, it was several days before we went. In 1945, folks didn't drive fifteen miles on a whim, because gas was rationed and money was scare and . . . "Money doesn't grow on trees, young man." I waited, impatiently. We finally made the trip to visit Aunt Lillian on Saturday; I walked ten blocks to Woolworths, but I was in luck. They had a balsawood modeling kit identical to the Cub that landed in town. I paid seventy-nine cents for the kit and rushed it home.

Twenty models hung in various attitudes from my bedroom ceiling, but this kit looked to be more difficult that I had planned.

It contained only three pieces of flat balsawood with markings stamped on them; it didn't look anything like an airplane. I would need to cut out each part with an Xacto knife before even beginning to glue them together, but I was persistent. I knew I could build that plane, and I knew it would fly. Bob had the same idea, only I didn't know it. He also talked his mom into driving to Red Wing—another one-upmanship tactic on Bob's part. But he was out of his sandbox domain this time. He was in mine. Sandbox Bob had met his match.

We walked to school on Monday morning toting our *Weekly Readers* and lunch buckets—peanut butter and grape jelly sandwiches, oranges, Ry Crisp crackers—but Bob didn't say a word about buying an airplane. I did. "Hey, Bob, you remember that Piper Cub we saw land behind Mary's place? Well, I bought a modeling kit of it, and I'm going to build me a genuine Piper Cub model."

"Oh, is that right?"

"You betcha. I'll have that baby done by the end of the week."

"Huh! Bet you don't, and even if you do, it won't fly!"

"Betcha back it will."

"I bought a kit, too," Bob said haughtily.

"Huh! I'll bet you did."

"Well, I did and I can build a better model than you, Jimmy, and it will fly farther than your dumb old plane."

"Bob, you never built a decent plane in your life. The only thing you can do is build sand mansions. What makes you think you can build a Piper Cub, and even if you can, what makes you think it'll fly farther than mine? You sure are dumb!"

Bob didn't back off at all. "Betcha I'll have mine done by Saturday and it will fly farther than yours."

"Betcha it won't."

"Betcha it will."

Bob was pressing me. He was good at arguing; I wasn't getting anywhere. I needed a different tactic.

"Betcha I'll have my Cub built by ten o'clock Saturday morning, and what's more, it'll fly farther than your dumb airplane. After I serve Mass, we'll take our planes to the church lawn;

we'll just see whose plane can fly the farthest. Betcha a double chocolate malt at Swenson's. So there!"

"Okay, betcha back," Bob huffed. The airplane challenge was on. We were going to duel. We would find out very soon who could build the best model.

After school I rushed home to my bedroom taking three steps at a time up the stairway, emptied the kit on my bed and was suddenly struck with fear.

How am I ever going to build this plane and get it to fly and beat Bob in one week?

What had I gotten myself into? Why was I forever doing things like this? Why didn't I just say, "Nice plane, Bob. She's a real humdinger. I'll bet she'll fly like a bird." But no, I didn't say that. I never said that. I was forever setting up a challenge. I should have kept my mouth shut with Lyle "Noisy" Rusch that stormy night on water tank hill—more about that later—but I didn't. It was too late now. I would have to learn, quickly, how to build a good balsawood airplane. Could I get help? Brother Tom didn't build airplanes. Rose Marie didn't build airplanes. I was in this alone.

But wait! Remember the Dinky. I . . . think . . . I . . . can, I know . . . I . . . can.

Suddenly, I felt better remembering our courageous little train. If the Dinky could pull up Hay Creek hill, I could build my airplane and it would fly farther than Sandbox Bob's, that's for sure . . . I think.

As I read the instructions, they became clearer. I was gaining confidence. I began to visualize the plane. Yes, I was going to do it. "Time for supper, Jimmy," Mother called from the foot of the stairs.

"Oh, Mom, I can't come down now, 'cause I'm building a plane."

"You get down here right now, young man, if you know what's good for you, or I'll *plane* you!"

"Oh, Mom."

I hurdled down the stairs, hurriedly washed my hash down with a couple glasses of milk then vaulted back upstairs to begin cutting out wing struts.

Careful! It's so thin. Damn! I cut a strut right in half!

No problem. I glued those two pieces together so they were as strong as ever. I looked through my window across the lawn into Bob's bedroom. He was hunched over a table with a quizzical look on his face.

Hmm, looks like Bob is having a problem. Maybe he doesn't know how to cut out wing struts.

By bedtime I had cut out struts for both wings and the fuselage. I was sure I could build a plane that would fly farther. I think I was sure. "Time to put out the light and go to bed, Jimmy."

"Oh, Mom, I need to work on my plane a little longer."

"I'll *plane* you if you don't turn out the light and go to bed."

"Okay, Mom, I'm going to bed now, g'night."

"Goodnight."

I had difficulty getting to sleep. Bob's light was shining through the apple tree and he was still hunched over his kit. It wasn't fair that I had to go to bed while he worked on his plane. The next morning, we strolled to school together. "How's the plane coming?"

"Great. How's yours?"

"Not so bad. She'll beat the pants off your old plane."

"Huh!"

I worked on the plane after school. I worked after supper. I worked until bedtime. I worked the next day and the day after that. I was making progress.

By now all fifth- and sixth-graders had heard about the challenge. Excitement spread throughout the school. Classmates began taking wagers. They bet their oranges and peanut butter sandwiches on either Bob or me. By Thursday it was eight peanut butter sandwiches and six oranges for Bob, seven peanut butter sandwiches and seven oranges for me. Mrs. Wood heard about the challenge and decided it would be a good opportunity to teach the class about aerodynamics in science class: "Bobby and Jimmy! Would you like to bring your planes to school tomorrow to show to the class?"

"Golly, I don't know Mrs. Wood. I've a lot of work to do yet. Don't know if she'll be ready," I said nervously.

"I don't know either, but I assume I can finish it," Bob
smirked.

I had completely glued the wings and fuselage together as
well as the tail and rudder, but I needed to fasten wheels to the
underside of the fuselage then cover the entire plane with tissue
paper. Then I needed to sprinkle the paper lightly with water to
tighten it so it would fly straight and fast and beat Bob's old
clunker. I also needed a rubber band for the propeller from Jesse's
Hardware. It had to be powerful to beat one-upmanship Bob.
Could I get it all done by science class?

Instead of running straight home after school, I ran downtown
to Jesse's. I knew he had rubber bands scattered around his
workbench; I hoped he would give me several strong ones. He did.
I ran out the back door and across the alley through Mans and
Benda's tire pile, petted ol' Buck the Black Lab lounging in the
shade under the barber pole, vaulted a rain barrel behind the Corner
Bar and made a beeline for home. I didn't even stop for a Hershey
Bar. I hurdled the stairs and looked through the window. Through
the leaves of the apple tree, I saw him hunched over his plane.

I had difficulty hooking the rubber band between the propeller and rear tail strut. Jesse had given me a strong rubber band, one
he used to hold the cover on a box of sixpenny nails, so the first time
I connected it, I broke a supporting balsawood strut. I strengthened
it with a double strut, then successfully hooked the rubber band in
place. Would it hold this time? I cautiously wound the propeller
counterclockwise only five times for a test. The propeller fluttered
to life. I relaxed. Then I wired the landing gear in place and covered
the skeleton-strutted plane with tissue paper. Tissue paper was
better than Heaney's meat-wrapping paper, because it was lighter,
and with water sprinkled over it, it became sleek and taut—good
for flying straight, fast and far.

Mother knew about the challenge by now, so she didn't bother
calling me for supper; besides, she was serving liver and onions.
It was bad enough that I had to smell it, much less eat it. I would
have a bowl of Wheaties later.

I finished at eleven o'clock. She was a beauty. I knew it was
better than Bob's, but could it fly?

We met under the apple tree the next morning to walk to school, each carrying lunch under one arm and an airplane covered with wrapping paper under the other. I couldn't see his plane. "Hey, Bob, how's it going?"

"Not so bad, could be worse."

"Let me see your Piper Cub."

"Naw, think I'll wait till we get to school. So, let me see yours, then."

"Naw, think I'll wait till we get to school."

The unveiling came at ten. Mrs. Wood brought us to the front of the room at the beginning of science class. Bob took his wrapping paper off first. His Piper Cub was completely yellow except for the black propeller. I was stunned when I saw it.

That's better than I expected. Bob doesn't usually build one that looks that good. Did his dad help him?

The class burst into applause. "Way to go, Bob!"

"Hecukva plane, Bob!"

"Great job, Bob. Not too shabby!"

It was my turn. My knees were shaking.

I didn't know Bob could build a plane like that.

"Come on, Jimmy, show us your plane," Bettie Lunde yelled from the back of the room. Slowly, I began unwrapping. I removed the Scotch tape from the right wing, then the left wing, the tail, the rear rudder and the landing gear until my Piper Cub was completely uncovered. It was so quiet that you could have heard a pin drop. My heart was beating so fast that it was ready to explode from my chest. Why was the class so quiet? In five years of school, I had never seen them this reserved. Abruptly, they burst into applause. "Great going, Jimmy, beauty of a plane," Mary hollered.

"Yeah! Jim, I really like it," Janice yelled.

Mrs. Wood was too much of a diplomat to choose Bob's plane over mine, or mine over Bob's. Instead, she said they were both lovely and that she couldn't choose between them. That was all right with me, because I was still stunned that Bob's plane looked so nice. I thought I had built a better plane, but the real test would come tomorrow morning on the Holy Trinity lawn.

I didn't get much sleep, and I don't think Bob did either. I could see him through the crooked branch of the apple tree as I glanced through my window. It looked as if he was making final adjustments late into the night.

All night long, I had visions of flying. I dreamed of falling through space and flying high over town without wings. I dreamed of jumping from the Elevator and flying to the water tank, nearly nicking the steeple of the Methodist Church. I tossed and turned, flying . . . falling. Finally, I awoke—Saturday morning, Mass, the big airplane challenge. I had difficulty concentrating during the *Kyrie* and the *Sanctus*, but before I realized it, Father had intoned *Ite, missa est*, (The Mass is ended), and I was standing at attention with George O'Reilly in the sacristy being dressed down by Sergeant Father Smith for moving the missal to the wrong side of the altar during the *Benedictus*. Droplets of sweat ran down his bloated face from temples to chin, dripping onto his purple vestments. He hollered at George and me in both English and Latin; he slurped coffee from a Thermos and chomped on a peanut butter sandwich during his harangue about the missal, but I had my mind on other things.

After Sergeant Father hollered, "Fall out!" I hurriedly hung my surplice on a nail, bowed, rushed from the sacristy, made a half-assed genuflection and sign of the cross as I passed the crucifix, raced down the isle past the Stations of the Cross, *Forgive me, Lord, for being so rushed in your time of need,* splashed holy water across my face and down my shirt, and banged through the front door to get my airplane. It was half past nine, only a half hour until the challenge. I made a couple of final adjustments on the propeller and the rudder before racing back to Holy Trinity. Bob was already there, and he had brought Pat and Mike with him for support. Patricia Ryan came. Janice Cook came. Lee Johnson came.

Bob and I didn't know how well our planes would stand up, so we decided to make the challenge a one-flight contest. We would stand at the sacristy end of the church while sending our planes flying toward the vestibule end. One flight with the wind at our backs and the Lord in our souls.

Fortunately, it was a nice spring day. A light breeze was gusting from the south making the morning feel warmer than forty degrees. The sun was shining brightly through the evergreen trees . . . a good day for flying. All the winner's plane needed to do was fly the farthest distance from the sacristy. When the flight ended, Lee would measure the distance with a painter's tape measure I had borrowed from Casey Ryan. Bob or I would have not only the prestige of being the winner, but also the recipient of a large Swenson's chocolate malt.

Lee tossed a buffalo-head nickel into the air to begin the challenge. Bob won and elected to fly first. He strutted briskly to the starting line, wound his propeller counterclockwise about twenty times, gently lifted his plane above his shoulder and with a firm thrust, let it fly into the heavens. The plane took off beautifully. I was stunned. I didn't think Bob could do it. I didn't even expect his plane to fly; I thought it would nosedive into the ground. Pat and Mike cheered. Everyone cheered, except me. The plane gained altitude and flew straight as an arrow toward the vestibule. Suddenly, a wind gust pushed it sideways nearly causing a crash, but the propeller surged with extra power, like an act of Providence, and pulled the plane out of its spin. It tipped an evergreen branch, stabilized itself and made a soft landing, fifty-two feet from the starting line. Fifty-two feet! I didn't think Bob could do it.

My turn. I was scared.

Jesus, Mary and Joseph, pray for me.

I plodded to the starting line while trying to keep my knees from shaking. The wind was dying down, only a gentle breeze whistling through the pine cones. I slowly and carefully wound the propeller seventeen times as I had practiced.

Just a few more turns to get more power, but be careful not to wind it so much that it breaks a strut.

Bob had had a good flight. I would have to do my very best to beat him. I inhaled a long, deep breath, adjusted the rear rudder a notch to the right to compensate for the breeze and the evergreen tree, lifted the plane above my right shoulder, and with a mighty thrust and an extra, "Jesus, Mary and Joseph," thrust it toward the vestibule. I sent it on its way with a prayer and a song . . . *Coming in on a wing and a prayer.* It surged from my hand startling me. I had dreamed of it soaring through the sky, but I was still stunned to actually see it fly. For twenty feet it was the most beautiful flight I had ever seen, but then it veered violently toward the ground. What was happening? I had carefully tuned the aileron and stabilizer. Why was it spinning out of control?

Oh, no, this can't be happening. Please don't let my plane crash, St. Jude, patron of lost causes, help my little plane.

It came up one foot before hitting the ground, dipped its left wing, stabilized itself while gaining altitude and headed directly toward the evergreen tree.

It can't hit the evergreen. The tree is only fifty feet from me, and if it hits, Bob will win and . . .

It flew directly toward the tree when, suddenly, fate or Saint Jude willed that *something* had to move, either the evergreen or my plane. Let me tell you, we hadn't seen any miracles in town; it wasn't likely the tree would suddenly vault skyward like a rocket. But my Cub veered upwards, dipped its wings to the right and missed the evergreen's trunk by a heart beat, but it did nick a pine cone just above the cockpit. The plane tumbled toward the ground. As it was about to crash, a gust of wind thrust it forward another couple of inches where it collided with the ground, tumbling to a halt. Was it far enough?

Lee measured. Forty feet, forty-five feet, fifty feet.

I don't know if I can stand this.

Fifty feet, fifty-one feet six inches, fifty-one feet eleven inches. Then, yes! Fifty-two feet two inches. My plane did it. We outflew Sandbox Bob by two inches. The plane was crumpled, but I was joyous. I had met the challenge.

Bob and I shuffled home together, a smile on one face, a frown on the other. "Nice flight, Jimmy. You beat me fair and square."

"Thanks, Bob, you didn't do so badly yourself."

"Want to go to Swenson's for a couple of malts?"

"Yeah . . . guess that wouldn't be such a bad deal. And . . . aah . . . Bob? Your airplane was prettier."

2

A Tree House For Boys Only

As next-door neighbor Bob and I grew up, we spent less time in the sandbox. I periodically ventured back to reclaim my territory, but it wasn't the same. I moved on to ball games and tree houses.

There was a sweeping, thirty-five foot elm behind our house that must have been growing for fifty years. It had a thick trunk with heavy branches reaching all the way to my bedroom window. When the wind blew hard on stormy, thunderstruck summer nights, its branches scraped the panes creating a frightening sound. Yet, it was the perfect tree for a tree house.

Building a tree house offered me the first opportunity to have a place of my own where I could be by myself. By age eleven, I was anxious for that independence. I didn't have any because of sharing a bed and bedroom with Tom. After sleeping with a brother in an unheated upstairs bedroom under fifteen feet of quilts through a sub-arctic Minnesota winter, I was ready for even a tree house.

I began acquiring the necessary building materials as I meandered around town. I thought I could find wood for the floor and walls at Streater's Lumber yard, and Dennis Heaney usually had lumber scattered around his cattle pens behind the Locker Plant. I needed twenty-five feet of strong rope for a pulley system to hoist materials into the tree. I had seen a coil behind Majerus' Gas and Appliance. I would ask Bert for it. I remembered a rusty can of nails in the alley behind Marshall-Wells. If I were lucky, it would still be there.

I was walking to the lumber yard for the wood, kicking an empty Grain Belt can through the dusty alley behind the International Harvestor shop, not thinking about anything in particular when a huge, mean-looking, hell-bent-for-election pig squealing to high heaven roared around the corner of the Locker Plant. Close on its tail came Dennis Heaney, Bump Schinnert and Dave Franklin all hollering, "Sooey, sooey, here pig!"

"Hey, Jimmy! Stop that damn pig," Dennis hollered. The pig was bearing straight down on me, and although I had no real fear of pigs, this looked like a three hundred-pound hog coming on fast, kicking up more dust than I was. I had no intention of getting in its way, but I did wave my arms, hollered "sooey" a couple of times, then jumped out of its way as it roared past me like a steam-belching locomotive, creating a swirl of dust so dense I was momentarily blinded. Its hind quarter brushed me on the leg, knocked me down and sent me sprawling into the ditch. I was wiping my eyes and picking grit out of my mouth when the posse ran past hollering their fool heads off. As the dust slowly settled , I knew they were no match for that pig.

You see, it wasn't a dumb pig. Bill Ryan brought it to the Locker Plant from Belle Creek to be butchered; it knew its fate. When Bump inadvertently left the gate open, it headed for open territory. That hog wanted out of Goodhue. Down the alley and across the street it barreled knocking over a water can as it circled the Shell Station dashing past Marshall-Wells followed by the Locker Plant Gang all huffing and puffing for more oxygen in the dust trail being left by the pig. The posse had picked up Luverne Haas as the pig roared through the gas pumps almost knocking him down. It bolted into the middle of upper street and ran head-long into John Berlinski's meandering pickup. But that collision didn't slow it down at all. It darted right, then left like a Minnesota Gopher tailback as it took to the grassy area between Ebe's Barber Shop and Marshall-Wells. Bump was the fastest runner, so by the time the pig passed Ebe's he was only ten feet behind those hoped-to-be pork loins. Dennis was tiring at fifteen feet; Luverne was gaining on Dennis and Dave was finished. He wasn't used to running, so when the pig broke left around the hardware store, he gave up the chase. "Get that damn pig, Bump!" he hollered while catching his breath sitting on the curb.

The pursuers lost Dave but picked up Bump's brother, Tom.

Now, Tom was strong and fast, and he accepted a challenge when confronted with one. He had been sitting on a bench in front of Eddie's Drugstore whittling on a hickory stick when he first saw that cloud of dust rising behind the Locker Plant. He watched the pig darting up the street causing more commotion than usual in the drowsy village. He was ready. By the time it broke left at Ebe's, Tom was off the bench and in full stride. Within twenty feet he had passed Dennis and was closing fast on Bump . . . and the pig.

But the pig was fast, too. When it passed Ebe's, it was at top speed and a sight to behold. Actually, pigs running free weren't that much of an oddity. Since the village began as a tiny railroad stop, cattle, pigs and sheep had frequently roamed its streets. It took many years to convince early settlers that letting cattle roaming at will wasn't in their best interest. But Bill Ryan's hog was creating bedlam on this sweltering July afternoon.

The motley band of panting pig pursuers ran across the alley toward Swenson's Cafe. In the summer, Heinie Swenson permitted the boys to drink 3.2 beer behind the cafe, because it was beastly hot inside. It was illegal, of course, but Hank Befort, the village Marshal, didn't get excited about enforcing that ordinance; there were more important things to do than make a few good ol' boys go inside to drink their beer. Well, the boys were out back when the hog headed toward the cafe. It sped around the corner so fast the Grain Belt boys didn't have time to properly react, their reacting time already slowed by a couple of brews. The pig caught Erv just as he was lifting his bottle. The bottle flew from his hand, sprayed beer from Goodhue to Bellechester and hit Red on the side of the head sending him hurtling headlong into three empty cases of Schmidt. Red and the beer cases rolled into the alley. Heinie rushed through the screen door to see what was happening at the same time the pig decided to execute a one hundred eighty-degree turn. It hit Heinie hard sending him sprawling toward Erv, Red and the spinning bottles. Regina Swenson heard the ruckus, rushed through the door, slipped on the foaming brew and hurtled headlong into Heinie. By now the pig was rightly confused; it didn't know whether to break left, right, or stay where it was. Tom took advantage of its momentary confusion. He was coming up fast, now leading the motley band of pursuers having passed Luverne, Dennis and Bump. He closed rapidly on the pig. From the curb, heavy-breathing Uncle Dave watched the entire mess unfold. Luverne was gasping and swearing a blue streak at the pig. If cuss words could have stopped that pig, those tangy words radiating from his mouth would have done it. They didn't. Those *sonofa-bitchs* and *goddamns* had no effect on that porker, but you couldn't blame Luverne for trying. He could swear better than run, but that wasn't the case with Tom who was now only three feet behind the confused hog, and he knew he had a chance when, for a brief moment, the confused pig stopped abruptly. Bump was in front of Tom but Tom acted instantly. He hurtled over Bump sending him sprawling toward Regina and Heinie. Tom was now airborne, on a flight path to the pig. The pig didn't see Tom's approach. Tom executed a three-point landing before it even heard the swish of air. Tom grabbed both hind legs, whipped his feet around that pig's head creating a viselock the kind of which had never been seen in the village. "That a boy, Tommy, you got him sure. Don't let him go," Dennis hollered as he huffed upon the scene.

Tom was a strong man, but he was being tested by that fighting-mad hog. Tom weighed in at two hundred fifty pounds; the pig went three hundred. The pig knew how to fight. It started dragging Tom toward a mud hole. By instinct it knew it would have a better chance of winning this bout if it could fight in its own environment. Tom saw the mud hole but couldn't stop the pig from dragging him. Dennis dove for its front legs but failed. Luverne yelled, "Stop that sonofabitch before it gets to the mud hole," but it didn't help. The pig dragged Tom to the hole, sloshed around a couple of times causing him to lose his grip. Luverne dove for the pig, caught a front shoulder, slipped and fell into the mud. Dennis grabbed for a back leg, and was rewarded with a kick in the groin for his efforts. The pig rambled out of the hole and headed for the last person between it and freedom—Bump. Bump wasn't as strong as Tom, but he had courage. He was the one who had left the gate open; he knew Dennis would "have his hide," if that pig got away. Bump didn't want to go through that.

As the hog roared toward him, he made his last stand. He

cornered the pig behind the cafe, lunged for it, caught it around the head, wrapped his feet around its slippery loins and held on for dear life. Dennis grabbed a rope, threw a loop around the pig's head, hog-tied that hog. The pig was squealing, Bump was dangling under the pig, Heinie was trying to emerge from under Regina who was slipping and sliding on beer foam. Red was sprawled in the corner wondering what in hell had happened to his Grain Belt; Dave was supervising the entire debacle from the curb, and Luverne was cussing that sonofabitchin' hog.

They pulled, tugged, wrestled and eventually secured the pig for the sojourn back to the Locker Plant. It was quite a sight— Dennis leading the procession pulling that pig every inch of the way, Bump full of mud from head to toe, stumbling along, and Tom, third in line, pushing Bump who was pushing on the pig's hind quarters. Dave had joined the procession by now offering everyone instructions on how to get the pig back to the pens.

About an hour later Heinie called the Locker Plant to place an order. "Hey, Dennis. I need two dozen pork chops, preferably from that damn hog you had down here this afternoon!"

After watching the holy mess with the pig, I resumed my journey to the lumber yard, going back to the alley where I located my dented kicking can. I found three two-by-fours at Streater's, a one-by-six plank behind the Locker Plant, a frayed, six-strand rope at Majerus Appliance, the Butter Nut can of nails behind Marshall-Wells, then trekked home with my treasures.

About nine feet up, the main trunk divided into three hefty limbs. I decided to build in that exact spot, because the floor would be supported by the limbs, and I would need only to build a couple of braces with two-by-fours, then tack the floor to the tree with sixpenny nails. The job proved to be more difficult than I thought, by myself. Bob was still playing in the sandbox, not interested in tree houses. Lee was flying kites, not interested, and Larry had other things to occupy his time. Brother Tom said, "Get lost!" But Dennis loaned me a block and tackle pulley setup from his wool barn to hoist my materials into the tree. "Just make sure you bring it back next week, Jimmy, because I need to hoist wool sacks."

"Okay, whatever."

Five feet above my floor was a branch to which I hooked the block and tackle permitting me to hoist two-by-fours, one-by-sixs, plywood, and a sheet of corrugated tin I acquired from behind Mickley's Garage. Surely, I would have the best tree house in the village. And when completed, I would live in it, eat, sleep, read, listen to my crystal radio set, look at my atomic ring and even talk to Bob on our Dixie Cup walkie-talkie radios.

Two days later, it began looking like a tree house. I nailed two-by-fours on each of the corners, tacked plywood on each side, left space for a couple of windows, placed the corrugated tin on top and it was done. I climbed down the two-by-four ladder nailed to the side of the elm, stepped back and filled my chest with pride.

But Mother wasn't happy about "that contraption" in the tree, although she knew I had to be a boy. She held her tongue. She was mostly concerned for my safety, "Now don't go and fall out of that contraption, because if you do, I'll have to take you to the doctor and that will cost a lot of money and your dad doesn't have much and you'll miss school," and on and on.

She wasn't concerned that our neighbors—the Hagas, the O'Reillys, the Gormans, the Heaneys, the Hennings, the Sawyers, the Swensons, the Bucks—her Bridge or Five Hundred Club would think it looked tacky. They didn't concern her. Money did. I could do almost anything if it didn't cost money. I grew up in the Great Depression when there wasn't any money! It hadn't been invented yet. Mother and Dad told us often, "We don't even have three cents to buy a stamp." Granted, we had little money, but I didn't realize it. We had food on the table, and clothes on our back. I didn't concern myself about it.

Word spread quickly that I had built a tree house. Bob, Lee, Larry and other friends, now wanted to see it. They rushed to the elm, climbed the ladder, and entered my special place. When I climbed up, it was already full and teetering toward Bob's sand-box. We could only sit cross-legged facing each other. There wasn't enough room to stretch out our legs, but I didn't complain. "Why don't we start a club with just the five of us," Larry said.

"Yeah, that's a good idea," Jack O'Reilly responded, "and let's have it only for boys. No girls allowed."

"That's a great idea," Bob O'Reilly declared.

"Yeah, but I don't know if I want my tree house to become a clubhouse. I just finished it and was figuring I would sleep here and eat here and listen to my crystal radio set, and besides, if we turn it into a club house, I won't have it for myself, and all of that."

"Come on, Jimmy, don't be a spoilsport. You can still have it to yourself even if we use it for a club house."

"Well, maybe it would be all right, if we don't have too many meetings."

"Way to go, Jimmy. You're a good buddy."

What had begun as my own tree house was now a club house. We decided to hold our first meeting that evening after supper. Larry was to bring two candles.

"Now that we're all here, what are we going to do?" Lee asked.

"We're going to have a meeting, you dummy," Bob hissed.

"About what?" Jack asked.

"Yeah. We can't just have a meeting. We've got to meet about something," I added.

"Well, our meetings can be about Beverly Hills," Bob said. "That would be fun. I could bring my movie star magazines, and we could start a fan club for Greta Garbo."

Larry became excited, "That's a great idea, and I can bring Lefty's *Life* magazines. They have many movie star pictures."

"I don't know. I'm more interested in cars than movie stars," Lee said. "Let's meet about cars; besides, I want to buy one when I get into high school. I've got magazines at home and dad would let me bring some of his, too. Let's have our meetings about cars."

Jack thought Lee had a good idea. "I like Lee's idea. I want to buy a '49 Plymouth when I get into high school, so I think we should have our meetings about cars, too."

"Do any of you guys like band saws and hammers and lum—ber?" I asked. "I've been buying *Popular Mechanics* at Eddie's and reading about those things. Let's have our meetings about building things. I could bring my *Johnson-Smith Catalog*, too; we could talk about two-way radios, and atomic rings and . . ."

"I don't like that idea," Bob said, rudely interrupting me. "I like my idea better, don't you, Larry?"

"Yup. I vote for a movie star club," Larry declared.

"I vote for a car club," Lee shouted.

"Me too," Jack yelled.

"Well, I still want our meetings to be about two-by-fours and nails and atomic rings and two-way radios," I said.

Silence enveloped us for a long time. Five, sixth-grade boys sat in the glow of two flickering candles, in a tree house, in Goodhue, in 1946 on a breezy, humid and shadowy summer evening trying to determine what to meet about. A stand-off. The only thing decided was—no girls.

Deathly quiet. Evergreen Cemetery quiet as we became mesmerized by the red and white flickering candle flames . . . "I got some girlie magazines at home," Lee whispered shattering our silence like a cannon explosion. Did I hear him right? Is that really what he said?

"Run that by me again, would you, Lee?" I sputtered.

"I got girlie magazines at home. I could bring 'em tomorrow night. We could look at 'em for our meetings."

"You can't have a meeting about girlie magazines," Bob snapped, "besides, who wants to look at them, anyway?"

"I'd kind of like to see them," Jack whispered.

I was nervous. I hadn't seen a girlie magazine yet, although I had tried many times to get to them behind the counter at Eddie's Drugstore, but he always intercepted me. "Yeah, I guess that would be okay if you brought them tomorrow night, Lee. It wouldn't be too bad of a deal if we looked at them." I was trying to be cool and calm, but the prospect of seeing girlie magazines was exciting, unnerving. "I guess that's it then. We'll meet tomorrow night at the same time. Larry, see if you can bring more candles. Bob, bring rugs to sit on. Jack, bring popcorn and I'll bring Kool-Aid. Lee, aah . . . I guess it would be all right if you brought your g . . . gir . . . bring your magazines."

The next day was a sultry July day. I made my daily trip to Swenson's to cool off with a chocolate bar and Nesbitt's orange soda. While sipping the Nesbitt's, Janice Cook and Bettie Lunde sauntered in. "Hi, Jimmy. We heard you guys have started a club. Can we join?"

"Naw, girls aren't allowed."

"That's not fair. What do you do at your dumb meetings, anyway?"

"Oh, not much. We look at *Popular Mechanics* magazines and talk about two-by-fours and cars and things like that, nothing you girls would be interested in."

"Come on, Jimmy, let us come to just one meeting."

"We don't have room in the tree house anyway. It only holds five. There wouldn't be room for two more."

"You're an old spoilsport. You're just afraid of girls anyway. I'll bet you've never kissed a girl, and I'll bet you've never even seen a girlie magazine," they taunted.

How did they know that?

"Uh-huh. Well, I'll be going. See you later."

That was close. We decided last night that we wouldn't let girls into our club, but now Lee is bringing girlie magazines, we sure can't. Maybe some other time.

The morning dragged on, unmercifully, hour by hour. I grew increasingly restless. It felt like Christmas Eve when I would wait impatiently for nightfall to open my presents. I was extremely nervous about tonight's club meeting and the magazines Lee would be bringing. I passed the afternoon by shuffling to the railway station to talk with Mr. Overby and to catch sight of a coal-burning freight train heading to Zumbrota. If I were lucky, I would catch a wave from the engineer, and if I were even more lucky, he would toot his steam whistle. If it were a very special day, he would let me climb into the engine as it took on water behind the Elevator. It was a treat to climb the steel-black stairs of the twenty-four-wheeler and gaze into the fire box and pull the throttles, especially a chance to tug the rope that blew the whistle. But it wasn't to be.

Engine 29 wasn't coming through town this day.

Instead, I kicked a can down the tracks toward the grain elevator, whistling and thinking, left foot walking the rail, right foot kicking the can twenty ties at a time. Maybe there would be some farmers there unloading wheat or barley. A boy can kick a can a long distance when he has a mind to. He can get pretty good keeping a can between two rails all the way from the railroad station to the Elevator. Besides, it took his mind off other things.

There was considerable activity at the Elevator when my can and I arrived. Some Belle Creek farmers were unloading trucks, dumping oats and barley through a steel grid into a holding bin where it was then augered into a silo for storage before being graded and loaded onto a freight car for shipment to General Mills where they made flour, bread, and Powdermilk Biscuits. As each farmer dumped his grain, a cloud of dust would envelope him and his truck, chaff covering his Dekalb cap, Oshkosh overalls, eyelids and whiskers; dirty work, but good as money in the bank.

I lost my kicking can in the grain bin, but replaced it with a stone as I ventured across the street to Mickley's Garage, preoccupied, head down, kicking the rock when I was startled out of my pants by a loud blast from a passing truck. "Jimmy! Watch where you're going," Les Banidt yelled as he sped by.

"How you doin', Les?"

Mickley was giving a '42 Chevy truck a ring job when I sauntered in. "Hey, Mick, what'cha doin'?"

"Just trying to make this bucket of bolts run again. Damn Chevys aren't any good. I don't know why I'm wasting my time trying to fix this piece of junk; don't know why anyone would buy a Chevy in the first place. They ought to drive Internationals like your dad, now that's a decent truck."

"You got that right. Dad does have a good truck. He's always liked Internationals; wouldn't be caught dead in a Chevy. Shoot! He said his International would out-pull a Chevy any day. Last winter, Bill O'Reilly was down there in the hills below White Rock and got stuck in a ditch with his Chevy . . . took three days to get out. Bill said that Chevy had less horsepower than Jack's bike. Took two farmers, three tractors and a mule to get that bucket of bolts out. Bill traded her as soon as he got the chance . . . driving an International now."

"You can say that again."

"Driving an International now."

Supper time was approaching. Time to be heading home. Central, the telephone operator, would be pushing the town siren button any minute to let everyone know it was six o'clock, time to quit work, go home and eat supper. I had just waved to Bill hunched over the anvil in the blacksmith shop when it blew. It wouldn't be long until the club-meeting.

I picked at my supper; Mother noticed. "You're not eating much, Jimmy. What's the problem? Bad stomach? Too much chocolate and ice cream?"

"I guess that's it. I ate two ice cream cones and a Nut Goodie bar. Sort of spoiled my appetite." But that wasn't the reason. I was hungry, but I was thinking about the magazines Lee would be bringing.

"What do you fellows do in your tree house?" Mother asked as she heaped more corned beef hash on my plate.

"Oh, not much, just sit around and tell stories."

"What's the name of your club?"

"Well, we're looking for a name. Can't decide, because we don't know what we want to meet about, yet. Bob wants to meet about his old movie stars, and Larry says that would be all right with him, and Lee wants to meet about cars and Jack said that would be all right, and I want to meet about lumber and nails and crystal radios. We can't decide."

"What are you going to meet about tonight if you haven't decided?"

"I guess Lee is bringing his dad's *Field and Stream* magazines. We're going to look at them and see if we want to talk about fishing and hunting."

"That would be nice, and something you fellows would probably be interested in."

"Lee said they were good magazines and that we would really like them, so I'm looking forward to the meeting."

"Just be careful. Don't burn the tree house down, and whatever you do, don't fall out of the tree, because I'd have to take you to Dr. Liffrig and that costs money and . . ."

"I know, Mom. I'll be careful. I see the guys. Bye."

Jack arrived first, then Larry, then Bob scurried up wiping peanut butter on his sleeve yelling back to brother Pat, "Stay! You're too young to be a club member. Go back in the house." But there was no sight of Lee. Was he coming? Couldn't he get the magazines?

Larry lit a candle as dusk gave way to darkness. With a smirk on his face, haughty Bob said, "It looks like Lee isn't coming; let's meet about movie stars. I brought these magazines. Here are some pictures of Hollywood Boulevard."

I sighed, "I wonder what's keeping him? He said he'd be here."

"Look at this picture of Douglas Fairbanks in his convertible, and look who's sitting next to him—Greta Garbo."

"Oh, Bob, I'm not interested in your movie stars. They're just a bunch of rich people in Hollywood, and they don't have anything to do with me, and we'll never be rich like them. So there!"

"Well, I'm going to be a movie star and be rich," Bob asserted.

"Hush up. How are you ever going to get all the way from Goodhue to Hollywood?"

"After I graduate from high school, I'm going to California to get a job as a waiter at the Hearst mansion, because that's where movie stars are. One of them will see me and I'll get a part as an extra and I'll become a star. Just you wait and see."

"Where in the heck is Lee? He said he was coming . . ."

"Hey! are you guys up there?"

Lee's voice. We looked down to see him climbing the ladder, magazines sticking out of his back pocket as he climbed slowly, hand over hand into the tree house.

"What took you so long?" Jack shouted.

"I had trouble finding the magazines and sneaking them out of the house. Mother kept hanging around so I couldn't get them from under Dad's bed, but I got 'em. Look at these babies!"

Lee took the magazines from his pocket and spread them on the rugs. The candles were flickering, cascading a soft, yellow glow on our anxious faces. Lee opened the magazines to photos of women in bras and panties, but they were smaller than what I had seen in the Sears catalog, much smaller. "You ever seen these, Jimmy?"

"Heck yes, see 'em all the time."

"Huh, I bet you do!"

Is that what girls look like underneath their dresses? Wow!

Then Lee said, "Wait till you see this!" He flipped a few more well-worn pages. In the shadowy darkness of my tree house, the wind blowing through the rustling leaves, candles casting eerie shadows on the walls and ceilings, I saw my first picture of a naked woman. Quiet, only heavy breathing and the wind invaded the silence . . . . Lee broke it, "What do you guys think of that?" No one spoke. We stared at the pictures, mesmerized by the nakedness. "You guys ever seen a naked woman before?"

"Oh, sure," we all said in unison.

"This ain't no big deal, Lee. We've seen pictures of naked women before," Jack blurted out. But I hadn't. I don't know if Jack or Larry or Bob had, but not me. My mind thought puzzling thoughts, my tummy felt odd. These photos weren't the same as photos in *Popular Mechanics.*

"I got to go now, have to get these home and put them under Dad's bed before he comes home," Lee whispered. "Maybe I can bring them again."

"Yeah, I have to go, too," Jack said.

"Me too," Bob said.

The guys climbed down the ladder leaving me alone in the tree house, alone with the moonlight and the wind blowing gently through the elm, leaves singing a sultry song as they rustled in the breeze. I sat there for a long time gazing at the candle's shadows dancing across the corrugated tin roof, looking at the moonlight as it slivered through a window. I thought about those naked woman I had just seen. They were different. I stayed for an hour not being able to get those pictures out of my mind. The dancing shadows on the roof soon became dancing women. The candle's flame and shadows were transformed into sensual, writhing women. "You up there, Jimmy?" Mother called from the kitchen window.

"Yes, Mom, I'm here."

"Well, what are you doing?"

"Oh, just thinking about Lee's *Field and Stream* magazines. They're pretty good you know, nice pictures."

"Maybe you and your dad can go fishing tomorrow."

"Maybe we can."

"Come in the house now, time for bed."

"Okay, Mom, I'll be right down."

From my bed, I looked through the window to my tree house and thought about what had happened tonight. I looked at the moonlight shining through my window, shadows from the elm dancing on the ceiling—women dancing, running through wheat-fields, naked and they were . . . sleep . . . gentle . . . peaceful . . . kind . . . sleep . . . .

Chapter 4

Class of 1954
Grade School Years

Grade School Classes of '53 & '54 in 1948

T HERE WERE FIVE, ONLY FIVE OF US IN FIRST GRADE.
Goodhue School didn't offer kindergarten in 1942, so it was
directly into first grade with us. I should not have started, because
I was barely five, but there I was, walking to first grade with Bob.
It was good I had him, though, because not only was he my

neighbor, he was also my buddy. And moms didn't walk their children to school on the first day. Children were expected to take care of themselves; anyway, we wanted to act grown up.

___1

The Five

I bounded out the back door, met Bob by the apple tree, then skipped across our back lawn through the pine trees to first grade. We met our three classmates, Mary Benda, Janice Cook and Bettie Lunde by the flagpole. The Five were the only children born in the village in 1936, but Mary and Janice were almost an entire year older than me. The school needed students, however, and Mom didn't want me around the house anymore, ". . . off to school with you, Jimmy." She didn't even ask me if I wanted to go, didn't ask if I was tired of playing in the sand box, tired of climbing the apple tree, tired of kicking stones. If she had I would have said, "No, Mother, I'm not yet tired of playing. Actually, school might wait another year." We entered first grade on a golden, sun-drenched September morn', five children beginning twelve years of education starting the Class of '54.

Goodhue erected a new school building in 1936, so we walked into a school that was built the same year we were. It was made of brick instead of wood, had shiny terrazzo floors instead of wood planking, and was two stories high. Grades one through eight met on the first floor while the high school grades convened on the second. The entire school district was housed in that one building. Some folks might snicker at our small class and school, but we weren't *that* small. Many of our parents had attended one-room country schools out in the townships where five children constituted all eight grades. We were bigger than that.

The Five were seated that first day at over-sized desks with ink holes on the upper right side. I don't know who decided first grade children needed ink bottles, but it was a mistake. First- and second-graders didn't need ink, but the hole was there, just in case. The Class of '54 didn't begin writing exercises with Schaeffer ink pens, but classes before us had used the ink wells, because blue stains were embedded in the carved names of village students who had preceded us. Class of '48—David Swenson, Terrence Shelstad, Elroy Rusch; Class of '49—Junior Lunde, John Stueber, John Yungers, Arlene Bremer; Class of '50—Richard Cook, Harold Lensch, Donnie Luhman, Jimmy Ryan, Genevieve Shelstad, Jo Ann Majerus; Class of '51—Rose Marie Franklin, Marilyn German, Jimmy Lohman, Mary Lou Majerus, Mary Ann McHugh, George O'Reilly, Mary Jean O'Reilly, Lyle Rusch, Elaine Shelstad, Jane Yungers; Class of '52—Bill Center, Tom Franklin; Class of '53—Larry O'Reilly, Jack O'Reilly, Beverly Moran, Dallas Diercks, George Lee Johnson, Dale Jonas, Jo Anne Mans.

> *See Dick, see Jane.*
> *See Dick kick the ball.*
> *See Jane catch the ball.*
> *See Dick and Jane run.*
> *How fun to see Dick and Jane run.*

Dick and Jane. A reading book. Dick and Jane, so clean. See Bob so clean. See Jimmy so dirty. See Mary, Janice and Bettie so clean. See their pretty dresses. Pretty pinafores. Pretty bows. They look pretty like Jane. Bob looks smart like Dick. See Jimmy's dirty fingernails. See Jimmy's scuffed shoes.

> *See Dick jumping rope.*
> *See Jane playing hopscotch.*
> *Dick and Jane are good children.*
> *See Dick's dog chase the ball.*

Dick and Jane was our beginning reader, an updated but less effective version of *McGuffey's Eclectic Readers.* But we learned to read, learned to write. Above the teacher's desk on the wall were the Palmer Method writing charts, upper- and lowercase cursive

letters of the alphabet flowing across the front of the room like
waves in an ocean. Our teacher taught us to write like the Palmers.
After reading *Dick and Jane* we would get our pencils, sharpen
them, retrieve two sheets of grade-one paper, writing paper with
wood shavings sticking out of it and lines two inches apart, then
attempt to write like the Palmers from Minneapolis or Chicago or
Kansas City or wherever they lived. I don't recall how the class'
penmanship developed, but for me the Palmer Method never
caught on. I tried but couldn't get my hands and fingers to move
in a flowing motion . . . A A A A A A A A A A A, B B B B B B B B
B, c c c c c c, d d d d d. "Hold the pencil softly, Jimmy; don't grasp
it so hard. Move in a flowing motion like this . . . up and around and
down and left. Doesn't that look nice?"

"Sure does, now let me try again."

I couldn't do it. My A's looked like boxes, my B's like
distorted circles. But I took my writing papers home to show to
Mother; of course, she said they were beautiful, but I knew better.
She was just being a mother. I walked home with Sandbox Bob and
I saw his papers. They looked like the Palmer charts. I knew. But
I loved Mother just the same for telling me how nice they were.
That's what moms are for.

Sometime during that first year we succeeded in memorizing
the alphabet and completing *Dick and Jane*, Book One. Our teach–
er told us wonderful adventure stories about places outside of
Goodhue County we had never heard of, and she showed us
pictures of Africa and Australia. We were on our way toward
receiving an education.

Reading and writing were all right, but I actually liked recess
the best. Once in the morning and once in the afternoon we dashed
to the playground to play on the swings and the merry-go-round,
and do whatever first graders do when they aren't tied to ink-hole
desks. We had swings, rings, a high bar and a teeter-totter. We could
also tease girls by pulling their hair, throwing stones, and doing
those things that annoy girls.

There was a cherished bond between us, five little squirts
born on the tails of the Great Depression, five kids thrust into the
hungry belly of southeastern Minnesota. If we could have chosen

when to enter the county we might have chosen a different era. We weren't baby boomers; we were FDR's kids. We didn't know there was an era better than ours, but our parents did. They had known an era before The Depression—an era when they had a few extra dollars in their pockets. They Charleston'd around the county during the Roaring Twenties and the Jazz Age. They had some good times before that fateful day in 1929. But as long as The Five had food on the table, hand-me-downs on our backs, a *Dick and Jane* book to read and the Palmer Method writing charts, we weren't doing so bad. We were post-Depression babies but we weren't depressed. There's a difference.

Grades one, two and three passed rapidly. The Five learned addition tables, division tables, multiplication tables and subtraction tables. We became better readers, spellers and writers, and my penmanship progressed to the point where Mother could tell I was trying to write the letter B instead of two circles.

2

The Five Expanded

We were a unified class those first three years, but the situation changed dramatically in the fall of 1945. The first day of fourth grade, Bob and I walked to school with new pencil cases, notebooks and gum erasers, polished Buster Brown shoes and rolled up jeans, but changes occurred that day for The Five. When we entered the classroom it was obvious something was very different. We saw Janice, Mary and Bettie, but others, too, strange-looking kids with funny faces and funny clothes and funny odors and funny names—Neil, Joleen, Pearl, Rita, Virginia, Gladys, Gloria Mae, Duane, Janet, Marilyn, Donna, David, Thomas Patrick, Beverly, Roy, Michael. I looked at Bob. Bob looked at me. We were bewildered. We looked at Mary, Janice, Bettie. They looked back, puzzled. What was happening? We looked at our teacher, but she didn't look puzzled. She said, "Welcome to fourth grade, children. We have many new children in our class this year. Students who have been attending school in the country schools of White Rock, Welch, Belvidere, Belle Chester and Belle Creek will now attend our school. We are so happy to have them here that I want the village children to give the new students a big round of applause and say, 'Welcome to Goodhue School.'"

I didn't want to do it. I didn't want any new classmates. I didn't want to attend school with Virginia and Roy and Michael and Neil and David and . . . . I was happy with The Five. *We* were the Class of '54. Where had these intruders come from? I thought The Five were the only children born in 1936. Why had these kids with funny faces and funny clothes and funny shoes and funny aromas come to Goodhue? Why didn't they stay in the country and go to their own schools? We were doing fine without them. "Now, would the village children, Mary, Janice, Bettie, Bob, and Jimmy please come to the front of the room to welcome our new class-mates?" Very slowly, I shuffled to the front of the room, Bettie tugging me all the way. "These are your classmates who have been the only children, to-date, in the Class of '54. They live in town, but I'm sure they are all very happy to have new classmates join them. Would you children now extend a big welcome to your new classmates from the country, and show them how happy you are to have them join you in fourth grade? Mary?"

"Welcome to the fourth grade class. You're welcome."

"Janice?"

"We're happy to have you in Goodhue. You're welcome."

"Bettie?"

"I am most pleased to have new classmates join us in the fourth grade. I am sure we will become the very best of friends and continue our education throughout the next several years to be the best class ever in Goodhue High School."

Oh, God, that's enough, Bettie, don't gush so much. You're overdoing it.

"Bob?"

"I'm very happy to have new classmates. Welcome to Goodhue Grade School."

"Jimmy?"

"Well . . . aah . . . um . . ."

"Go ahead, Jimmy, extend your welcome."

"Well, you see, I was actually doing pretty well before these country kids arrived. I wasn't actually looking for new classmates, so it's kind of caught me off guard, but I guess as long as they're here, it won't be too bad a deal. Welcome, to the new country kids."

The Class of '54 was no longer The Five. We were now more like fifteen. I had never seen that many students in one classroom before. Bob and I had been the only boys, but now we had to share with Roy and Michael and Thomas Patrick and Duane Curtis. But gradually, I learned to share and like my new classmates. It didn't take long to develop new friendships, to enjoy their stories about living on a farm. They had yarns and used words we had never heard. They talked about cultivating and tilling and plowing and mulching and fallowing and harrowing and fertilizing and sowing and inseminating and harvesting and gleaning. They talked of milking cows and feeding sheep and baling hay, and of cows 'doing it!' They talked about coming out to their place. They talked about breeding and growing and hatching and feeding and fattening and milking and saddling and hitching. They talked about bellybands and martingales and cruppers. They talked about Rhode Island White chickens and quarter horses and Palominos and Brown Swiss cows and Herefords and Holsteins and Shropshire sheep and Berkshire hogs and every kind of animal imaginable. They talked about driving balers and windrowers and pegtooth harrows and combines and tractors and four-bottom plows and corn pickers and disk harrows. They used words Bob and I had never heard before.

The Fifteen passed through fourth- and fifth grade before another major change occurred. Goodhue School purchased their first two orange school buses to transport those country kids into town. We felt important to now be a school with buses like Mazeppa, Cannon Falls and Zumbrota . . . made us proud to have buses with *Goodhue* written on both sides.

We learned together, played together, spent the next eight years together molding our characters while finding out about friends and girls and boys and dating and sex, and well . . . we grew up. We had begun innocently enough along an arduous journey through reading, writing, geography, social studies, arithmetic, algebra, history, English, physics, chemistry, basketball, football, baseball, band, chorus, the junior play, the senior play, the operetta, the autumn dance, the spring dance, the prom, the first date, the first kiss, the first . . . well . . . you get the idea.

Chapter 5

GHS Basketball
Team of 1944

District Champions, 1944

Wᴴᴇɴ Gᴏᴏᴅʜᴜᴇ Hɪɢʜ Sᴄʜᴏᴏʟ ꜰɪᴇʟᴅᴇᴅ ᴏɴᴇ ᴏꜰ its most successful basketball teams to-date in 1944, Dad used his truck, the same one in which he hauled cattle to the South St. Paul Stockyards, to transport local fans to Kenyon, Northfield or Rochester for the basketball tournaments, because travel was restricted due to WWII gas rationing, and those two orange school buses hadn't been purchased yet. What travel folks did was necessary travel; certainly not for pleasure. Vehicles displayed gas rationing stickers on the windshield indicating the amount of allocated gas. Doctors, ministers or priests were allotted more, but if you couldn't claim a profession like that you received the minimum. Driving ten miles out of town seldom happened; of course, driving to a basketball game was a different story. Imagine standing in the back of a cattle truck for twenty-five miles in a Minnesota winter to attend a basketball game. I wore my heavy Mackinaw coat, a cap with wool ear laps, my heaviest pair of mittens, and four-buckle snow boots.

_____1

Our Dream Team

The '44 GHS basketball team was our dream team. There had never been a team like it in the history of Goodhue sports. The feat they were to accomplish wasn't duplicated for another twenty-nine years. Gerald "Lefty" O'Reilly, Burt Eppen, Phil Ryan, Eugene Haas and Dick Eyestone were the starting five. There were others: Toby Buck, Willie Eppen, Hank Bartel, Bill and Elroy Schulz. Karl Tomfohr took late afternoons off from his implement dealership to coach, and Davie Franklin took time off from Heaney's Market to be team manager. For this boy, they were the best basketball players in the world.

Lefty would set up at the top of the circle, place both feet together, loft a two-handed set shot toward the basket causing the fans to go wild as his shot split the net. Phil, one of the taller players, pulled down every rebound in sight and could shoot a dazzling hook shot. The talk around town was that Phil taught George Mikan how to shoot the hook shot that made him famous with the Minneapolis Lakers. I did say the *Minneapolis* Lakers, not the *Los Angeles* Lakers. The Lakers were Minnesota's team and have always belonged to the Land of 10,000 Lakes. They're called the Lakers aren't they? How many lakes does Los Angeles have? The Lakers had Slater Martin, George Mikan, Jim Pollard and Vern Mikelson, the world champions of basketball. And to think Phil Ryan taught Mikan how to shoot the hook. Then Mikan taught it to Kareem Abdul Jabbar. What a lineage and it all started at GHS.

The basketball season was electrifying for the village. The team was so good that they even generated excitement throughout the county. Even our neighbors in Wabasha and Olmsted counties heard about the boys. Prior to 1944, GHS had lost regularly in the first or second round of the subdistrict tournament. Our teams usually played well during the regular season, but seldom succeeded in the tournaments. And to return home a loser from tournament play made the remainder of the winter very long. But 1944 was different; even the winter was different.

The team gained confidence as the tournament approached. Phil was playing exceptionally well pulling down almost every defensive rebound plus tipping in rebounds from his teammates. Lefty was uncanny hitting those long set shots from beyond the free throw circle, and that was long before the three-point play. He would have been Goodhue's all-time scoring leader if basketball had had the three-point play in '44. The team finished the regular season with only two losses, one to Kenyon, the other to our nemesis Wanamingo.

A week before the tournament there was considerable exhilaration at the Corner Bar, Taylor's Eat Shop, Heaney and Gorman, Mans and Benda's Shell Station, the Goodhue Elevator, the Goodhue County Tribune, Campbell's Hardware, Shelstad's Cafe, Swenson's Cafe, Husbyn's Hatchery, Majerus Gas and Appliance, Eppen's Electric Shop, Eddie's Drugstore, the post office, the International Harvester Shop, Sidney Berg's Shoe Repair and every business in the village. They could hardly wait.

The subdistricts finally arrived, but I had difficulty concentrating on school. How great it would be to beat Wanamingo. They won during the season, but we would have our revenge. There was no question in my mind that the team would "... win over all."

I dashed out the door when school ended. By half past four Dad had hosed down the floor of his cattle truck and parked it beside the Goodhue Hotel, ready to drive a load of fans to Kenyon. Packed like Herefords, we motored across frozen roads not unlike what county immigrants had done a hundred years earlier when they trudged the frozen tundra in 1844. The game with Wanamingo was hard-fought, but by the final buzzer Goodhue had prevailed. I was ecstatic. Even the cold ride home couldn't freeze my spirits.

A few days later we met Kenyon for the subdistrict title. Kenyon usually won, but not this year. Lefty, Phil, Dick, Burt and Eugene were our salvation. The game began with our team immediately falling behind. It looked bad. I wanted a Pepsi, but it was Lent. I was nervous when Ryan suddenly pulled down a big rebound, threw the ball the length of the court to Eyestone who dropped it in for a lay-up. Two points. We were only five points behind and I could see the spirit rising in our lads. That lay-up gave us pep, and I even forgot about the Pepsi. By halftime GHS had tied Kenyon at 19 points. That was the correct score. Basketball teams didn't score much in the forties. I felt relieved. We had tied Kenyon, and I just knew our boys would prevail in the second half.

The GHS Band struck up the school march, and the Goodhue fans burst into song.

> *Hail, hail the purple and white,*
> *Wildcats in spirit, Wildcats in fight . . .*

We were going to fight; there was no question about it. The Kenyon Band played Clyde McCoy's *Sugar Blues*, but I knew Goodhue wouldn't have the blues tonight.

Neither team scored during the first five minutes of the second half. The Goodhue fans became increasingly agitated. Then Kenyon scored to go two points up. Goodhue missed an easy lay-up. Kenyon rebounded and went the length of the floor to score another two points. We were four down. I felt queasy. A scramble for the ball—we had it. Deliberately now, Goodhue moved down the floor. The gymnasium had become as quiet as a Lutheran wake as Burt dribbled slowly down the middle of the floor, one eye on the ball, the other on the clock. Bounce passes from Burt to Lefty to Eugene, back to Lefty, then to Dick. Then a loft to Phil—two points!

Kenyon 23, Goodhue 21.

Kenyon quickly dribbled the length of the floor. Oh, they were good. Swift pass to the key, then to the corner and a bounce pass along the baseline. Two points!

Kenyon 25, Goodhue 21.

O'Reilly to Eppen, down the floor—a shot, no good. Kenyon rebound, quickly up the floor, into the corner—a shot, no good. Ryan rebound; long pass to Eyestone under the basket— lay-up. Good!

Kenyon 25, Goodhue 23.

Kenyon pass into the corner. Back out to the top of the key, interception! O'Reilly stepped right in front of that pass, dribbled eighty feet to score.

Kenyon 25, Goodhue 25.

Heebie-jeebies. I couldn't stand it and I had take a leak so badly I was ready to wet my pants, but I couldn't leave. Fifty-seven seconds to play—all tied up. Suddenly, Eyestone toppled to the floor. It looked like a bad ankle sprain. Despair.

No! This can't happen now. God, please listen to me. GHS has to conquer over all. We have to beat Kenyon. Anyway, they're only Lutherans. You're Catholic aren't you? Fr. Smith said you were. If you are, surely you'll help us beat the Lutherans.

Eyestone was up but hurting badly. Elroy Schulz substituted for Eyestone. Oh, what could Elroy do? The other cagers were seniors, but Elroy was only a sophomore.

55 seconds.

Kenyon's ball. Pass into the corner, back out front, then to the side. Good defense. Loose ball and scramble around the circle, two players on the floor. Jump ball.

23 seconds.

Elroy and a taller Kenyon player jumped. There was a wild scramble but Phil came up with the ball.

18 seconds.

Ryan to O'Reilly. O'Reilly to Schulz. Schulz to Eppen.

Be careful now, we only need one basket.

8 seconds.

Ryan to Schulz. Schulz bounce pass to Haas. Haas to O'Reilly, almost intercepted. O'Reilly saves the ball.

2 seconds.

Set your feet, Lefty. Only two seconds left, but you've got time—don't hurry. Don't listen to the crowd. Just look at that basket. You can do it, Lefty; you can make the shot. Let it go. Send it on its way . . .

1 second.

The ball darted from Lefty's sweaty hands to form a beautiful arc to the basket twenty-one feet away. It rose gracefully until reaching its pinnacle, then began a gentle descent. It was such a beautiful shot. If it had been colored it would have been a rainbow. The ball seemed suspended in the air, hardly moving. In slow motion it descended toward the basket, but was it on line? Would it split the nets giving Goodhue its long-awaited victory over Kenyon? Fans were on their feet hollering and yelling as it floated closer and closer to the basket. There was nothing Lefty could do now, so he just stood there watching the trajectory of the ball. Closer now, even closer. Then, yes! It was good! The ball split the middle of the basket sending the net flipping up over the rim. Goodhue had won.

0 seconds.

We won the subdistrict tournament. Champions. Lefty and the team and an eight-year-old boy's prayers conquered Kenyon. After years of frustration we finally had won a subdistrict championship. After years of losing to Wanamingo or Kenyon, Goodhue finally prevailed. Our armed forces were still fighting in France, Germany and the South Pacific, but for a moment, the war wasn't quite as important. Tonight, we were victorious on our own front. We rode home with our hearts full and heads held high, comfy in Dad's truck.

The victory over Kenyon had been on a Saturday night. It would be a long wait until the start of the district tournament the following Tuesday. District tournament, just imagine it. Even the old-timers couldn't remember the last time we had been to the district. Did we even have a chance? Goodhue had been playing Wanamingo, West Concord, Pine Island, Zumbrota and Kenyon for so many years in the subdistricts that we were unfamiliar with the teams in the district tournament—Morristown, Faribault, Northfield, Owatonna. Where were these towns?

On Sunday we heard Goodhue would play Morristown in the first game, a town I had never visited because the war was on and there was gas rationing and Dad's Model A didn't travel far from town. We only drove five miles to St. Columbkill's in Belle Creek, or to Red Wing to visit relatives, but *never* to Northfield, Faribault, Owatonna, Morristown. Suddenly, I needed to become familiar with those bigger district-tournament towns.

Population was important to our citizens. Only four hundred fifty people lived in the village, whereas most towns around us were bigger. Zumbrota, Red Wing, Rochester, Kenyon, even Wanamingo was bigger. We thought students from other towns were bigger, smarter, prettier, more handsome, better basketball players. We were apprehensive about playing those larger schools. Well, maybe the team wasn't, but I was. Were Morristownians Lutheran, Methodist or Catholic?

The districts were held at Northfield High School. I don't believe anything that big had happened in Northfield since Jesse James and his brothers held up the Northfield State Bank in 1876.

They sauntered into Northfield, Jesse riding up front on his white stallion, his brothers flanking him on both sides. They didn't ride fast; in fact, they trotted very slowly as they rode into town from the east. It had been a tiresome, stifling hot, dusty ride across southern Minnesota. Their throats were parched and their rumps were sore. They were tired, hungry, thirsty and broke. They needed money and food, and they needed it now.

Northfield was a sleepy jerkwater town in 1876; surely they could rob a bank with no trouble and then be on their way west to the Rockies and gold! Jesse squinted at his watch and noticed it was high noon, a good time to rob a bank, because most folks would have gone home to eat a little lunch. Even so, the James Gang had robbed many a bank and never took their work lightly. A person could run into trouble robbing banks and Jesse knew it.

They slid around the corner, four horses abreast, trotting slowly until they saw the bank down the street. It looked good to Jesse, but Frank was nervous; something didn't seem right. Jesse wanted to get the job done and get out of Northfield, get out of Minnesota. The gang stopped a block from the bank to water their mounts and get a better view of the layout. Frank thought they should wait a couple of hours until the sun went down, but Jesse was restless and wanted to get on with it. He was the boss—he won the argument. "Let's get on with it, boys."

They mounted their steeds, sat high in their saddles and headed toward the bank. There was only one sway-backed mare and wagon tied to the hitching post in front of the bank. Two old-timers were dozing on a bench in front of the Gilded Garter Saloon across the street. The sound of an irritating out-of-tune piano filtered out of the saloon into the powdery street. A gust of wind kicked up a spiral of dust causing the gang to tie bandannas around their faces. They rode up to the bank, dismounted and walked in, guns on hips. A stooped, little lady was at the teller's window as Jesse strode up, shoved her aside, stuck a Colt 45 in the teller's face and demanded all the money. Will Jones, the teller, was so nervous he hurriedly placed the money in a bank bag. Five thousand dollars. It was easy. The other gang members were covering the windows—nothing happening on the street, just those old-timers sleeping, and that damn piano . . .

It was too easy. They walked out, mounted their horses and trotted down the street. Suddenly, a shot

*rang out. "Where in hell are those shots coming from?"
Jesse screamed. A bullet ripped into Frank's leg. He got
so mad he dismounted and began firing back at the
bank. Tom Wilson lived upstairs over the bank and
happened to look out the window as the gang was
making its getaway. Tom was mad. He had all of his
savings in that bank and the James Gang wasn't going
to escape without a fight. For fifteen minutes, a great
gunfight erupted. There was considerable shooting,
but little killing. Tom Wilson got nicked on the hand;
Frank James hit in the leg, but other than one dead
horse, all the James Gang escaped. They raced out of
town with Tom's money, never to return to Northfield,
and that damn piano player was still playing.*

The gunshot holes are still visible in the walls of the Northfield State Bank. It was a big day that day the James Gang rode into
town, probably the biggest day Northfield had ever seen, but that
was all to change. March 15, 1944 would now be the biggest day.
Goodhue was playing Morristown.

I had been fearful of larger towns, but I found out later that
Morristown was only a little burg, a hole-in-the-wall town west of
Faribault. Surely the Goodhue Wildcats could conquer them. We
did. Phil, Burt and the boys had no trouble defeating Morristown.
The Wildcats were wild indeed as they roared through the first
game of the district tournament, but things would be different
against Northfield. There was another shoot-out coming, Jesse.
The game would be a battle between David and Goliath. Goodhue
versus Northfield. How could David succeed against Goliath,
again?

The ride to Northfield was frigid and frosty in the back of
Dad's International. Although I was only four-foot-six and could
huddle between the adults, I was still cold. I tried to keep my mind
off the cold by saying a rosary for victory, but I didn't want to take
off my mittens to run the beads.

The Goodhue boys played poorly during the first half. I
believe they too thought they didn't have a chance against North-

field. The Wildcats entered the game with preconceived ideas: surely, a little farming-community team didn't stand a chance against city slickers. Our team had trotted onto the floor with timid looks on their faces and fear in their eyes, but coach Tomfohr had encouraged them to be courageous. He said farm and village boys could beat city slickers any old day of the week, but throughout much of the first half, it didn't look as if he had convinced them. They lost the ball time after time and couldn't even make a lay-up. The score at the end of the first half was Northfield 21, Goodhue 14.

Now, Karl was normally a mild-mannered man when selling tractors or cultivators at his shop, but not during that halftime in the locker room. He was mad. He knew Goodhue was a better team than Northfield, so he barked at his team. He said they were a bunch of wimps and why did they even bother coming to North-field. He said that if the James Gang had been wimps they would have been killed before they rode out of town. He said their skeletons would still be sprawled in front of the bank and that damn piano player would still be playing out-of-tune boogie-woogie. He yelled, "JESSE JAMES WASN'T A WIMP AND NEITHER ARE YOU!" That team trotted to floor with bank-robbing vengeance in the second half. GHS captured every loose ball, every jump ball, shot better than the James Gang then rode out of town.

Goodhue 39. Northfield 37.

To wait until Friday night for the finals was almost more than I could stand. I certainly couldn't think about arithmetic, reading or geography. The only thing I could do was pray for a victory in the finals against Waseca. How many victories did God have left? I was convinced that it was Phil's rebounding and Lefty's shooting and my praying that were securing these wins. Maybe God would come through one more time.

Friday. Dad finished his milk route early, made a quick trip to the South St. Paul Stockyards with a load of squealing hogs, then hurried back to hose down the truck. He parked the International by the hotel at four o'clock. Thirty-five fans jammed into the cattle truck standing back to back, belly to belly like a load of hogs going to market, but we were going to Northfield hoping for a different kind of slaughter.

The Goodhue contingent filed into the gym and took the seats in the south bleachers. Some villagers with better gas rationing stickers drove to Northfield in the comfort of a warm car. They were in the bleachers when we entered. Those Waseca boys sure looked huge. How could we hope to beat them and win our first district title?

The first-half was rugged. Goodhue wasn't as intimidated as against Northfield, but these Waseca boys were very good. Back and forth, jump, shoot, struggle, fight.

Hail, hail the purple and white
Wildcats in spirit, Wildcats in . . .

Halftime score, 31 to 31. Was it really possible to win?

The second half began with the teams racing up and down the floor. Two points didn't separate them throughout the third quarter. With the score tied at 42 and only a minute left, Waseca had possession of the ball on the far sideline. It didn't look good for us. Waseca was so good and they could dribble so well that I was sure they would be able to keep the ball away from us until the last few seconds when they would then shoot and win. They attacked down the floor. Pass left, then right. Bounce pass into the corner, then back out to the top of the circle.

15 seconds.

A pass under the basket for a lay-up. No good! Eyestone picked off the rebound.

7 seconds

Time-out, Goodhue.

The team approached the bench and surrounded Karl. He looked directly into their eyes—calm, deliberate, strong. The players shifted from one foot to the other looking at the floor. Karl said firmly, "You can do it, fellas. We can beat Waseca. Now here's what I want you to do. Dick, take the ball out; throw a bounce pass to Phil in the corner. Phil, pass to Lefty out front, then Lefty, fake one of your famous two-handed set shots. As your defender comes toward you, toss a bounce pass back to Phil on the baseline—he should be open. Phil, put 'er in for two points and the win. Let's go."

The play worked perfectly. Lefty got the ball, faked, passed to Phil on the baseline and Phil lifted a five-footer toward the basket. It was good from the moment it left his hand.

GOODHUE WINS THE DISTRICT TOURNAMENT! GOODHUE 47, WASECA 45!

Jesse James, stay out of town. Goodhue owns Northfield now.

My joy was unbelievable. I believed in the power of prayer, but I never knew it was this powerful.

The village erupted after the district finals. Fans headed to Shelstad's Cafe on lower street for a celebration. It was already packed when Dad pulled his truck up to the front door to unload more fanatics. Everyone was rejoicing, having a few beers, and for me, a Pepsi. I was caught up in the excitement of the reveling, eating more candy than I should have. But it didn't matter. GHS had won its first District Four Basketball Tournament in the history of the school. David had beaten Goliath . . . again. On to Rochester and the regional tournament.

If I had been in a dither about the districts, I was absolutely frenetic about the regionals. They were only two games away from the state tournament in Minneapolis where the Golden Gophers played. I absolutely could not comprehend that.

GHS drew Rochester in the first round. Imagine! Goodhue versus Rochester, a city of thirty thousand. We didn't have that many folks in the entire county let alone one town. *David* was still small but *Goliath* had suddenly grown much larger. How many victories did God have left?

Dad parked his International by the hotel again to transport fans to Rochester. We were scheduled to play in game one, followed by Austin versus Mountain Lake. If we could beat Rochester we would meet the winner of the Austin-Mountain Lake game to progress to the state tournament.

The team was exceptionally nervous. I could tell they were in awe of the immense Auditorium. Our gym held only one hundred fifty people packed to the rafters, but Rochester Auditorium held four thousand. The team had momentarily lost its sense of space. During warm-ups, Lefty couldn't hit his set shots because he didn't have a reference point. Eugene had the willies.

Goodhue quickly fell behind, 10 to 0. Every shot they attempted missed the basket. Not only didn't they go in, they didn't even hit the rim. The auditorium was too big. Karl called time-out. "Boys, we're having a little trouble getting our aim and distance right. I want you to relax. Pretend all these people aren't here and we're just playing in our own gym. Don't look into the seats; concentrate on the floor and the basket. Let's go."

Eugene scored Goodhue's first two points. The ice was broken. Rochester was good and very experienced at tournament play. They had developed good teams, year after year, and had even won the state tournament several times. How could our team ever beat them?

Halftime score: Rochester 35, Goodhue 22.

Karl encouraged the boys in the locker room. He was soft-spoken, simply saying they were a fantastic team and fantastic boys. He was proud of them. He said if they could keep their concentration they could beat the former state champions. "Let's go, boys. Get a victory for ol' GHS."

Burt sank a ten-footer, then Phil dropped a hook shot; Lefty drilled a twenty-foot two-hander. Goodhue quickly closed the gap to 35 - 28. We had a chance. The teams dueled fiercely through the third quarter, but the Wildcats could never quite catch the Rockets.

Fourth quarter. Rochester kept attacking, getting rebounds and dribbling quickly down the floor. It didn't look good for us.

Two minutes remaining. Rochester 41, Goodhue 37.

We were trailing and not catching up. Down to the final minute now. A basket by Eugene, then Rochester scored again. Only a few seconds left . . . *Oh, Lord, it doesn't look good.*

Seven seconds . . . six . . . five . . . four . . . three. Oh, no, this can't happen, can it? Two seconds . . . one . . .

Just one more miracle.

0 Seconds.

"No! We have more time, don't we? The clock's wrong, isn't it, Dad? Tell me the game isn't over. Tell me we didn't lose."

The drive back to Goodhue was bitter, freezing, endless, grave-digging cold. Tears froze on my nose and mouth even though I huddled between the moaning adults.

The team had come a long way. It was the best GHS team we had ever seen. But I saw things more accurately from that time on. Oh, I kept praying but I realized even though God could do anything he wanted, maybe sometimes he chose not to. I realized that he liked Lutherans and Methodists, too. I realized he wasn't only a Catholic God; he was just God, everybody's God.

"God, bless the boys from Goodhue; oh, yes, bless the boys from Rochester, too."

Our season ended, but there were still a couple of weeks of tournament play remaining. The regional winners would meet at Williams' Arena on the University of Minnesota campus to crown the new state champion. State champion was every boy's dream, but it was not to be for the Goodhue team this year. Wait until next year, or the year after, or the year after that. Maybe . . . a lifetime.

Chapter 6

Clarinet Soliloquy

GHS Concert Band, 1947

I DON'T KNOW IF IT WAS THE SONOROUS SOUND OR THE glistening silver that first led me to the instrument, or maybe listening to Benny Goodman or Artie Shaw on a distant-city radio station from Chicago, New York or Kansas City while reclining in bed on a Saturday night watching the moonlight slither through the apple tree, but I certainly was enamored by the clarinet. I knew that when Mother and Dad let me begin band I would choose it.

_____1

Squeaks And Squawks

I wanted to play like Benny Goodman, Artie Shaw and Woody Herman. There was to be no loud, obnoxious trumpet playing for me. That wasn't my style. The soft pearl-shaped melodious tones that spun from Benny's clarinet are what I wanted to hear and play myself someday. Benny would set the clarinet in his mouth, hold it gently with one hand while counting off the beat for his band, and then swing into *Sing, Sing, Sing* or *Let's Dance,* or *Don't Be That Way.*

I was concerned about the multitude of keys, holes and mechanisms on the clarinet, though. I didn't understand, in sixth grade, how I would master all of them. I'll admit there was a moment when I considered choosing the trumpet, because it had only three valves to operate. That certainly looked easier than mastering twenty-five keys and levers.

Charles Wood was Goodhue's music man in 1947. He drove into town from County Road No. 9 in a '42 jalopy singing *Ah, Sweet Mystery of Life,* and Nelson Eddy songs from Sigmund Romberg's *Student Prince.* He played French Horn themes from Richard Wagner's *Die Meistersinger*, and peddled his wares. "We're going to start a band, folks, right here in Prairie City. We're going to have a band, and I want you children to look at these shiny new instruments. Step up. Look at them, touch them. Look at our new band uniforms with braid and chevrons and pants with shiny stripes, and look at this hat! When wearing it, any boy or girl will be the pride of Minnesota. That's right, I said the pride of Minnesota. And when you wear this uniform, playing clarinet, marching down the street past the hotel and Art's Bar and Diercks' Market and Jesse's Hardware, everyone in town will stop, look, and listen. You'll be a hero, the toast of the town!"

What child could refuse a pitch like that? I was already hooked just looking at the instruments, but when Mr. Wood began talking about being a hero and the toast of the town . . . well, that was the icing on the cake. That's all I needed. "I want to play the clarinet, Dad."

"Do you really think so, Jimmy? Looks difficult to me."

"Yes, I'm sure that's the instrument I want to play, but . . . on the other hand . . . I don't know. I like the cornet, too. Bobby Hackett plays it, and Louis Armstrong is good . . . it might be fun."

"It looks easier to me than the clarinet with all those keys and levers. Shoot, we had farm machinery on the home place that didn't have as many levers and rods as that clarinet. You think you could manage all that hardware?"

"Uh huh. That's the instrument I want, because I want to have a band of my own someday. I want to play on the radio at night, and buy a bus to travel across country playing in dance halls. And I want to make records and have my picture on music books. Let's buy the clarinet."

My formal music life began that September evening. Little did I know what impact choosing the clarinet would have on my career. But it was a good choice. How many times can we look back on choices we made and say it was a good decision.

Dad purchased a Conn clarinet for $69.95. At home that evening, I didn't know what to do other than look at it. Three sections were set in individual compartments, and there was a part Mr. Wood said was a mouthpiece, also a Legionnaire or ligature or some word like that. I didn't understand. He said to take it home and look at it, but not try to put it together before our first band lesson Monday morning. That was a lot to expect—to buy a clarinet and then not be able to play it? Well, of course I was going to play it. I was anxious to get a head start on being the toast of the town. I was going to be Goodhue's answer to Benny Goodman.

"Ladies and Gentlemen! From Gorman's Dream-land Ballroom overlooking downtown Goodhue, we

*bring you the sweet sound of Jimmy Franklin and his
orchestra. Jimmy has put together a wonderful band
for your listening and dancing pleasure. I hope you
enjoy our broadcast tonight brought to you by the folks
at Heaney and Gorman's Meat Market. Remember,
when you're passing through town, don't stop without
buying some of that delicious, salty, tangy Heaney's
dried beef, and while you're at it, pick up some sausage
too!*

*And now, here's what you've been waiting for . . .
Jimmy Franklin!"*

"Jimmy, it's getting late. Time for bed. You've been looking
at that clarinet for an hour. It'll be there in the morning."

"Oh, Mom, just a little while longer. Don't you think I could
put it together just once?"

"Mr. Wood said you could only look; besides, you don't know
how to assemble all those pieces, and we just paid $69 dollars of
hard-earned money for it, and you know money doesn't grow on
trees around here!"

"Come on, just one time."

"You just run up to bed. You can play in band class on
Monday."

I couldn't sleep. Would you expect a boy who has just
received a new clarinet to sleep, a boy who would soon be sitting
on a band stand with Benny or Artie or Woody or maybe even
Louis? I vaulted the stairs, flew into bed, turned on my Setchell-
Carlson radio and picked up New York's Waldorf-Astoria broadcast. "From the Starlight Roof high atop the Waldorf-Astoria Hotel
in New York City, we bring you the sounds of Sammy Kaye and his
orchestra—Swing and sway with Sammy Kaye." I became drowsy
listening to the sweet, dulcet sounds of Sammy's orchestra. I felt
I was being transported out of my bed, through the apple tree, over
the catawampus cross of Holy Trinity, over the baseball diamond
and out across Elmer Bremer's beanfield.

Soon, I was passing high above Minneapolis, then onto Chicago. I looked down to see the Liberty Bell in Philadelphia, and before long, I was floating over New York City, bearing down on the Waldorf-Astoria.

"Ladies and Gentlemen. We have a special treat for you this evening. Along with the Sammy Kaye Orchestra, we are going to feature a young new talent coming to us all the way from Minnesota, one of those cowboy states. But this little fellow isn't a cowboy, I'll tell you that. He doesn't rope calves and steers, but I'll tell you one thing he can rope. That's your heart. Wait until you hear him play. Here is Jimmy Franklin."

I stepped to the front of the band, looked at Sammy, and set my clarinet. The dancers had gathered in front of the bandstand looking directly at me. I was nervous because I'd only had a couple of lessons on this thing and . . . here goes. I closed my eyes and let the music flow like the smoke from a Chesterfield cigarette, slowly curling through the chandeliers . . .

I was playing at the Waldorf, but my music was being sent over the airwaves to that prairie where the cowboys roam and the cattle feed on prairie weed . . .

Mother and Dad tuned in in the middle of the broadcast . . . "Tom, do you recognize that new clarinet player with the Sammy Kaye Orchestra?"

"No, but he sure has a good sound."

"I didn't know Sammy had a clarinet player that sounded like Goodman. Benny won't be too happy when he hears about it."

"You know, Lucille, I think I recognize that sound."

"It does sound familiar now that you mention it."

"I feel I've heard that silvery-tone before. It's round and mellow, even a country quality to it."

"He sounds a little like the clarinet player in Whoopee John's Orchestra, but what would he be doing playing with Sammy Kaye?"

"I agree but even more familiar than that."

"Lucille, have you checked on Jimmy lately? Did he go to bed or is he sitting on the porch?"

"I think he's in bed. I'll check."

Mother trudged up the stairs, found me asleep with my new clarinet beside my pillow, a picture of Benny Goodman on the bed. She placed the clarinet on the dresser along with Benny's picture, then went back downstairs. "He's asleep . . . had his clarinet on the bed along with Benny's picture. He's probably having good dreams. You know, that really is a sweet clarinetist with Sammy."

Reality struck Monday morning during my first lesson with Mr. Wood. The sounds I had dreamed about didn't come easily. It appeared that becoming another Benny Goodman wasn't going to be as easy as I had imagined. Mr. Wood helped me assemble the clarinet then showed me how to place it into my mouth. He said something about forming an *armchair* or *embouchure*. I didn't understand the word, but tried to get my teeth and lips around the mouthpiece. Then he told me to blow air through it as if I were blowing out candles at my birthday party. I didn't see the similarity, but I gave it a try.

In retrospect, I don't know how Mr. Wood tolerated teaching music to me and other beginners. He entered the profession because he enjoyed music, but ended up listening to cacophonous sounds beyond his imagination. Why would he want to do that? What did he get out of hearing a kid squeak and squawk through lessons? How did he have any confidence those discordant sounds would ever turn into music?

By the end of lesson one I had learned how to assemble and disassemble the clarinet, how to place a reed on the mouthpiece, how to form an embouchure, and how to squeak and squawk. I was happy. The sounds weren't what I had anticipated, not sounding anything like Benny, but they did sound a little like music I heard Saturday nights in front of Anderson's Hall downtown. I was going to be the toast of the town; however, the look on Mr. Wood's face didn't reflect my exuberance. "Gee thanks, Mr. Wood. I'm going to like this clarinet, see you in a couple of days."

"All right, Benny, I mean Jimmy. Practice hard now."

Squeaks and squawks gradually gave way to reasonable sounding tones. Random foot beating gradually gave way to steady eighth, quarter and half notes. I worked my way through the *Belwin Band Builder, Book One*, through *Frere Jacques*, and *Three Blind Mice* so by the time I finished my first year of lessons I could even play *Lightly Row* on page thirteen of *Rubank Book One*. That was significant because *Lightly Row* had been the benchmark for Goodhue's fledgling instrumentalists. Many aspirants started lessons on clarinets, flutes, trombones, tubas, snare drums and cornets, but never progressed farther than *Lightly Row*.

The song wasn't that difficult, but Noisy Rusch never progressed beyond *Lightly Row*. He honked in band for many years, but *Lightly Row* was his high water mark as a musician. Glen "Sunkist Orange" Dankers and his cornet did progress all the way to *Humoreske* with dotted-eighth and sixteenth notes at the end of the book. John Stuber passed *Lightly Row*. He played clarinet almost as good as Benny. He was a high school senior playing first chair clarinet in band when I was a sixth grader. John progressed all the way to Carl Maria von Weber's *First Clarinet Concerto*. He didn't stop at *Lightly Row*, but Noisy did. That was all right for Noisy, though, because he wasn't interested in playing the written notes anyway. He just liked setting that tenor sax mouthpiece and blowing. He thought that if he produced considerable noise— Noisy Rusch—things would be fine. Placing notes in the right place at the right time wasn't a great concern to him, although it was to Mr. Wood. "Lyle, do you think you could play those quarter notes more carefully?"

"Sure, Mr. Wood, I can do it. No big deal."

But he never did . . . never changed his ways with that sax.

2

Less Than Endearing Charms

The Five joined band in sixth grade, all beginning that same September evening. Bob, Bets Lunde and I chose the clarinet, but Mary Benda and Janice Cook chose the trombone. We honked, squeaked and blatted, but persisted, miraculously even playing a few recognizable tunes by the end of the year. I loved my clarinet almost as much as my basketball. I improved enough that Mr. Wood asked me to play a solo at the spring band concert. "I guess so, but I'm not sure. I might get nervous and Mother and Dad . . . Mother would probably cry . . . can I think about it for awhile?"

"Yes, Jimmy. If you decide to do it, I would like you to play *Believe Me, If All Those Endearing Young Charms*. You like it, don't you?"

"Sure, Mr. Wood, it's nice, but I would rather play *Stompin' at the Savoy* or *King Porter Stomp*—one of Benny's songs."

"You're ambitious, but I think we better wait a couple of years for those. I think *Believe Me, If All Those Endearing Young Charms* would be just right for your first solo."

Mom and Dad encouraged me to play the solo. I decided to do it, but thought Benny's first public solo wasn't *Believe Me, If All Those Endearing Young Charms*. It probably was *Sing, Sing, Sing*, or *Down South Camp Meeting*. But it was the way I began my performance career.

For the next month my routine was school, sack potatoes, eat supper, practice my solo. Believe me . . . *Believe Me, If All Those Endearing Young Charms* had lost all its charm by the time the spring concert arrived. The family had had about as much charm as they could tolerate. There wasn't any *dear* left in *Endearing*. After my first days of practice the house would suddenly become quiet as I began practicing. I initially thought they were being nice to me by being quiet, but one day I needed a drink of water and when I went downstairs I found the house empty.

Believe me, if all those endearing young charms,
Which I gaze on so fondly today,
Were to change by tomorrow, and fleet in my arms,
Like fairy gifts fading away.

Again: Smoother on the C to D. Play the eighth notes more evenly. Don't rush. Is this the way Benny started?

Finally, it was one day before the concert. I was nervous, in an accelerated state of worriment.

How did I get myself into this predicament? I don't like Believe Me, If All Those Endearing Young Charms. *Can't I play* King Porter Stomp?

It should come as no surprise that Goodhue didn't have a local symphony orchestra, and it was a long drive to Minneapolis to hear one; consequently, the townsfolk had to tolerate the school band for their musical entertainment. And most people didn't own a phonograph in 1947, either. Maybe that was good, though, because they couldn't compare our band to other ensembles.

The GHS Concert Band began the program with the finale to Dvorak's *New World Symphony.* Poor Dvorak. But the audience liked it. They clapped, hollered and stomped their feet. Next, we played selections from *Die Meistersinger*, an opera about German singers. Mr. Wood thought it would please those of German ancestry. Then a Norwegian hymn for the Norwegians, a Swedish march for the Swedes, and finally *Londonderry Air* for the Irish. The *Air* brought the house down. Our audiences weren't very cultured in the forties, but they knew what they liked and weren't afraid to demonstrate it.

Much too soon, it was time for my solo. After the shouting and whistling died down, Mr. Wood looked at me in the clarinet section, and with his eyes, asked me if I was ready. I glanced into the audience to see more people than I wanted to see. I had been practicing alone in my bedroom, accustomed to playing for myself. I had never played in front of so many people before. Yes, I had played for Grandmother Franklin when she visited, "Play us a nice song, Jimmy."

"Oh, Mom, do I have to? I want to go out and play baseball."

"Just one. How about *Lightly Row*?"

Every child who ever took music lessons went through the ordeal. Every grandmother and grandfather who ever sat through a piano or clarinet solo went through the ordeal.

I looked back at Mr. Wood with fear written on my face. My eyes were saying, No! My body was saying, No! My Sahara-dry mouth was saying, No! My trembling hands were saying, "No! We can't find the keys," and my feet were saying "No! We can't stand up." Everything I owned was saying, NO! NO! NO!

John Stuber leaned over to whisper in my ear, "Come on, Benny, show them your stuff."

"Did you call me Benny?"

"Yeah, come on, Benny. Get up there and show them your stuff with *King Porter Stomp*."

Did John really think I was that good? He was my idol and could play Mozart and Carl Maria von Weber and I could only play *Lightly Row* and part of the *Clarinet Polka*. I was hoping desperately I could play *Believe Me, If All Those Endearing Young Charms*.

"JIMMY! GET UP THERE AND GIVE THEM HELL!" Noisy hollered from the saxophone section.

"Come on, Jimmy, you can do it," Jimmy Lohman whispered from the cornet section.

From the clarinet section I heard Sandbox Bob whisper, "Go for it, Jimmy."

I rose from my chair. I don't know how I did it. I don't think I did it on my own, because my legs weren't working that well, but I shuffled toward Mr. Wood. He gently put his hand on my shoulder and led me to the front of the band. I was terrified. All I could see were faces and legs and arms and . . . Mother crying, tears welling up in her eyes, running down her face . . . *Jesus, Mary, and Joseph, help me through this.*

She had her rosary out, lips moving rapidly. She had been

saying a novena on my behalf for the past month; she wasn't about to stop until this was over. She had been attending Saturday morning Mass, and had spent a fortune on special intention votive candles. I didn't know if she would make it. I didn't know if I would make it.

Mr. Wood stepped onto the podium. He glanced at me. I gave some kind of motion that apparently indicated yes, and the band charged into its first notes. After sixteen measures it was time for my entrance. It didn't happen. I started in the right place, but when I blew into the clarinet nothing came out. After a couple of attempts Mr. Wood stopped the band, came over to me and asked if I was all right. "I can't get any air to go through this thing."

"Just relax and loosen your embouchure. You're pinching the reed too tightly."

I could see Mother moving rapidly through her beads. Mr. Wood again gave the downbeat, the band began its introduction once again.

Two more measures till I enter. God, please help me get a note or two out.

Nothing, not a single clarinet note broke the stale air of that auditorium. I huffed and puffed and blew and farted until I was red in the face, but nary a sound emerged. There was more air coming out of my butt than my clarinet. I was passing more gas than Northern States Power. Mr. Wood stopped. The band stopped. Mother's heart stopped! Terrible silence hung over the auditorium. I looked at my clarinet. Why couldn't I get any sound to come out. It had worked all right an hour ago in my bedroom. I felt a light touch on my shoulder. I looked up. John was standing beside me. He bent over to whisper in my ear. "Benny, you're the best damn little clarinet player in Goodhue County. There isn't a clarinet player that can even come close to you. I can play Mozart and von Weber, but you've got style. You can play *Believe Me, If All Those Endearing Young Charms* just like Goodman plays *King Porter Stomp*. Go for it. Make your mother proud of you!" I turned to Mr. Wood with renewed confidence. I told him to give another downbeat. He did. The band played the introduction for the third time. Four measures until I come in . . . three . . . two . . . one . . .

Ladies and gentlemen! From the great city of New York and the beautiful Waldorf-Astoria Hotel, we present to you the Benny Goodman Orchestra with special guest clarinetist, Jimmy Franklin. Chesterfield cigarettes and Ivory soap bring you this special broadcast. Pick up a pack and a bar and enjoy the sound of Jimmy Franklin with the Benny Goodman orchestra . . .

My clarinet tones soared above the Waldorf, above the skyscrapers of New York, above the Hudson River and the Empire State Building. My tone was beautiful as the melodies floated over the audience on the dance floor, over the airwaves to Minnesota.

Benny stood in the corner directing the band and listening to me in amazement. He was transfigured. He knew he was an excellent clarinetist, but he was awestruck as he heard me play. He set his clarinet down, stopped conducting the band and just listened. He had never heard a clarinetist play so beautifully, so cleanly, so rapidly. He had never heard such a clear, distinctive melody. He had never heard technique and improvisation like this. The dancers stopped dancing. The band stopped playing. The waitresses stopped serving. The bar tenders stopped tending. Everything and everyone stopped, except me. I just kept on playing . . .

My fingers were doing things I didn't know they could do. I heard chords and harmony and melody and music I didn't know I had in me. Where were these melodies coming from? I played on and Benny listened, the band listened, the dancers listened, the waitresses listened, the bartenders listened. My fingers left my hands. They were magical.

I played into the stratosphere of the clarinet range. I played notes that weren't on the clarinet, and then I stopped. Silence filled the Starlight Roof ballroom. For fifteen long seconds, there was deathly silence, but then it was suddenly broken by tremendous applause. A roar enveloped the dance hall. I had transported those people into another world. I had transported them into the world I was in. They loved it. I loved it. I looked at Benny in the corner. He was sad. He didn't say a word, but instead, slowly took out his clarinet case, wiped his reed, put his clarinet into the case and plodded out the back door toward the Hudson River.

Mr. Wood looked at me two measures before my entry. I had a smile on my face. He knew I would be all right this time. I came in, on time. From the first note, I charmed the audience. I looked at Mother and saw tension leave her face, color return to her brow. The melody flowed from my clarinet, gently rose over the balcony and into the farthest corners of the auditorium. The normally boisterous folks from Bellechester and Belle Creek were silenced. My simple little melody touched their hearts that night.

Thou would'st still be ador'd, as this moment thou art,
Let thy loveliness fade as it will,
And around the dear ruin each wish of my heart,
Would entwine itself verdantly still.

Thanks, John. Thanks, Mr. Wood. Thanks, Benny.

3

Benny, Louis, Tommy, Woody—The Band

Music performance grabbed me tightly that night and never let go. Oh, I still liked dribbling my basketball; in fact, I became adept at bouncing a basketball and playing clarinet simultaneously, at least left-handed clarinet. I could play the first few notes of *Believe me* . . . with my left hand while bouncing the basketball with my right. That was my routine—balls and music, music and balls. It might have been better had I selected only one activity, but it wasn't to be.

In Goodhue, in 1948, playing sports was a passage into manhood. I had a dilemma. The music spirit was embedded deep in my soul—no one was likely to get it out.

Our family didn't own a phonograph, so my music listening was relegated to late-night radio broadcasts from far off cities. Many radio shows in the forties were dedicated completely to music. When I couldn't pull in a music show, I would shuffle down to Mary Ann McHugh's house to listen to records on her 45 rpm player, one of the few in the village.

A couple of years after I began clarinet, I decided I needed an official music stand. I had difficulty practicing on the bed, and that wasn't the way Benny Goodman, Glenn Miller and Jimmy Dorsey did it. They had real music stands— *The Benny Goodman Orchestra*, *The Glenn Miller Orchestra*, *The Jimmy Dorsey Orchestra*. I wanted a music stand like that.

I asked Dad to make one. He began building a stand like Glenn's and Benny's. He purchased a sheet of plywood, drew some pencil marks, then cut out the bottom section. He screwed in two hinges so the stand would fold in the middle, then made a slanting top to hold my music. It was beautiful. He even let me paint it. I chose yellow for the bottom, red for the top; bright colors for a music stand, but just right for my orchestra. On the front I hand-painted, *Jimmy Franklin and his Orchestra: The Sweetest Music in Goodhue County.* I moved my practice sessions from my upstairs bedroom to the downstairs living room. My playing had improved considerably; consequently, the family didn't leave the house anymore when I began. I would set up my stand by the Heatrola, get out music and launch into a session playing for hours, or at least until it was time for a ballgame—Benny Goodman versus Mickey Mantle. Artie Shaw versus George Mikan. One minute I was playing clarinet at the Waldorf-Astoria, the next I was sinking a jump shot for the Lakers against the Boston Celtics. I jumped from bed not knowing whether to put on my basketball shoes or clarinet reed.

Seated behind the stand, caressing my clarinet, I could be playing anywhere. I had a big imagination. I could be playing Dixieland in New Orleans, Chicago-style jazz in Chicago, blues in

Kansas City, or sweet music in New York City. Closer to home, I could play with Fez Fritch and his Polka Dots from Zumbrota, the Kufus Brothers from Rochester, or Whoopee John Wilfart with his St. Paul band at the Prom Ballroom.

As quickly as Glenn Miller and I finished In The Mood, *we launched into* Moonlight Serenade *and* Stairway to the Stars. *No one had a reed sound like Glenn. He developed a unique voicing when he arranged his music with the clarinet on top of the saxes as the lead instrument. No one else had done that. It became the tonal trademark of the Miller orchestra. I was there with my music stand. I played that lead clarinet on* Stairway To The Stars!

My magical music stand permitted me to play with the great swing and jazz bands of the thirties and forties. I played with Louis Armstrong's Hot Five Jazz Band. I played with Sammy Kaye and Glenn Miller and Jimmy Dorsey and Tommy Dorsey. I played clarinet as the Modernaires crooned ballads. I backed up Frank Sinatra in the Tommy Dorsey Orchestra, and Tony Bennett in the Sammy Kaye Orchestra. I even played clarinet and cowbell for Spike Jones and his City Slickers. I swung on some of the great recording sessions with Woody Herman and his First Thundering Herd. I backed up Harry James when he recorded Ciribiribin. *I played alongside Stan Getz, Zoot Simms and Flip Phillips with Woody Herman's Four Brothers. I played duets with Benny all over the country as we rode the bus from the east coast to the west coast doing one night stands in every podunk town from Pennsylvania to Nebraska on Route 66. I played in more local opera houses than Richard Wagner. I was on the road every night. I was in heaven.*

I stood in front of the Jimmy Franklin Orchestra while muted trumpets played a cool riff and trombones blew lush harmonies underneath my solo. Gene Krupa played a four-to-the-bar beat on the bass drum as Teddy Wilson played obbligato counterpoint. It was a good band. We swung. We grooved.

*After soloing, my sax section played full five-part harmonies, running through the chord changes, singing a sweet vibrato that melted the hearts of the neighbors who had come to hear us play. All the great players of the forties played in my band. Every night they found their way to Goodhue to play in the Jimmy Franklin Orchestra. I don't know how they managed to find our house, but they did. Some rode the Dinky into town. Some drove in from County Road No. 9 while others mysteriously appeared with horn in hand. Woody Herman brought two arrangements—*Apple Honey, *and* Woodchopper's Ball. *A few years later Stan Kenton arrived with* Intermission Riff, *and Tommy Dorsey sat in on trombone while we played* The Song of India. *Brother Jimmy arrived with his arrangement of* So Rare, *and one special night Count Basie brought his entire orchestra to play earthy blues that filled our house with moaning saxes in the living room, lonesome trombones in the dining room, wailing trumpets in the kitchen and pulsating rhythm on the front porch. The Count let me play with his reed players. Duke Ellington arrived with* Prelude To A Kiss. *They all came.*

I was in Carnegie Hall with Goodman, Krupa and James. I swung Benny's One O'clock Jump *feeling the riffs driving, driving. I listened as Benny reached the top of his clarinet while the saxes, trumpets, and trombones played counterpoint behind him. I was right in the middle of that band. And I was at the Stardust Ballroom with the Glenn Miller Orchestra when we played* Johnson Rag, Chattanooga Choo Choo *and* I've Got a Gal in Kalamazoo. *I didn't know where Kalamazoo was but I could play the arrangement. I was in the clarinet and sax section to hear Tex Benecke solo and sing in* Tuxedo Junction, *and listen to the Modernaires*

'Don't Sit Under The Apple Tree With Anyone Else But Me.

I played Memories Of You *with Benny, Teddy and Lionel in the Goodman Sextet, solo clarinet with the Duke, duets with Woody, and Buddy De Franco. I played* One O'clock Jump *with Count Basie, and even some early Goodman tunes with the Fletcher Henderson Orchestra. I played* Ain't Misbehavin' *with Fats Waller.*

One Saturday evening in 1948, I received a phone call from Chicago. Benny had come down sick with the flu, and his manager wanted to know if I could make the 10 P.M. show at the Sherman House in The Loop. I said I probably could, but that I would have to ask Mother first. She didn't know I had received the call, so I was out of the house and out of town in a minute.

The boys in the band were worried about the date, but after they heard my first tones, their fears were set aside. After I finished my solo in Stompin' At The Savoy, *they gave me a big round of applause. What a great night. The mayor of Chicago came; Mr. Wrigley brought his gum. They had come to hear Benny, but left having heard Jimmy.*

Get out of town, Benny!

"Time for bed, Jimmy."

"Oh, Mom, I can't go now. We've got another set to play, and I'll be letting the boys down if I have to leave now."

"You just tell the band that Jimmy's mother said it's bedtime."

"I don't think they'll understand that, Mom."

"Well, I'll 'understand' you if you don't put your music stand away and get to bed. You have school tomorrow."

"I've got to go, boys. Got another job to play before this night is over. Hey, Benny! Let's swing out with Let's Dance, Stompin' at the Savoy, King Porter Stomp, One O'clock Jump, Avalon, Don't Be That Way, Sing Sing Sing . . ."

Chapter 7

Heaney & Gorman

Heaney & Gorman, 1951

I BECAME FAMILIAR WITH HEANEY & GORMAN ABOUT the same time I entered first grade. Hamburger, round steak, pot roast, headcheese, sweetbread, ham, pork chops, hog jowls, rump roast, bologna, liverwurst, spring fryers, herring and bread aromas attacked my nostrils when Mother took me to the store in 1942. I saw sawdust around the butcher's block, Procter & Gamble soap and Hill Brothers' coffee on the shelves, and twisted, sticky fly strips dangling from the ceiling imprisoning unwilling flies. Will, Dody, Dennis and a few more Heaney family members worked at the store. Cousin Davie Franklin was also a standard fixture for years. Little did I realize at that young age what an impact the Heaneys and that store would have on my life.

1

Will Heaney's Brood

The store had a wood floor, two butcher blocks, a refrigerated meat counter, and cones of string hanging from the ceiling behind the meat counter, above the butcher blocks, above the dairy case and over the produce. Pre-packaged foods had not been developed. Everything was tied with string.

Will Heaney used heavy waxed paper to wrap meat, then tied it with six feet of Heaney's best string. Some years later that same waxed paper provided me with the finest kite-flying paper in the village. Dennis would give me a long strip of paper from the dispenser behind the meat counter, then I would stretch it across two quarter-inch crucifix-shaped strips of pine wood, fasten it to a string perimeter, purchase eight hundred feet of kite-flying string from Jesse's Hardware to send that kite soaring. Meat-wrapping paper was the best kite-flying paper.

Will and Johanna Heaney, with the help of Mary Kelly, raised six children—Dennis, Josephine "Dody," Gerald, Richard, Mary Catherine and Elizabeth. There were more Heaneys than pork chops. Will and Johanna were decreed by the pope to raise a big family. They did. And they needed to fill that spacious two-story house on Second Avenue.

Dennis and Dody stayed in the village after graduation to work in the store. Elizabeth and Mary Catherine moved to Belle–

chester and Belle Creek to raise more Heaney offspring. Gerald and Richard escaped Goodhue's boundaries entirely. They left the rutted dirt streets, the sole one hundred-watt street light downtown, the lonesome Sunday afternoons, the surrounding golden wheatfields and tasseled fields of corn to move to greater fields in Duluth and Washington D. C. But they didn't really escape. They only *thought* they did.

You can't take a child away from his hometown. You can't have grown up in the village and not taken it with you. Goodhue is hard to discard. It's a part of you. You went to school there, were educated there. The stores, churches, water tank and school are imbedded in your memory forever. How could I ever forget Finney's Woods, County Road No. 9, The Goodhue Elevator, Jesse's Hardware, Diercks' Grocery, Eddie's Drugstore, Sundberg's Food Store, Stemman and Buck's Meat Market, Ole Haga's Furniture and Undertaking, Nei's Blacksmith Shop, Faye's Beauty Shop, Shelstad's Cafe, Sidney Berg's Shoe Shop, The Creamery, Postmaster Otto Drenckhahn, Bill Huebner's Blacksmith, The Goodhue Tribune, Diercks and Lunde Grocery, Arlene's Apparel Shop, The Streater Lumber Company, Eppen's Electric Shop, Rosener's Blacksmith Shop, Majerus Gas and Appliance, Uncle Dave's City Dray Line, the Goodhue Hatchery and Produce Company. Forgetting Lodermeier's Repair Shop, the Goodhue Laundromat, Holm Brothers Construction, Allers Construction, Goodhue Produce, Lohman's Standard Oil, Bremer's CO-OP and Inez's Beauty Shop just isn't possible. Erasing Ebe's Barber Shop, Faye's Beauty Shop, Buck's Cafe, Taylor's Eat Shop and John Berlinski's Corner Bar from my memory would be tantamount to sin of the worst kind. You can try to kick the dust from your boots, but you won't succeed. Many people leave their hometown never to look back, but that is to their disadvantage. They can move away, but they can't get away. Roots are important. "Hey! Scab."

"How ya doin' there, Ace?"

"Could be worse."

"How's she running?"

"Not so bad."

"Heckuva deal."

"Gettin' much?"

"Naw."

"So, you gonna get married, then?"

"You betcha."

"So, who you marryin', then?"

"Marryin' one of the Thomforde girls."

"A guy could do a lot worse."

"You got that right!"

Heaney's Market burned to the ground on a snowy, bitter cold January evening in 1945. But the family had been in the meat and grocery business since 1895; they weren't going to let a little fire stop them. They set up temporary quarters in a vacant building next to Swenson's Cafe on lower street until the new store was ready for occupancy in 1951. Heaney's Market moved back to Third Avenue across the street from Mans and Benda's Shell Station and Tomfohr's International Harvester Shop. Dody Heaney married George Gorman. They changed the sign to: Heaney and Gorman.

The new store was roomy with new meat, poultry, and dairy cases, spacious front glass windows, a walk-in freezer, and a toilet in the basement, a story in itself.

Dennis, Dody, George, Kelly and eventually ten or more Gorman children were my neighbors. Heaney and Gorman offered me my first regular job when Dad died suddenly in 1951. I worked daily after school, Saturdays and summers. They offered me a job, and a way for Mother to make ends meet.

2

Graveside

The cold, piercing rain pelted my face, stinging like a swarm of voracious mosquitoes. It mixed with my tears until they became one, tumbling down my cheeks, over my nose and mouth until they dropped in the mud beside the grave.

It had rained forever or so it seemed. Normally, Goodhue County didn't receive excessive rain, but this downpour was different. It was bad enough that Dad had died suddenly of a heart attack, but it was particularly horrible to be burying him in this torrential downpour on such an overcast, bitterly cold day. I shifted from one foot to the other and held on to Mother's hand as she wept violently while struggling to maintain her balance. On the other side of her were Rose and Tom, crying. Everyone was crying in the freezing rain. I looked at my mud-covered shoes as I peered down into the depths of the grave as Ole Haga slowly lowered Dad's coffin into the saturated ground. This was an awful day, a terrible day to be standing in the freezing rain and mud burying my dad. Any day would be a bad day to bury your father, but at least a sunny funeral day would have been better. A shining sun wouldn't have brought him back, but it would have made it a little easier for our family, Grandmother Franklin and Dad's friends—the volunteer fireman, Knights of Columbus, American Legion, his fishing buddies. It wasn't to be.

The wind blew harshly through the rustling corn stalks surrounding Belle Creek Cemetery causing the mourners to huddle together like cattle in an open pasture as Fr. Smith intoned over Dad's grave. I didn't really hear Father's words. I heard Latin being spoken, but I still didn't know what it meant. I shivered in the mud, staring into the grave. That was Dad down there. What had happened? I had known him only a few short years. How could he be gone so quickly? Fourteen years weren't enough for a boy to know his dad. Where would he be when I needed help? How could I learn to drive a car, fix my bicycle, and learn about girls without him? How could he be in a grave? It didn't make any sense.

". . . May his soul and the souls of all the faithful departed, through the mercy of God, rest in peace. Amen."

The rain turned to snow creating a gray, lifeless sky from horizon to horizon as American Legion members fired four volleys over his grave sending echoes rolling across the cornfield, and shudders through the huddled mourners. Dad had served in Germany during WWI, but the guns didn't help. Dad was dead. I didn't need guns to make it worse, but they were only doing their duty.

Mourners converged on Mother, "Come on, Lucille. It's all over now. Let's go home." She didn't want to leave the dark, cold graveside. She wanted to stay there forever and die with Thomas Bernard Franklin. She pushed the mourners away.

"I don't want to. Let me stay here with Tom."

"Come, Lucille. It's freezing here; you'll catch pneumonia."

I didn't want to leave either. It was snowing harder now, icicles forming on my face. My toes were freezing. It was so cold and wet in that grave. I didn't want to leave my dad down there. How could I go home to a warm house and leave him in the grave? That's not fair, God. If I left now, I would never see him again. Leaving the graveside would be final.

He had died three days ago. We received the bad news that he had had his third heart attack within a week. We drove furiously to St. John's Hospital, walked to Ole's mortuary to pick out his casket, chose his best suit to bury him in, greeted neighbors and relatives as we waked him in our living room for three nights, and prayed the rosary twenty times. With all of that activity it didn't really seem like he was dead, maybe just on a fishing trip for a few days. But now he was in his casket, in the vault, in the cold grave. This was for real. "I don't want to leave, Mother. Just let me stay here a while longer," I cried.

"Come on, Jimmy, you'll catch the death of cold. Your dad is all right now."

I took a step backwards and slipped in the mud, falling to my knees by the side of the open grave. As I slipped, mud tumbled into the grave sprinkling Dad's vault. I took more mud in my hands and tossed it into the grave. I fell to both knees grabbing big chunks of mud and tossing it into the grave. Uncle Dave came over and tried to lift me to my feet, but Mother said, "Let him be, Dave, let him be." I worked faster grabbing mud and furiously tossing it into the grave. The mourners huddled together, watching. I was covered with mud from head to foot. Then Tom joined me, then Rose, finally Mother bent over slowly and grabbed a handful of mud tossing it into the grave. Then the mourners sloshed through the mud grabbing handfuls of mud tossing it into the grave. Tears had turned to ice on my face, and as I attempted to wipe them away, I smeared my face and head, but I felt better. I slowly raised to my feet, tossed one last handful and whispered. "Good-bye, Dad. I'll be seeing you . . ."

3

Sacking Potatoes

One week after the funeral I began my first regular paying job at Heaney & Gorman dumping one-hundred-pound sacks of potatoes that towered to the ceiling, then sorting and packaging them for customers, many of Irish or German descent. Those folks loved potatoes. They couldn't serve a meal without potatoes.

We sold tons of potatoes at the store in a year's time. I would finish school, stroll downtown kicking a few stones along the way, give ol' Buck a pat behind his ear as he relaxed by the jail, stop at Swenson's Cafe for a chocolate cone, then trek to the store to spend the next hour dumping one hundred-pound sacks onto the floor, filling paper sacks with five, ten, fifteen pounds of spuds. It was a good job for a boy who had just lost his father.

Sacking potatoes taught a boy a lot about life. First, there was a knack in finding the correct string to open the sacks, and once it was emptied onto the floor there was a skill in scooping them into individual bags. You see, potatoes aren't just potatoes. They have character. Potatoes are like cats—no two are the same. Potatoes are like feathery snowflakes—no two entered Goodhue the same shape. George Gorman thought I was merely sacking in the back room, but little did he know I was gaining an education. There was a special type of potato I sacked for Mary Haas; Agnes O'Reilly received another type; Fr. Smith received holy potatoes, and I usually saved the worst for the Lutherans, because they were going to hell anyway. Why waste good potatoes?

I became so adept at bagging taters that George promoted me to head potato sacker and chief garbage boy. I was now also in charge of toting garbage to the incinerator each evening. Here was a boy moving up. While Bob, Jack, Lee, Larry, Bettie, Janice and Mary went home and studied after school, I sacked potatoes and toted rubbish. Two good jobs. Some people might laugh and say that burning the garbage wasn't much of a job, but a job is what you make it. You can either do a get-by job or you can do it with style whether you're a musician, a potato sacker or garbage boy.

I lugged towering loads of lettuce, peach, pear, meat, Campbell's soup and general refuse boxes to the incinerator behind the wool shed. I would carry as many boxes at one time as I could, because in that way I would get the job done sooner. Yet Dennis didn't see the logic in this procedure. He called it a lazy man's load. That never made sense to me. I grunted all the way to the incinerator thinking I was working hard while Dennis was saying it was a lazy man's load because I was carrying the garbage in one trip instead of several. What he didn't know was that if I made one trip instead of three, I would have a little more time to stand around the incinerator and rest for a few minutes. I was actually saving time. One heavy load to the incinerator, two or three minutes of relaxation, a leisurely stroll back to the store, and I had some spare time.

The job was a beginning—and it paid. Sacking potatoes and toting garbage paid fifty cents an hour. I was rich. Two hours every night after school plus eight hours on Saturday gave me enough money to gorge myself on all the ice cream I could eat at Swenson's, plus a little left over to help Mother meet those ends.

Donnie Luhman, George O'Reilly, Tom Franklin and Davie Franklin all worked at the store at one time or another during my tenure. They were my mentors. They taught me all the tricks of the store. They taught me to write my name in every conceivable place—on the basement beams, in the toilet, in the storeroom, under the butchering block, in the smokehouse, in the wool shed, and in the freezer. Writing your name for posterity was important. It might have been more important than sacking potatoes, toting rubbish or stocking detergent. If a fellow could find a clear place to write his name on the toilet walls, so much the better. To leave our names in a place that would last forever was like writing our own obituary. They're still there, in the basement, in the toilet . . .

Donnie Luhman, 1948.

Tommy Franklin, 1951.

Scab O'Reilly, Goodhue vs. Wanamingo, 21 points, 1951.

Ace Franklin, 1948.

Davie F, 1944, Team Manager.

Lefty O', District Champions, '44.

Jimmy Franklin, 1952.

Then years later, a different generation, a new bunch . . .

Tommy Gorman, 1963.

Charlie Gorman, 1964.

Helen Gorman, 1961.

Dickie Gorman, 1967.

Mike Gorman, 1962.

Ernie Gorman, The Greatest!

O'Reillys, Franklins, Luhmans, Gormans. Every one of us who worked at the store, every fellow who was nurtured there left his name. We didn't want to be forgotten when our working days had passed. We had been part of something important.

The working history of many boys and girls can be traced by going into the basement to read the names. Next time you're traveling Minnesota Highway 58, maybe on a Saturday night, slow down for a moment, turn into Goodhue, drive past the silo and over the railroad tracks a couple of blocks to the store. Ask if you can go to the basement, to the toilet, to read the names of the children who passed that way some years before.

4

Saturday Night In The Village

Saturday night was the biggest night of the week in our secluded hamlet. Farm families journeyed to town in the jalopy to buy a couple of bolts for the threshing machine, a pound of nails for the chicken coop roof, a bottle of aspirin for mom, adhesive for grandmother's false teeth plus milk pails, troughs, skillets, spatulas, binding twine, feed supplement, thread, crochet hooks, overalls, roast beef, sauerkraut, maybe even a couple of Hamms brews at Art's Bar. Load the children into the pickup, drive to town, drop them off at the free movies on lower street then head to George Diercks' General Merchandise, or Frieda Vieths' General Store, or Heaney & Gorman to buy groceries. Buy a lot because you wouldn't be back in town until next Saturday evening.

It was a good night to work at the store, because so many folks came in to buy groceries and chat. We sold Folger's coffee for ninety-nine cents, three pounds of hamburger for thirty-nine cents, and Heaney's special summer sausage for only twenty-nine cents a pound. You couldn't drive into town without buying sausage or dried beef. I helped Bump and Dennis and Tom and George make that sausage. I wasn't the boss by any means, but I contributed by turning the crank after each hog casing was slid onto the hollow pipe. We would get a regular assembly line going putting on a casing, then ten, then twenty, then fifty, then one hundred. Hang the fresh sausages on the rack and roll them into the smokehouse. Load the smokehouse with hickory wood to get the smoke rolling, tumbling and billowing until it permeated those sausages to a tasty, tangy, melt-in-your-mouth flavor. Folks drove from Red Wing, Oak Center, Zumbro Falls, Lake City, Pine Island, Wanamingo, Kenyon, Nerstrand, Hader, Dennison, Stanton, Cannon Falls,

Vasa, White Rock, Hay Creek, Welch, Wacouta, Frontenac and even Bay City, Wisconsin for that sausage. They couldn't buy sausage like that anyplace else.

I enjoyed selling groceries and sausages, but it was the talking I most enjoyed. People didn't just drop in to purchase their weekly groceries. No, sir, they came to chat. There was a potbellied stove, a bucket of coal, a stack of wood, a bench, several oak rocking chairs and a spittoon where folks rattled on. Around that stove I was enraptured by the yarns of Uncle Dave. Around that stove, I heard the epics of Frank O'Gorman and Vince O'Reilly and Thomas O'Rourke and other wise tale-spinners. Shoppers only incidentally left with a car of groceries. They could get along without food for a week, but not without talking. They had to hear what was happening in town and what their neighbors had done during the week. The store and the potbellied stove provided that opportunity.

Uncle Dave always had stories to tell. He had the gift of gab, that's for sure. If he didn't have a ready yarn he made up one. He told tales about the difficulty of digging a grave in the Belle Creek Cemetery when the ground was frozen solid and he needed to *store* the corpse in a barn until spring. He could make a chestnut like that scary. I could imagine that corpse shivering in his casket waiting for spring. Dave could hold your undivided attention. And he told stories about his courting days when he was a young whippersnapper himself. He spun outrageous stories of how he courted Tres. I believed him. He told stories about working on Bookie Bucholtz' pea viner and supervising the lads who pitched vines and boxed fresh, green, juicy peas when they were running fast and furious in the fields. He was a master story teller.

Uncle Dave had moved off the Belle Creek homestead in 1938, came to Goodhue, bought a dray line business and told stories for the next forty years. He sold his horse and wagon business in 1947, but before his time was up, he held about every odd and even job in town. He had a knack for getting jobs and making them fit his lifestyle. He knew how to get himself into a supervisory position regardless of his title. He often persuaded George O'Reilly, brother Tom and me to work while he supervised us. In the summer of 1952, Dave and I painted the bulk tanks for the Co-op Oil Company down by the Great Western tracks. Dave got the job then hired me to help him. We did a good job. He worked me all over those thirty-foot-tall tanks painting up, down and around while he supervised, but he said his nephew was a good worker. Words like that from an uncle were important to a boy.

While parents were buying groceries and talking, their children were watching free movies on lower street. The screen would flap in the southerly breeze as the movie was projected onto the side of the Great Western Depot. Children found a place to sit on blankets as Abbott and Costello performed their antics: "Who's on first?"

"I don't know who's on first."

"What's on second?"

"No, he's on third."

"Who's on first."

Gene Autry galloped across the Texas panhandle to wrestle a cattle thief, later to sing *Tumbling, Tumble Weeds* with the Texas Playboys by a roaring fire.

Saturday night free movies were special. The village didn't have a movie theatre, television hadn't been invented, and folks didn't travel far from home for entertainment. If they could get by driving only five miles to Goodhue instead of ten or fifteen to Red Wing, Zumbrota or Cannon Falls, they did.

With so many people in town the village absolutely hummed with activity. Even ol' Buck couldn't get a nap with the commotion. He would leave his spot by the jail about six o'clock and slowly meander toward Mickley's Garage seeking a quiet spot under a junked Reo truck. He knew enough to stay out of the way on Saturday night.

5

Slaughtering

After the sociability of a typical Saturday night at Heaney & Gorman, Mondays were long butchering days, the day farmers trucked plump hogs and fatted steers to town for slaughtering and processing. I never toiled in the slaughter house. I don't know what Dennis saw or didn't see in me, but he never assigned that job to me. George O'Reilly, Tom Franklin, Bump Schinnert, Dody, George, and Sally Schinnert butchered but I never did. Maybe Dennis thought I would faint when he would string up hog after hog and slit its neck, blood splattering throughout the slaughter house, or when Bump would tie a steer's neck to the floor and place that sledge hammer in the precise spot between its eyes. Maybe he thought I was so good at cleaning the block that he didn't want to spoil my expertise by slaughtering. But I did trim pork bellies and wrap hundreds of sides of beef after the slaughtering.

After butchering twenty steers and thirty hogs, the remainder of the week was devoted to cutting, trimming and wrapping. Dennis would hoist a quarter of beef onto his shoulders in the cold storage room, carry it to the cutting room, flop it onto the block, then run it through the bandsaw to cut round steaks, sirloin steaks, chuck steaks, tenderloin steaks, rump roasts, chuck roasts and shoulder roasts. He would toss the cuts to the wrapping table at just the right angle to miss my head. I would take over by wrapping, taping and stamping the cuts for the owner. I wrapped, marked, and taped beef and pork until I had nightmares. I went to sleep thinking pork and beef, beef and pork. Huge hogs devoured me during the night. Row upon row of beef rolled at me during my dreams . . .

Faster, Jim. Don't make a mistake. Don't give Bessie Benda's pork chops to Leone Ryan. Don't send pork chops to Laura Mans.

Dennis could work non-stop. Once he revved that cutting saw up to speed, there was no stopping him. Don't get in front of his bandsaw unless you want to end up in Locker No. 259.

I became the expert block cleaner at Heaney & Gorman. Dennis said that of all the boys who ever worked for him, no one ever did a better job of cleaning the block than me. What makes a boy seek a particular skill be it pork chop wrapper, meat trimmer, floor sweeper, potato sacker or block cleaner? I just liked cleaning the block. When Dennis hollered that it was time to clean up for the day, I would head for the block. After using it throughout the day to cut up chops, ribs, pork bellies, it was rewarding to clean it to a radiant sparkle. Dennis couldn't assign just anyone to clean it. George wasn't good at it. Tom wasn't good at it. Davie wasn't good at it. Donnie wouldn't do it at all. Maybe I acquired it by default.

Press hard—Left, right.

Start on the upper left edge, then work down to the right.

Apply the right amount of pressure.

Push the wire brush at just the right angle.

Push harder.

Make that block shine.

"There, it's done. Isn't it beautiful? Look, everyone! The block is clean, ready for tomorrow."

Such a small thing to the world. Such a big thing to a kid.

"Nice job, Jimmy."

"Okay, Dennis. No big deal."

6

Mackinaws In July

One of the most ludicrous summer sights in the village was two brothers walking to downtown, temperature ninety-five degrees, humidity ninety-five per cent dressed in Minnesota's finest winter clothing of four-buckle overshoes, Mackinaw coats, gloves, Russian-style wool caps and scarves. Why would normal boys be dressed like that? Didn't their mother teach them anything? But Tom and I knew what we were doing. We were going to the Locker Plant to work on one of Dennis' annual jobs—emptying lockers in the below-freezing freezer.

When farmers had a steer or pig slaughtered they usually left the processed meat at the Locker for cold storage. Few freezers were available in the late forties and early fifties, so people rented a locker, devices similar to giant safety deposit boxes at the bank, or cold storage bins at the morgue, pull-out drawers where valuables are kept. Pork and beef stock were valuable. Although the drawers were large they couldn't hold an entire side of beef, so Dennis' procedure was to store a customer's overflow meat in wire cages above the lockers. Each customer's packages were stamped with a number, so we knew who they belonged to even though the cages held meat for many different renters. When Nick Matthees came up short on round steak, and Bill Ryan searched for more side pork it meant their individual lockers were getting empty. It was time to transfer packages to their lockers.

Dennis had the best job. He *was* the boss standing on the top rung of the stepladder, grabbing several packages from the storage cages, calling out the numbers, then tossing them to Tom, George or me to place in the proper individual lockers located deep in the catacombs of the freezer. For several days we emptied cages during the blistering, sultry summers of southern Minnesota, ninety-five degrees in the village, twenty-five degrees in the catacombs. Spend the morning filling lockers, take off your four-buckles for lunch, then back to the freezer for the afternoon.

There was considerable frivolity while emptying the cages, however. We tried to keep up with Dennis, but not at the expense of eliminating foolishness. By nature, working at the locker plant and grocery store subjected you to varying degrees of frivolity and pranks. What would a day of work be without a good prank! You couldn't be around Dennis Heaney, Dave Franklin or Lefty O'Reilly very long without being subjected to a caper. Here is how one was foisted on me . . .

Jimmy Ryan was selling knives, pots and pans to earn money

for his college education at St. Thomas. Pots for boiled potatoes, pans for roast beef dinner and cooking boilers for moms' favorite hotdish were good sellers. It was on a beautiful April Saturday morning as I was wrapping a side of beef for Frances McNamara that Jimmy sauntered into the cutting room peddling his wares. Pots pans and knives hung everywhere on his body. He even had an aluminum boiling pot sitting on his head like a World War II helmet. Knives of every size and shape dangled from his belt, shiny silver blades and cherrywood carved handles that fit into your hand like a pork-belly glove. "Got some new knives here, Jimmy. They'd make an awfully nice Mother's Day gift."

"Naw, I don't think so."

"Just think how much your mother would enjoy a nice knife like this to cut up her chickens and slice her roast beef."

"Naw, I'm not interested."

"Look at this lovely butcher knife. Now that's a knife!"

"Well, I've seen worse. How much is she selling for?"

"Seven-fifty for the butcher knife. What do you think?"

"Well, I haven't bought her a gift yet. Maybe it wouldn't be such a bad deal." The deal was struck. Jimmy Ryan, Dennis, Lefty, Uncle Dave and other supervisors had entered into a conspiracy to pull off one of the store's most infamous pranks.

Jimmy carried only samples with him as he peddled his wares. He didn't have his inventory in town. They needed to be ordered from the Cutco plant in Chicago. That meant I needed to wait a week or two for my knife, all the while hoping it would arrive in time for Mother's Day.

Golly, this is going to be a wonderful Mother's Day. The knife sure will beat the can opener I gave her last year. This will be the best gift I've ever given her.

It was always excruciating to wait for a package to arrive at the post office. Most items I owned had arrived through the mail. We didn't have a Sears, Penny's, Coast to Coast, Ben Franklin or Woolworth store. We had necessary stores that sold bolts, nails, paint, aspirin, hamburger, gasoline, and four-buckle overshoes. Our merchants didn't sell custom-carved-cherrywood-handle butcher knives.

The wait was long and painstaking. Would it arrive in time? It cost seven-fifty, a whole week's pay. Buying that expensive knife meant fewer chocolate cones and hamburgers at the Greasy Spoon. I stopped at the post office every day on my way home from work and peered through the beveled glass in Box 58 to see if there was a package notice for me. Mother's Day was only a few days away. While I waited impatiently, the pranksters were sitting back in the shadows having the time of their life. The prank was working.

Two days. I wrapped, taped and marked meat packages after school. "Hey, Dennis. I need to run up to the post office for a minute. That be all right?"

"Sure, but hurry back. We've got more cutting and wrapping to do before you clean the block."

"No sweat!"

I darted out the door, hollered to Luverne at the Shell Station, waved to Sidney in his shop, petted ol' Buck relaxing by the jail, waved to Eddie Fisher in the drugstore then rushed headlong into the post office almost knocking down Mrs. Hennings. I peered through the window to see a yellow card—Turn right to R, then left to W, and finally two more turns to C, click open—indicating there was a package for me. It had arrived. I was saved. What a great day Mother's Day would be.

Well, Lefty was the assistant postmaster in addition to being a fine story teller around the potbellied stove. He saw me rush through the door; in fact, he'd received a hurried telephone call from Dennis, via Central, that I was on my way. I hurried to the window to claim my package. Lefty brought me a package that was going to give Mother her best Mother's Day ever. I couldn't wait to see the knife, so I hurriedly ripped open the package. To my dismay, I held a knife so ugly that Dennis wouldn't have used it for slaughtering. I held a knife so ugly Jesse wouldn't have sold it at his hardware store, Marshall-Wells wouldn't even have carried it in stock, B.C. Majerus wouldn't have even used it to cut sewer pipe rope. I held an ugly knife. The blade was bent, rusted and pitted, and it certainly didn't have a cherrywood handle. The pine-wood handle was stained and cracked with rivets only half set. What had gone wrong? Where was the beautiful knife Jimmy had shown me. I was stunned, horrified. I trudged out of the post office in a daze trying to determine what had happened.

They were all down the street behind Sidney's in the shadows, out of sight. They saw me leave the post office with head down, tears in my eyes, that ugly knife dangling in my hand. They were laughing and having the time of their life. The prank was working. Oh, it was working beautifully.

I walked into the cutting room with my head down, a rumpled corrugated package under my left arm, an ugly knife in my hand. Moisture trickled from my left eye. "Did you get your knife, Jimmy?" Dennis asked, out of breath, from behind the bandsaw.

"Let me see your Mother's Day knife, Jim," Uncle Dave smirked appearing from nowhere.

"Naw, I got it, but I don't think you want to see it."

"Show it to us," they said in unison. Reluctantly, I set the knife on the butcher's block.

"Hell! This doesn't look like the knife Ryan sold you. This knife is ugly!"

"What happened, Jimmy? Where's your cherrywood-carved knife with the silver blade?" George inquired. I couldn't think. I didn't know. How was a fourteen-year-old boy supposed to understand? He had only wanted to buy his mother a nice gift for Mother's Day, but now he stood there, hands in his pockets, a despicable knife on the block.

Jimmy Ryan walked into the room. "Did you receive your knife, Jimmy?"

"Yes, but it isn't the one you showed me. This knife is ugly."

"Let's see that knife. Hey, this isn't so bad. I'll bet your mom will like it just fine."

"No she won't. This is a gruesome knife." Lefty had rushed from the post office and casually sauntered into the room. They were all standing around the butcher's block like chicken hawks waiting to pounce on a road kill out on County Road No. 9 . . . looking, leaning, smirking, smiling. Everyone knew about the unfolding prank. Erv Richter was sitting by the potbellied stove, smiling. Uncle Dave was standing by the meat counter, laughing.

George and Dody were glancing over their shoulders to keep tabs on the proceedings. Then, suddenly, everyone disappeared.

It was time to wrap more pork chops for Bessie Benda. I didn't feel like wrapping. I thought only of that ugly knife, about how much I had planned, how much I had spent to get Mom a nice gift, and now it had all failed. It wasn't a good afternoon at the wrapping table. I mismarked Bessie's beefsteak as pork chops, her pork chops became round steak.

Just before closing time, after I had returned from toting the garbage, there was a package on the block. I was startled as Dennis spoke, "Jimmy, there's a special delivery package for you. Why don't you open it?"

"Oh, it can't be for me, I already received my package."

"Go ahead, open it."

It was addressed to Master Jimmy Franklin, Box 58, Goodhue, Minnesota with a return postmark from Chicago. I cautiously retrieved a cutting knife from the block and carefully slit open the package. On the inside of the wrapping was a beautifully packaged box with CUTCO KNIVES stamped on it. My heart began to thump wildly. I looked up. Standing alongside me around the butcher's block, appearing from out of nowhere, were Lefty, Dave, George, Dody, Erv, Dennis and Jimmy. No one spoke, but they watched me intently, slight smiles breaking their faces. I tore at the package. Before my eyes were *two* of the most beautiful cherry-wood-carved-custom-handle carving knives I had ever seen. As I lifted them the blades sparkled and glistened like silver. A big round of cheering arose throughout the store. The prank had worked.

Mother's Day was wonderful.

_____7

Pay Day

After my seven-fifty Mother's Day gift I needed money. Dody distributed weekly pay checks on Saturday night. At seventy-five cents per hour my check totaled about fifteen dollars, enough to buy hamburgers, fries, malts, Pearson's Nut Goodie bars for an entire week, and a little left over for Mother's ends. I didn't save a cent. That money was meant to be spent. Saving was simply too difficult. If I worked all week I deserved to spend it on junk food, or so I believed. Dody would hand me my check and I would be out the door. She knew where I was going. I would be sitting on a stool at Swenson's in two minutes ordering a malt and burger. I would be broke by next Saturday night.

Actually, my monetary habits proved to be valuable, however, because they had considerable impact on Dody and George. I pre-dated their ten children by several years, so they had an opportunity to use me as a pre-test kid for their children. They were able to observe me and say to themselves: *Jimmy should be putting some of his money in the bank. We won't let our children spend money like he does when they're growing up. We're going to require Helen, Tom, Charlie and the rest of our children to save* some *of their weekly pay.*

If it hadn't been for my free-wheeling spending habits, the Gorman children wouldn't have saved money either. I did them a tremendous service by spending every cent of my check. Dody and George wouldn't have thought of it on their own. I saved the Gorman brood considerable money.

Dody and George set up a policy later which stated: "Children won't receive their entire weekly pay check. One-half goes into a savings account." They probably didn't fully realize what they were doing at the time, but in effect, they were developing a college fund, an employee saving plan. They were way ahead of their time. They taught their own children thriftiness and money management at an early age. I certainly was a good influence on their children.

8

. . . Lift That Bale

Once a year, usually under a sizzling summer sun, the wool-shipping season began. In addition to selling meats, groceries and processing meat, Heaney & Gorman operated a wool business as if butchering, processing, smoking hams, cranking out sausages, curing bacon and making dried beef weren't work enough. Dennis purchased newly-sheared wool from farmers. In late July or early August, sheep coats would have grown thick and heavy indicating it was time for shearing. Dennis collected the wool, then shipped it to Cedar Rapids, Iowa.

He had constructed a twelve-foot tower that held a tall gunny sack. I stuffed wool bundles into those sacks, but it took at least three fellows to operate a wool-sacking session, plus Uncle Dave and Erv Richter as informed observers. The village always had a surplus of observers and supervisors. You could always count on guys with strong opinions hanging around offering advice. There was a plethora of advice, a paucity of assistance. If Luverne was fixing potholes on upper street, guys were standing right there observing him, offering suggestions he didn't need. If Leonard Lodermeier was overhauling a tractor, guys were standing alongside giving him advice. If the volunteer firemen were putting up the annual Christmas tree, guys were right there providing counsel. The village was never left wanting for unsolicited advice.

The wool-sacking operation had Dennis as the *official* super-visor, George, Tom and me as tossers and stompers. The work was hot and tiring, so we would alternate tossing and stomping throughout the day. When it was my turn to stomp inside the sack—being the shortest—I couldn't begin stomping too soon because I would have been buried alive. Mischievous George and Tom would toss bundles on top of my head while I was in the sack. To counteract, I usually sat on top of the tower until the sack was filled to six feet. Then I would jump in to stomp the bundles down and pack them tightly. Jump in, jump out, jump in, jump out. We stomped bundles in the sultry summer days by the wool shed. After the bundles reached the ten-foot level, Dennis would sew the top shut, place it on a dolly and load it onto the truck. Then we would hook another sack to the tower for more stomping, more tossing, more frivolity. When the truck was loaded, Dennis drove it to the railroad station where we then loaded the sacks into a box car. Those sacks were so large and heavy, weighing three hundred pounds, that I don't know how we ever managed to load them into the one hundred-degree box car.

Pranks, puns and more chiding than one could ever imagine permeated the Heaney & Gorman enterprise. You grew up fast. You had to hold your own. If you didn't stand up for your beliefs and opinions, you would have been defeated. You learned to talk and think and defend yourself, because everyone who worked there was assertive. If you started talking, you had better be able to defend your statement.

My years of working, joshing, talking and listening to the old-timers by the stove have had a major impact on my life. The Heaneys, the Gormans, the Franklins, the O'Reillys, the Luhmans and all the others who passed that way during the forties and fifties are embedded forever in my memory.

Chapter 8

Pastimes in the Village

Baseball by the Apple Tree

MINNESOTA WINTERS WERE HARD, BITTER AND endless, but if we could get through March, we had hope the pitiless winter would eventually end. Late March brought *hoping* signs—trickles of melted snow, inquisitive ground hogs, skinny red-breasted robins looking for spring nightcrawlers, tender blades of Kentucky Blue Grass sprouting through the dingy, crusted snow, or a precocious purple tulip lifting its petals on the south side of the house where it was warmed by an elusive winter sun.

___1

Atomic Rings And Crystal Radios

One of my activities during the endless winter months was reading the Johnson-Smith Catalog, my *bible*, my connection to the world. Goodhue didn't have stores where I could buy gadgets like those from Johnson-Smith. Our merchants didn't sell atomic rings that glowed in the dark.

I spent January and February reading the catalog, deciding what I couldn't live without. It advertised wonderful gizmos a boy needed—atomic rings that glowed in the dark, lighted bow ties that blinked on and off like a Christmas tree, bow ties that squirted water through a long rubber tube from a squeeze bulb in my pocket. When I strolled up to a girl or an annoying sister to say *hello*, I could squeeze the bulb to squirt water into her face. I ordered windup buzzers for the palm of my hand. When I shook hands with a girl I could give her the buzz of her life causing her to jump back three feet. I bought marked playing cards, magnetic dogs that fought each other when placed on a table, microphones I connected to the radio so I could sing like Bing Crosby or Perry Como. The catalog advertised crystal radio sets that would receive radio stations from around the world. I ordered one, assembled it, strung a long antenna from my bedroom windowsill to the tree house, and spent two weeks trying to make it work. Never did. The most I received was static, and I believe that was a result of Mother's Maytag motor. But it set my anticipation to working.

Any moment now, I'll be pulling in a radio station from Chicago, Kansas City, New York or Del Rio, Texas.

I paid $1.35 for it—surely it would work. In the meantime, I ordered another gizmo. After several weeks of impatient waiting, I finally received a brown package from Cleveland. I rushed home to my bedroom, opened it and stared at my broadcast microphone. I only needed to determine how to connect it to sing and talk through our radio. I liked tinkering with switches and electricity even though I knew little of what I was doing. I experimented with everything Mother and Dad permitted. They had faith in me.

The brief instructions said to dismantle the back of the radio, hook up the black wire to the negative terminal, the red wire to the positive terminal. That seemed easy enough. But there were so many terminals inside the radio that I had difficulty determining the correct ones. Connecting the black wire was easy, but when I connected the red, sparks flew from the radio sending a surge of electricity up my arm, spewing brown, yucky wax from my left ear. I was knocked to the floor, dazed. It was only the first of many electrical shocks I would receive over the years. But experimenting was a way to learn—trial and error. I was going to confession weekly, so even if I touched the wrong wire and was jolted all the way to the Belle Creek Cemetery, I would get into heaven, at least purgatory.

The microphone never worked. I placed it on the shelf to collect dust alongside the crystal radio set, the atomic ring, the water-squirting bow tie, the walkie-talkie and the hand buzzer.

By the end of another tiresome winter, my friends and I had spent countless hours in outside activities. It was impossible to stay cooped up for six months with only my Johnson-Smith Catalog, even though it was teeth-chattering cold outside. But none of us had lived in a different state, so we didn't know there were climates more temperate than Minnesota's frigid winters and steamy summers. We didn't know there were warmer states—California, Arizona, Texas, Florida—where snow didn't cover the ground five months of the year. If we had fifteen feet of snow and twenty-five degrees below zero cold, wet, freeze-your-nose-off weather from November to May, then surely everyone did. Without television we couldn't watch the sunny California Rose Bowl game on New

Year's Day. If we had seen that we would have all left Minnesota. The only living creatures remaining today would be walleyed pike, loons, deer and snow rabbits. Minnesotans would have abandoned the state. But we didn't. We skated and sledded in the brutal, freezing, stick-your-warm-tongue-on-a-cold-sled-handle winter.

On most nights we headed for water tank hill for sledding. I would rush out of the house leaving the dirty dishes to Rose or Mother, amble up water tank hill, grease my runners with a bar of wax, run for fifteen feet, thrust my Flexible Flyer into the air, land with a belly whopper and zoom down the hill. If the snow was particularly good and my runners were well waxed, I could glide all the way to the school. That would be a ride.

2

Encountering Lyle "Noisy"
Rusch Up On Water Tank Hill

Sometimes a boy does dumb things. It's not always his fault, though, because there are usually older boys offering suggestions, teasing, taunting him to do something he wouldn't normally think of himself. A grown man can consider himself lucky to have navigated childhood without doing too many, and if those few lame brain acts weren't life threatening, he would have been even more lucky. At times a boy's decisions are downright stupid. I made one. I made a stupid decision in the subarctic winter of 1948 up there on water tank hill.

We were into our tenth run down the hill. The night was pitch-black, snowing heavily with an icy, scary wind howling through Evergreen Cemetery. But we were having fun, nonetheless, sledding in spite of the below-zero temperature. To this day I'm unclear how it started, but some of the older fellows—Tom Franklin, George O'Reilly, Harold Lensch, Terry Shelstad, Lyle Rusch— began talking about tongues sticking to cold metal. Now, why they would talk about that with youngsters like Bob, Lee and me around I'll never know. Noisy said he had been at his uncle's farm in Featherstone Township last winter when a calf accidentally stuck its tongue on a metal grain feeder out in the back forty. He said that calf was there for a week before anyone found it froze to death, because when it touched the feeder its tongue stuck the calf to its icy death. They found it frozen like a statue, standing up, tongue welded to the feeder. And Noisy said it loud enough that Bob and I heard him. I hadn't had any experiences with sticking tongues; besides, I was a doubting Thomas. I didn't believe what someone said just because they said it, because they felt like running at the mouth. I believed Fr. Smith because he was backed up by the Vatican, but Noisy or Terry or Harold weren't. You can imagine what happened. I had to find out for myself.

"Hey, Noisy!" (We called him Noisy for two reasons: 1. He had a leather-lunged voice that could be heard from one end of town to the other, particularly on cold winter evenings when the air was clear and brittle; 2. He blew that tenor sax with unmitigated vigor.) "I don't believe your story. I don't believe a calf's tongue could get frozen to a metal feeder so hard he couldn't get it off."

"Well, it's true. And if you don't believe me, go ahead and stick *your* tongue on the metal handle of your Flexible Flyer there?"

"I could do it but I'm not going to just because you said so."

"Scaredy cat, aren't you? I know you're just a chicken shit little kid."

"I could do it if I wanted to, but I don't believe you, and I'm not going to do it." Then George chimed in.

"Yeah, Jimmy, if you don't believe Noisy's story, go ahead and stick your tongue on your sled." Then Harold said it and Terry said it and finally it became too much of a challenge. I couldn't back down now. I had a reputation to uphold, so even if I was only a little fart with those older fellows taunting me, I couldn't dismiss the challenge. When challenged you had to stand up to it. If you backed down, everyone in town would know. You would go to school the next day to find the story floating throughout the entire school. Girls wouldn't talk to you in the hallway. Teachers would look the other way during class; they wouldn't call on you at all. You would go to basketball practice and no one would throw the ball to you. It would be hard and all because the word had spread that you denied a challenge. "Did you hear that Jimmy Franklin backed down from a challenge by Noisy, George and Terry?" I couldn't do that. I would have to meet it.

I faltered bending over to pick up my sled, hands freezing, trembling. Slowly, I brought the handle toward my mouth. I was a doubting Thomas, but I was now doubting Jim.

What if Noisy is right? If he is, will I have this sled stuck to my tongue for the rest of my life? Will I die standing up like that calf?

The metal handle was coming closer.

God, how did I get myself into this mess? I wish I hadn't been such a skeptic. I wish I would've said . . . "Hey, Noisy, that's quite a story about the calf. You know, I really do believe it."

But I didn't say that and now it was too late. The taunters moved like Eskimos circling for a seal kill, watching intently to see if I would do it. They were my witnesses even though they had difficulty seeing me through the frenetic snowflakes. The wind had increased, now approaching blizzard force. Snap! My warm, soft, red tongue was out of my mouth too quickly and the piercing, bitter metal handle met it. The bonding was instantaneous. My tongue lurched forward, drawn to the sled like a magnet, and in an instant, welded to the metal. I was stunned. I tried to pull my tongue back but the sled came with it. I tried to push the sled away but my tongue went with it. I was petrified, filled with fear. The Eskimos began laughing, rolling in the snow like slaughtered seals, moaning, pointing fingers at me, taunting, screaming. Hysteria. Tears flowed from their eyes and formed icicles on their hissing faces from laughing so hard. I stood at the crest of water tank hill in a freezing, howling snow storm holding my Flyer to my face feeling horror throughout my entire body. "SEE! I TOLD YOU SO, YOU DUMB KID," Noisy screamed.

"Why would a kid be so stupid as to stick his tongue on a cold sled?" George bellowed.

"Boy, I've seen everything now," Terry hissed.

Tom didn't say anything. He suddenly realized the severity of the situation and even though the others were his friends, I was still his tag-along little brother. He began feeling sorry for me, realizing the sled wasn't going to come off. I believe he had visions of his brother spending the rest of his life walking around town holding that sled up to his face. Tom didn't want to go through that. "Come on, Jimmy, I'm taking you home."

"Unnh, aah, unnh . . ."

He took me by the arm and began walking me down the hill, but it was too steep and icy. I slipped, fell and nearly lost the sled and my tongue at the same time. Tom picked me up, set me on his sled and towed me home. I rode holding the Flyer to my tongue. We cautiously made our way down water tank hill, and even when we reached the bottom I still heard Noisy yelling at the top of his leather-lunged voice from the crest of the hill. "I TOLD YOU SO, YOU DUMB LITTLE TURD!"

Tom towed me home, then ran into the house to get Mother. She vaulted out the back door, saw me sitting on a sled with another sled stuck to my tongue and cried out, "Jesus, Mary, and Joseph, what have you gone and done?"

"Unnh, aah, unnh, aah."

She took one elbow, Tom the other. I held the sled as they carefully walked me into the kitchen, holding on to the sled for dear life, because I knew what would happen if it slipped from my grasp. I held it so tightly the circulation in both arms stopped. My hands were turning blue but I wasn't about to let go. "Let's get you into the kitchen. When you and your sled get warmed up we should be able to get your tongue off."

"Unnh, aah, unnh."

She tossed a couple of logs into the stove, took off my boots and sat me in front of the wood burner. I wondered what would happen to my tongue. Unfortunately, while sitting there, I had time to think and I was being hard on myself.

Why do I always have to be a doubting Thomas? Why couldn't I have believed Noisy's story? If I had this wouldn't have happened. I would still have my tongue. Maybe I'll never talk again. Maybe my tongue will come completely off when it warms up. Maybe I'll end up dead just like that calf.

Then I felt a gradual tingling sensation in my tongue, like Novocain leaving my mouth after a trip to Dr. Knutson's dentist chair. Mother and Tom held the sled. Nothing was moving, nothing that is except my heart which was beating at a furious pace. A minute went by, then another and ever so gradually, I felt the bitter-tasting metal releasing me from its grasp until it was finally gone. I was free of my sled. I sat there with my tongue dangling from my mouth like a panting dog, not feeling it, but knowing it was there. Could I talk? Would I ever again be able to eat a Hershey or chocolate cone again? Fear swept through me as I pondered these thoughts. But then, for a brief moment, I experienced joy.

If I can't talk, I won't have to go to confession!

"How does it feel, Jimmy?"

"Unnh, aah."

"Your tongue is bleeding. Here, let me put something on it."

"Unnh, aah."

Mother went for the dreaded Mercurochrome bottle. It fixed everything, but stung fiercely. She took the dropper out and gently placed a couple of drops on my placid tongue. "Ouch, owe! . . . that hurt!" I could talk, my tongue worked! I could eat peanuts and ice cream and . . . I could still go to confession. I made a vow at that very moment—in the future I would try much harder not to be a doubting Thomas. It was a stupid thing to do up there on that freezing hill, but I was learning. I was growing up.

For a change of pace from sledding, we skated at the ice rink adjacent to Mickley's Garage. The volunteer firemen flooded the lot each winter for young skaters. Ice froze solid and deep in Goodhue's bleak winters making it easy for the firemen, but it was so beastly cold during January and February that water often froze before it even gushed from their hoses! The ice was good, but it was difficult skating in that Siberian weather. We could only skate for ten minutes before needing to thaw out. Many of us spent more time in the warming house than on the rink; consequently, I never became a good skater. When I did get onto the ice, I had consider-able difficulty standing up, because I never had a pair that fit, never owned my own skates, always wore a pair of two-sizes-too-big-hand-me-downs. I tipped to the insides of my skates onto my ankles, looking like a pigeon-toed whooping crane from the backwaters of the Mississippi. I was better at sledding than skating, as long as I kept my mouth shut.

Old Man Winter eventually had mercy on us, so that by the third week of May the snow disappeared heralding springtime in Minnesota.

3

Springtime On The Prairie:
'Crocodiles' And Peach Box Racers

The Mississippi flowing past Red Wing was our nearest river, but in the spring there were temporary rivers around the village. So much snow had usually accumulated during the winter that when it finally melted, creeks and streams were transformed into rivers. Jack O'Reilly, Lee Johnson and I would trek to the outskirts to find a normally placid creek roaring with water. For several weeks we had our own rivers on the prairie.

A favorite activity was spearing *crocodiles*. We built spears out of broom handles by hammering a sharpened nail in one end, filing the head to a point, then tying a long rope through a hole at the top of the handle. We would find a few logs, walk up stream, toss them in and run back to the bridge to spear the *crocodiles* as they floated by. Jack speared a ten-footer for the village record.

As spring rivers gave way to summer dust, two-wheeled scooters, clamp-on roller skates, balloon-wheeled bikes, and peach box racers made their appearances. Every boy needed a peach box racer including me. I was experimenting again with something I knew little about, but it was safer than electricity. I wanted a racer that would speed down water tank hill without loosing a wheel, and would roll all the way to the school house to beat out Jack and Lee.

My peach box racer had four wheels, a wooden platform to sit on, a steering wheel and a Del Monte peach box grill from Heaney's. Jack's had a Libby's peach box from Frieda's, Lee's a Sunkist peach box from Diercks'. Attached to the peach boxes was a plywood steering wheel cut out by Ole Haga. Ole owned the only band saw in town, and only a band saw could cut a circle. From the steering wheel through the peach box was a two-foot length of doweling to which was attached a rope wrapped several times around the doweling—one end connected to the right wheel, the other to the left. If all worked as designed, the racer could be steered. The theory was good, but in practicality it was difficult to accomplish. We were our own engineers as well as drivers. Trial and error prevailed. We didn't research our designs, but that's what boys do. Just build it.

By the time we had assembled steering systems, fastened wheels to axles with a couple of Jesse's cotter keys and built floorboards, they resembled peach box racers. We toted them to the top of water tank hill, counted down, then sped all the way down to the high school without a steering assembly falling apart or wheel falling off. Jack came in first, Lee second, me third. But it was close.

4

John Yungers' Rubber Gun Special

By 1948 WWII was over but the boys of the village still engaged in war games just like our troops had done a few years earlier on the beaches of Normandy and Okinawa. Without television accounts of the war to see, we read about the GIs' battles and listened to Edward R. Murrow's radio broadcasts. If we were fortunate enough to see a movie in a real movie house in Red Wing or Zumbrota rather than at the lower street free movies, we would see Movietone News accounts of the war followed by maybe John

Wayne in the *Sands of Iwo Jima*. Afterward, we marched back to town to fight our own wars. This is how we did it.

About ten fellows would gather for a rubber gun war in the heart of the village. The attackers usually invaded from the Catholic Church while the defenders positioned their line of defense around the jail. Goodhue would be under siege from dawn to dusk on any given summer day. We had vivid imaginations and, rubber guns.

John Yungers made the best rubber guns. We all made them, but his were special. When you skirmished with John, you knew you were in for a battle, because he used sturdy walnut wood instead of pine to create eighteen-inch barrels, strong, stinging rubbers sliced from truck inner tubes, plus two extra strong clothespins for a trigger. His *bullets* zinged from behind a rain barrel or a coal cart catching you on the forehead—instant *dead*—leaving a red welt for several days. Score one for Yungers.

Making a good rubber gun took planning and talent. John made his Specials for the Eastside Lutherans, but the Westside Catholics had a few good gun makers, too. George O'Reilly made guns with zing. Tommy Franklin made guns that reverberated with a snap when fired. His developed a unique sound that scared his victim as much as hurt him. We would find wood behind Streater's Lumber Yard, discarded inner tubes in Mans and Benda's scrap pile, and clothespins in Mom's laundry bag. We would bribe Ole to cut out our guns by promising to mow his lawn first thing Saturday morning, then we would strap the clothespin to the handle with a strip of rubber, test fire a couple of rounds at Ol' Buck and we would be ready for battle—North versus South, Yanks versus Huns, Westside Catholics versus Eastside Lutherans.

Skirmishes were fought daily on the battlefields not unlike those at Appomattox, Bull Run or Utah Beach. I don't know where we learned our tactics, but they were surely better than those used at Gettysburg where Union and Confederate regiments simply lined up facing each other, advanced and fired point blank. The victor would be the regiment with the most men. Neither the North or the South took evasive action, electing to stand shoulder to shoulder while firing at their enemy. We didn't fight like that. We planned our battles better than those Gettysburg generals, or so we believed. We used tactics. We used evasive action. We attacked from behind the post office. We sought cover behind Ebe's Barber Shop, behind Husbyn's chicken cages, behind the Creamery's milk cans. We hitched a ride on Uncle Dave's wagon to the other side of town to attack our surprised enemy.

General George O'Reilly, captains Terry Shelstad and Tom Franklin, privates Jack, Bob and Larry O'Reilly and myself made up the Westside Catholic Army. General John Yungers, captains Harold Lensch and Lyle Rusch, privates Darrell Jonas, Lee Johnson and Fritz Schulz made up the Eastside Lutheran Army. An updated Crusade was about to happen, a battle made in heaven.

The entire village was our battlefield. The Westside Catholics used the defunct church basement excavation as headquarters. In 1934 the members of Holy Trinity decided they needed a new church, believing that their tiny clapboard church—formerly a chicken coop—wasn't suitable any longer. They petitioned the bishop. The existing chicken-coop church and parish house were on three acres of land, but there was considerable land available for a new church. The Knights of Columbus trucked in a backhoe, excavated for a new basement but the parish soon ran out of money. Construction stopped. For twenty years a basement-sized hole loomed next to the parish house, a perfect place for war games. We built a fortress from logs, lumber, twigs, branches and leaves. Our fort was impenetrable from the outside forces.

When we had finished assembling rubber guns, cutting inner tube *bullets*, tying twigs on helmets, applying charcoal-black burnt cork to faces for camouflage, and filling canteens with water we were ready to move out, ready to face our enemy. We fanned out cautiously, route-stepping single file across city park and through the *river* in McHugh's back yard, through the *minefield* in O.T. Parker's flower garden, across the *canyon* in Yungers' front yard, and over the *White cliffs of Dover* in Jim Ryan's rock garden. We maneuvered until we sighted the enemy barricaded behind the jail. If our planning and tactics were correct, we would be able to catch them off guard to strike the first blow. We weren't lucky. The Lutherans had placed their line of defense around the jail in order to be closer to their railroad station headquarters; consequently, they could retreat quickly if they needed to. And we were using a dangerous tactic. We were three blocks from our headquarters; if we fell into serious trouble we would have difficulty retreating. The Lutherans spotted us advancing around the Goodhue State Bank, detecting us before we crossed upper street.

The two armies collided in the middle of the street. The first Lutheran rubber fired by Darrell nicked Jack in his right leg as he was sneaking around the corner of Marshall-Wells. We had taken our first casualty and the rules of the game were that once hit, once *dead* you had to sit out for five minutes. The battle raged throughout the afternoon, Catholics advancing only to be driven back to the bank. We attempted a flanking attack from the blacksmith shop, but to no avail. They blocked our advance and at the same time inflicted more casualties from John's Specials. More Catholic soldiers out of the battle for five minutes.

Waging battle was fun, being *dead* for five minutes wasn't. At least the Catholics were honest about counting a full five minutes, because we couldn't lie, or weren't suppose to. Although it was only a game, there was a fine line between bending the truth and lying. If we told a lie we had to face confession, and even though lies weren't as hard to confess as impure thoughts, they still weren't easy. It seemed the Lutherans cheated on counting the full five minutes. We knew they didn't have to confess, so cutting off a couple minutes didn't make much difference to them.

We took many casualties with that flanking movement, enough to drive us beyond Huebner's Blacksmith shop all the way to the Creamery. We took cover behind milk cans on the south side of the building to regroup, to rethink our strategy. This wasn't working the way we planned it. Where was God when we needed him? Wasn't he on our side as he was when the Israelites fled Egypt, or when Moses led the Israelites through the Red Sea? "Hey, Bob, say a prayer so we can conquer the Lutherans."

"*Ite missa est*," Bob whispered.

"Shit, Bob! That means 'The mass is ended, go in peace.'"

"Well, that's all the Latin I know."

Jack offered another tactic. He suggested we split our ranks to put the pincer squeeze on the Eastsiders by attacking them from two directions simultaneously. No one had a better idea. We accepted his plan. Silently, we moved out from behind our milk can barricade, crawled around Jim Ryan's house on our bellies, crept down the alley behind LaVerne Diercks' house, snaked around the English Methodist church, dashed across the road through Edna O'Reilly's flower garden and maneuvered into our attack point behind Majerus' Gas and Appliance. One squad filed around the hotel to attack from the north while the other squad slid south through the alley behind Art's Bar. We planned on trapping the Lutherans in the alley behind Marshall-Wells. "Synchronize your watches. We'll commence the attack at 3:30 sharp," General George whispered. "Move out."

Both squads moved out without being detected by Yungers and his band of Protestants. We were confident. The tactic was working; that is, until one of the numerous O'Reillys made a mistake advancing around the bank. Jack thought he saw a Lutheran setting a land mine (a rutabaga from Emily Parker's garden) in front of the bank, but unfortunately, it was only Mrs. Hennings walking home with a sack of groceries. Jack fired. A direct hit. He caught Mrs. Hennings smack in the middle of her forehead. She dropped her groceries on the sidewalk—milk bottles shattered, oranges rolled into the gutter, eggs splattered onto her new summer pumps, yellow, sticky egg yolk ran down her left leg. She was stunned. Jack was stunned. He didn't know what to do. She froze— shell shock. Mrs. Hennings became one of the civilian casualties inevitable in war. Jack ran from the scene as fast as he could. We saw him running, so we ran. We could handle rubber gun *killings*, but didn't know what to do with this civilian situation. Mrs. Hennings would have to take care of herself; we still had an attack to complete.

Unfortunately, Jack's mistaken attack blew our cover. The Lutherans saw us advancing. They had positioned a squad by Sidney's Shoe Shop and another on the north side of the blacksmith shop. A trap. They waited, patiently. Oh, those Eastsiders were patient. Our squads approached from opposite sides, but the incident with Mrs. Hennings had delayed us so we weren't in position by 3:30, and Bob's watch was undependable. Our squad's watch was three minutes slower than Bravo squad's. We didn't get our attack coordinated. We were massacred. Jack was still so shaken because of the incident with Mrs. Hennings that he was daydreaming when he got hit by a direct shot from Terry. Then Bob was wounded in the knee by Lee. Suddenly, two soldiers out of action before we even attacked. Then Larry was wounded by a glancing shot from General John as he moved around the back of Marshall-Wells. I was crawling on my stomach, trying to move into a better firing position when Fritz suddenly appeared out of nowhere, caught me in a defenseless position, leveled his long-barreled J. Yungers' Special and fired. Snap! Swish! Zap! The shot hit me in the left rib cage. *Dead!* Five minutes *dead.* The Lutherans knocked us out of the skirmish. After five minutes we retreated, heads hung low, back to the safety of our headquarters. We lost today, we were humbled, but we would be back with a better battle plan. We wouldn't catch any civilians in the line of fire next time.

We didn't accept defeat well. Losing any battle was bad, but being defeated by the Eastsiders was particularly humiliating. We also suffered considerable chiding from the old-timers watching our daily skirmishes. Those fellows enjoyed our battles, casually watching out of the line of fire while sitting in front of Swenson's Cafe, the jail, Diercks' Grocery, Eddie's Drugstore, Julius' barber shop and Frieda's General Store. Sitting wasn't that unusual at any time in the village. Sit and talk or if you didn't feel like talking, just sit. Folks lounged on benches chewin', spittin', whittlin', talkin' and jawin' as they witnessed our battles. I never understood how those fellows could be so casual in the face of war. They were sittin' that day we lost to the Lutherans. We trudged past the old-timers sitting under Ebe's revolving barber pole—Erv, Red, Oscar—with our tails between our legs. We took considerable chiding as we plodded back to our church-hole fort like the Nazi's retreat from Stalingrad.

There was another battle two days later, only this time the Westsiders were victorious. We planned and practiced our tactics meticulously. Day and night training sessions were held at our headquarters.

The second clash was set for Saturday noon at the first whine of the town siren; we were ready by eleven o'clock. We had to succeed this time. It would be too humiliating to face the Lutherans, and the old-timers, in defeat. Our battle plan was to deceive the Lutherans by feigning a skirmish in the alley behind Florence's Eat Shop, but in reality, setting up an ambush at the grain silo near the highway. Our strategy called for Alpha squad to outflank the enemy by sneaking around the lumber yard, creeping through Lohman's Standard Oil bulk tanks, maneuvering across the railroad tracks to take up positions in the grain silo. Once there Alpha would climb the stairs to hide in the machinery room above the entrance and be at the ready with guns loaded and extra ammo. Bravo squad, in the meantime, would pretend they were attacking the Lutherans behind the Eat Shop, but at the last moment fall back and retreat toward the silo. If all went as planned, the Lutherans would follow Bravo squad to the silo where they would meet their final doom from our hidden Alpha squad.

Alpha moved into position at the silo without being detected. Bravo moved out cautiously pretending to attack the Lutherans from the Eat Shop, but didn't engage, only firing a half dozen long-range rubbers before retreating. Our retreat route was well planned, plus we had practiced it several times. We made a pass through Lodermeier's Implement lot climbing over the Allis Chalmers tractors, crawling under New Holland combines, sliding under John Deere manure spreaders, racing across the street and slipping through Heaney and Gorman cattle pens, climbing over wool bundles, donning gas masks while coughing through the smokehouse, filing through the lumber yard, rappelling Standard Oil bulk tanks and sneaking through the rear door of the silo. Alpha was already in position in the machine room above the grain dump, hidden from view. The Lutherans followed Bravo squad everywhere, pursuing us over the tractors, under the combines, under the manure spreaders, across the street, through the cattle pens, over the wool bundles, coughed through the smokehouse, ran through the lumber yard, and scampered over the bulk tanks to the grain silo firing rubber guns continuously. But we were too fast for them; besides, we knew the route. We didn't suffer any causalities. We were drawing them into the trap. We scurried through the rear door just as the Lutherans surrounded the silo. "All right, you mackerel snappers, this little caper is up. Surrender or die, you dumb Irish croppies."

"No Lutheran WASP can take us alive. We'll not surrender."

They began firing rubbers randomly. One bounced off the door, another skittered along the dirt floor kicking up a swirl of dust and nicking a Bantam rooster that had been sleeping in a corner. The rooster scampered out the door past the Lutherans who were momentarily startled as it cackled past them into bright sunlight. The dust settled slowly in the sweltering silo. It was stick-your-tongue-to-the-roof-of-your-mouth-peanut-butter-sweltering hot. It was mouth-full-of-cotton dry.

The siren blew—high noon. George hollered, "All right, we give up. You've got us surrounded." They took the bait, entering cautiously through the open doors, guns at the ready. Bravo squad was *surrendering* just inside the doorway on the ground floor while Alpha squad was above us in the machine room. The musty grain invaded Bob's nostrils and he felt a sneeze coming on just as the Lutherans reached the open doorway. If he sneezed now he would blow our cover. Jack whispered, "Hold on, Bob. Press your tongue to the top of your mouth, hard. You can't sneeze now." Bob held. Bravo squad dropped their guns and raised their hands into the air. When the Lutherans saw that, they rushed in, but it was a mistake. Alpha Squad opened fire from above. Rubber filled the silo. They were trapped.

Every Lutheran was *killed* at the Great Grain Silo Shoot-out. We marched back to our headquarters past the old-timers, heads held high.

5

Mr. Mischief: Naurice Husbyn

The village wasn't always under siege. There *were* places safe
from the raging rubber gun wars. Husbyn's Hatchery was one.
Naurice Husbyn moved to town from the vicinity of Northfield
where hundreds of Norwegians and Swedes had settled after
emigrating from their homelands across the sea. He was one of the
conquering hordes that settled in Goodhue County, a jokester,
mister mischief. He could see a kid coming from blocks away and
have a caper going in no time flat. He could generate a prank at the
drop of a hat . . . or an egg.

On a drowsy, muggy, corn-growing Saturday morning, I was
ambling down the street, one foot on the sidewalk, the other in the
gutter for variety when I stopped at Shelstad's Cafe for an ice
cream bar. I watched two old-timers play Cribbage, another
twosome playing shuffle board then moseyed across the street to
see what was happening at the Hatchery. Naurice saw me coming.
"So, how you doing today then, Jimmy? See you got yourself an
ice cream bar."

"Yup."

"So, how would you like to do me a favor on your way home?"

"Whatever."

"Mary McHugh called and asked if we could deliver a couple
dozen eggs to her . . . said she's baking an Angel Food cake and
needs the eggs as soon as possible. You wouldn't mind dropping
them off on your way home, would you?"

"Nope, wouldn't mind."

There wasn't any rush, at least in my mind, so I hung around
for awhile to hear stories I had missed out on. The fellows candling
eggs were as quiet as the sleepy village, though, so after half an

hour I decided to leave. Naurice brought me a box. He had wrapped it in the back room, so I didn't actually see the eggs, but I noticed a slight odor rising from the box, but that wasn't unusual at the Hatchery. I took the package, bid my good-bye and headed toward McHugh's to do my Boy Scout good deed for the day. I was working on that Tenderfoot badge.

Mary was waiting impatiently for me at the back door with hands on hips, because she couldn't proceed with her cake without eggs. As soon as I opened the screen door, she took the eggs from my hands, unwrapped the box, opened the cartons, and gazed upon twenty-four of the rottenest, god-awfulest smelling broken eggs I had ever seen. She scrutinized me over the top of her bifocals. I looked back. "Heavens to Betsy, Jimmy. Look at these eggs!" I glanced into the box and was considerably dismayed at the sight, and the smell. "Why would you bring me rotten eggs?"

"But . . . I didn't know . . . Naurice, he . . . ."

Mary was in on the caper. When Naurice saw me enter Shelstad's he knew I would be sauntering across the street for a visit in a few minutes. He placed a quick phone call to Central and asked her to ring Mary. She and Naurice set up the prank. Mary carried it to the hilt. "But, Jimmy, I ordered two dozen *fresh* eggs. These are rotten."

"Mary, you see I've . . ."

"Now, Jimmy, Naurice wouldn't send me rotten eggs. What have you done with my fresh eggs? Is this your idea of a prank?"

Cold shivers darted through my skin even though it was hot and steamy in her kitchen. All I had done was deliver the eggs. I was merely trying to be a good kid and get that Tenderfoot badge, but it wasn't turning out so well. I felt responsible for the rotten eggs. Where had things gone wrong? As I shuffled from one foot to the other, head down, trying to figure out the dilemma, the phone rang. Mary picked up the receiver. "Jimmy, it's for you. Naurice Husbyn is on the line."

"Hi, Jimmy, how you doing?"

"Not so good, Naurice. I've got a problem here."

"Well, what's wrong? Did you deliver the eggs?"

"Yes, but they're broken. I don't know what happened."

I heard laughter in the background as Naurice spoke. He was chuckling, Harold Lensch was roaring, Noisy Rusch was laughing his heart out. Oh, they did it again. "Hey, Jimmy . . . I made a mistake here."

"What's that?"

"I mistakenly sent the wrong eggs with you. The eggs I gave you were intended for the garbage. You took garbage eggs to Mary."

More laughter in the background. "Oh, that's okay, Naurice, no big deal."

As quickly as it started it ended. Mary removed her apron, gave me a big hug then kissed me on the cheek. Naurice said to come by the Hatchery tomorrow and he would buy me another ice cream bar.

6

Hank Befort's Jail

The village jail was located around the corner from Naurice's Hatchery, on upper street, a tiny red-brick building with a fire bell on the roof to be rung in the event of a fire. We often wondered what a person could possibly do to warrant getting jailed. Henry Befort, the village policeman, periodically left the outside door open so we could see the solitary cell, but I never entered any farther than the doorway. But I did see the jail used one time.

On a Saturday evening in 1948 some of the boys at the Corner Bar started a fight. They consumed too many Hamm's Sky Blue Waters, a brawl broke out in the bar then spilled into the street. It happened just as the free movie ended. By the time I reached upper street, Hank had apprehended an imbiber, placed him in handcuffs and was marching him to the slammer. Hank didn't even have the alleged culprit appear in front of the Justice of Peace. I don't know if the jail had ever been used before, probably, because when folks began partying, drinking and dancing it wouldn't have been unusual for fights to break out, especially with area Germans, Irish Swedes and Norwegians protecting their own kinfolk. Hank made that fellow stay in the cell all night . . . slammed the door and snapped on a heavy duty padlock. Folks milled around the jail for a couple of hours before Hank told everyone to go home. "You kids, go home now, git!"

"Aw, Hank, we just want to watch."

"Go home now, you hear. He's locked up for the night."

"Come on, Hank, just a little while longer. Can we stay?"

"Five minutes, then t'home with you."

Hank kept that rascal in jail all night until he sobered up. He released him at eight o'clock Sunday morning and told him never to cause any more trouble. That fellow left the jail and left Goodhue. He never stepped foot in town again. Hank was surely waiting for him.

____7

Gophers On The Prairie

My tree house had been weathered by Minnesota's heavy snows and summer rains, so that the roof was askew, the walls were bowed out and the floor was tilting toward the sandbox. It was in bad shape after a couple of winters. Dad kept suggesting I dismantle it, but somehow I never got around to it. I didn't climb up there much any more—the long disbanded club had never been named—and I found Eddie's Drugstore a good source for girlie magazines to replace Lee's. But on a late summer's night when rain fell softly on the tin porch roof outside my bedroom window creating a symphony of sounds, I could hear my tree house's corrugated roof squeak against rusty nails as it swayed in the wind and rain. It was a gentle and pleasant sound.

As summer months waned and nights became nippy my

interests turned to football and basketball. Autumn was our season for playing church-yard football, listening to the Minnesota Golden Gophers on WCCO, and watching early television-era games.

In 1948 there were only two television sets in the entire village—Art's Bar and Tomfohr's International Harvestor. Karl apparently saw the potential for television sales in its infancy; he began selling sets along with tractors and farm machinery. The first televised football game I saw was at his shop on a set in a corner behind a red International tractor. I'm glad someone told me beforehand that it was a football game, because I couldn't tell from watching the screen which was filled with snowy round blobs, supposedly football players but looking more like Pillsbury Doughboys. I didn't spend much time trying to watch television games, though; I found it more exciting to listen to the Golden Gophers on radio.

The forties were truly golden years for Minnesota football. Coach Bernie Bierman developed talented players—Leo Nomelini, Clayton Tonemaker, and Bud Grant who played football and basketball equally well years before he became coach of the Vikings. I would tune in WCCO Saturday afternoons to hear the Gophers playing for the Little Brown Jug against Michigan, the Floyd of Rosedale pig trophy against Iowa, a Wooden Bucket trophy against Indiana, or the Milking Cow statue against Wisconsin. It didn't matter who they played, though, because the Golden Gophers consistently beat the best of the Big Ten teams. I would keep my ear to the radio, then during a time-out or halftime rush out of the house to play a couple quick downs. Jack O'Reilly, Lee Johnson and I would get up a game on the Holy Trinity lawn, the Methodist Church lawn or possibly the German Lutheran lawn. We weren't fussy. Holy Trinity didn't care. The Methodists and German Lutherans didn't care as long as Jack didn't cuss excessively.

We wore heavy clothing to ward off the nippy November afternoons. Sometimes older fellows joined our scrimmages—George O'Reilly, Tommy Franklin, Lyle Rusch, Harold Lensch, Terry Shelstad, Dave Swenson, Jimmy Lohman, Jimmy Ryan, Junior Lunde, John Yungers—big guys who beat upon smaller fellows. Sometimes we would balance the teams by playing five little guys against two big, but usually we tried to play with fellows our own size; if we could get a game with younger and smaller fellows, we did. Occasionally, Pat O'Reilly, Smoky Shelstad, Tommy O'Reilly, Frederick Rusch and Fritz Schulz joined us.

Big Ten mascot names were interesting to me. We usually called ourselves the Gophers, but what was a Hawkeye, a Buckeye, a Wolverine? I knew why the Minnesota team was called the Golden Gophers, because all I had to do was walk along County Road No. 9 or No. 6 to see them along the roadside, little golden gophers standing with heads poking the air, always looking for something. I don't know what they were looking for—maybe for a way out of the county and Minnesota, maybe looking westward where summers weren't so sultry, where mosquitoes were absent, where winters weren't so bitter. Actually, gophers settled in Minnesota long before the Norwegians, before the Swedes, before the Irish and Germans, too. They were there first and they've stayed longer than many immigrants because gophers are hardy, intelligent and determined creatures. They probably originated in Canada or Alaska, then believing Minnesota to be warmer, followed Babe and his Blue Ox out of the Canadian ice glaciers to Bemidji. But the gophers, still seeking a warmer climate, kept traveling south, always looking. Could be true.

Today, it is obvious why the University of Minnesota named the team after those determined creatures; however, the team could have been named after the loons or the walleyed pike or the muskie, but those names wouldn't have worked out as well as *gophers*. Can you imagine the Minnesota team trotting onto the field . . . "And now, here they are folks, the Minnesota Walleyes; let's hear it for the Walleyes!" Or how about, "And now, today, playing against the Michigan Wolverines, we give you the Minnesota Muskies!" Or even worse, "Ladies and gentleman, today, playing against the Wisconsin Badgers, we give you the Minnesota Loons!" I'm glad those university folks used common sense.

Minnesota hats off to Thee,
To our colors, true we shall ever be,

Firm and strong united are we,
Rah, rah, rah for Ski U Ma,
Rah, rah, rah, rah, Rah for the U of M.

__8

Lakers In The Dining Room

The late November sun cooled rapidly as Thanksgiving approached, dipping lower on the horizon to become softer and mellower as it slid farther south. The disappearing sun was a sign the football season would soon be over, a sign fierce winter snowstorms would soon be invading Minnesota. When frost appeared on the garden pumpkins, it was time to winterize everything in sight. Old Man Winter would be blowing in soon. Snowfall would be heavy again bringing howling, bitter winds from the west. Streams and creeks would soon freeze. Duck hunters would build decoys and blinds. Pheasant hunters would dust off two-barreled shotguns, fisherman would begin preparing gear for the ice fishing season, and dads would buy baled straw to place around our houses in vain attempts to keep out arctic winds. Folks would wash outside windows, put up storm windows, place insulating strips around doors and windows, fill every nook with rags. Dads would fill fuel oil tanks, guys at the Shell Station would check antifreeze for twenty-five below zero saying, "Yup, she looks like she'll be a hard winter." For me it was time to store the football, time to say good-bye to the Gopher football team and welcome the basketball team. Without basketball, Minnesota winters would have been unbearable. Without basketball Minnesota would have been unlivable . . . for a boy.

By eighth grade Goodhue boys could play school basketball against Wanamingo, Mazeppa, Zumbrota, Kenyon, Cannon Falls and Pine Island. I liked basketball. I was short—five feet two inches—but we didn't have tall players, anyway. Being short wasn't so bad. If you were six feet, you were considered tall. Later, in high school, Dallas Diercks grew to six feet five inches, a giant. As a senior I was five-nine, still not tall for a basketball player.

I was inspired by the Gophers and the Minneapolis Lakers with George Mikan, Vern Mikelson, Jim Pollard and Slater Martin. Dad and I sat in the kitchen by the wood-burning stove on blustery winter nights listening to them. Mikan was the greatest Laker of all, my hero. Even at five-two, I wanted to play like him. No one ever told me I couldn't. Five-two was just as good as six-ten to me, particularly when I was playing basketball in our dining room.

I rigged a basket above the door sill, backboard made of plywood, hoop a ring from Mother's old coffee pot, net of Heaney's string. The hoop was four inches in diameter, the playing floor only five feet wide, but on that tiny floor using a tennis ball for a basketball I was Mikan. I could make a basket from anyplace in the dining room, hit a lay-up from the right side, a left-handed hook from the left side, a right-handed hook shot from behind the dining room table, a two-handed jump shot like Slater from beyond the sewing machine. I could swish a two-handed jumper like Mikelson from the china cabinet, and I could shoot like Pollard from the radio, the dining room table, the buffet. I could even flip a lay-up while running through the doorway to the kitchen. Oh, I could play basketball in the dining room . . .

Ladies and Gentleman! Tonight's Laker's game against the Fort Wayne Pistons at the Minneapolis Auditorium is being brought to you by Grain Belt Beer and Powder Milk Biscuits, two treats that we're sure you'll enjoy. Try 'em both, you'll like 'em!

Our starting lineups; the Fort Wayne Pistons . . .

And now, yooooouuuuurrrrrrrrrrrrr Minneapolis Lakers! Starting at guard, Slater Martin. At forward, Vern Mikelson. At the other forward, Jim Pollard. And starting at center, tonight substituting for the injured George Mikan, here he is, Jimmy Franklin!"

Hard first quarter. Fort Wayne is playing strong and leading the Lakers by three points at the end of the quarter. Lakers seem lethargic. In the second quarter the Lakers close the gap. Mikelson is beginning to score from the baseline and Slater has hit two long set shots. Franklin hasn't been much of a factor yet, but we're hoping he gets going as the quarter progresses. End of the half, Lakers down one point 42 to 41.

Whoopee John's Orchestra is providing halftime entertainment with those old favorites—Beer Barrel Polka, Mom and Dad's Waltz, *and* Red Wing, My Pretty Red Wing. *The audience likes Whoopee's music, but they're anxious for the second half to begin.*

Lakers come out strong at the beginning of the third quarter. Martin hits one from twenty-two feet, Pollard makes a jump shot from the key and Franklin finally gets untracked hitting both a left-handed hook and a right-handed hook from behind the sewing machine . . . 'er . . . I mean . . . the baseline! Lakers are playing better; they're ahead 53 to 49 and looking good. End of the third quarter, Lakers leading 59 to 55, but the Pistons aren't giving up.

Fourth quarter is a struggle with both teams trading baskets. Ft. Wayne for two. Lakers for two. Ft. Wayne for one. Lakers for two. Three minutes left, scored tied at 65. Mikelson has fouled out, Pollard has four fouls—the Lakers are in deep foul trouble. Ft. Wayne comes down the floor, Pepper sets, lets a twenty-two footer go. Swish, right through the nets. Ft. Wayne 67, Lakers 65. Laker's ball now, Martin to Pollard, Pollard to Mikelson, Mikelsen to Franklin, Franklin back to Pollard, Pollard lay-up. Good! Ft. Wayne 67, Lakers 67. Ft. Wayne down the floor, 59 seconds left, they lose the ball, Slater Martin scoops it away, dribbles the length of the floor, shoots the lay-up, no good! Ft. Wayne's ball, down the floor, into the corner, back out to the key, into the other corner, into the post, back out, 15 seconds, score tied, a long set shot—no good! Time-out, Lakers. 7 seconds.

Lakers huddle, they set up the play. Slater is to fake

a long set shot, but then pass to Franklin. Franklin is to take the shot. Oh, God, Jimmy, here's your big chance to be a star.

Time-in. Mikelson passes the ball inbound to Pollard in the corner .

Six seconds.

Pollard passes to Martin out front.

Five seconds.

Martin fakes the set shot but passes to Franklin.

Three seconds.

Franklin zooms out of the kitchen, around the dining room table, past the sewing machine, past the buffet, around the china closet, but oh! his mother is throwing up a tough defense; she's got him boxed in around the circle as she carries a load of dirty hotdish plates to the kitchen, but wait . . . Jimmy outmaneuvers her by the radio, throws up a left-handed hook shot. It's . . . good! Franklin scores. Lakers win!

"Time for bed, Jimmy."

"Okay, Mom."

"Who won the game?"

"Oh, the Lakers, we murdered 'em."

Chapter 9

Roots

Casper & Margaret Haustein, Catherine Franklin

MOST FARMS IN GOODHUE, BELLE CREEK, HAY Creek, Belvidere and Featherstone townships were settled by immigrants from Norway, Sweden, Germany, Ireland or Austria, pioneers trying to make good in a new country, because their homeland wasn't doing well. In the mid-1800s, economic depression, religious persecution and potato famines were quite common in European countries, so America appeared to be a better place to live for many of the persecuted. When they heard families could gain one hundred sixty acres of farm land through the Homestead Act, they boarded ships to sail across the sea. Most landed in New York, were processed by the authorities and released to find a place to live, work and raise a family in what they hoped was a better country than what they had left.

David Franklin and Joseph Haustein, my ancestral great-grandfathers, weren't any different from the hordes of other emigrants in the mid-1800s seeking that better life. David of Ireland and Joseph of Austria left their homelands with their parents to find a better life in America. It was a good idea to leave Ireland and Austria in troubled times, but their parents might have better planned the journeys. Ten-year-old David boarded a ship to sail from southern Ireland the same day eight-year-old Joseph left Imst, Tirol Austria. Four weeks later on an overcast, windy November day in 1853, the two boys passed each other in the New York Immigration Center, each intent on processing quickly and getting on with his life. Each hoped that this new land would be a more prosperous and forgiving land. Little did they know they would become intertwined in a countryside far from New York City, in a land west of the Mississippi River. They accidentally bumped each other as they stood in the processing line. For a moment each looked into the other's eyes, but their eyes didn't stay connected. It was immediately obvious to each that the other fellow wasn't of the same ancestry. But each had a feeling their paths would again meet. They did.

When the families departed their respective ships in New York City's harbor they had the entire country from which to choose, as there were only thirty-five million living in America in 1853. Their first decision was whether to stay in New York City or move westward across the hills of New York, Pennsylvania and Ohio. The Franklins and Hausteins might have chosen Arizona, California or New Mexico, warm states where there might be a nip in the air come September, but other than that, a decent winter. They didn't do it.

1

The Franklin Ancestry In Belle Creek

David Franklin and his parents processed through the Immigration Center, then passed through New York State to stop for a few years in Pennsylvania. But Philadelphia didn't satisfy the family. It was too unlike Ireland. After several years they packed their belongings to move farther west beyond Ohio, Illinois and Wisconsin until reaching Minnesota. Great-great-grandfather David stopped his oxcart a few miles west of the Mississippi River and said to his family, "This is it, I'm not going any farther."

It was September, so it didn't seem like a poor decision at the time with beautiful golden leaves quaking throughout the wooded Hiawatha Valley, but what David didn't know was the severity of Minnesota's winters. He had been told about Midwestern winters from his father back in Ireland, but this was only September, surely they couldn't be as harsh as his father said. Ireland was damp and foggy much of the time, so when David finally stopped the ox team for good in the fall of 1858, looked at the gentle rolling hills, saw a warm, yellow sun setting beyond the birch trees, saw rolling fields that looked good for plowing, planting and growing crops, and noticed only a few trees needing removal, he said to his wife, "This is a good place, the place we'll call home and set up our farm. We have a hill to the south, a rise to the north and we can build a log cabin here on this rise, a barn down there, a chicken coop over there, and all that land to the east can be pasture for our milk cows. We have healthy children to help us." He had stopped in Belle Creek Township, Goodhue County, Minnesota. (A meandering creek runs through this township flowing north-south from Vasa to Minneola Townships. *Belle* is French for *beautiful*—The beautiful creek.) He raised crops, cows and kids . . . was good at all of them.

David (great-grandfather) worked the land with his father in this place called Belle Creek, toiling the next several years to clear and develop the land. (Belle Creek Township was settled primarily by families who had also immigrated from Ireland. In 1854 the first tracts of land were placed on sale.) At age twenty-one, David married an Irish lass from down the road, moved her onto the homeplace and raised his own family, continuing the tradition his father had begun. He cleared more land, milked cows, raised chickens, raised children and attended church on Sunday. As the years passed his children—David, George, Celia, John—wanted more excitement than Holsteins and wheatfields and Sunday Mass. David (grandfather) became restless around the homeplace especially after the threshing was finished and the hay stacked in the barn for the winter. He began thinking about other things like young ladies. He went out and found a lass to share his life with. He found her at church on a sunny October Sunday as he shuffled to his surrey, accidentally bumping her as he was hitching his team together for the ride back to the Franklin farm. "Excuse me, ma'am. I was just trying to get this bridle on my team, didn't mean to bump you."

"Apology accepted, young man. What is your name?"

"David Franklin. We're farming north of here by a couple of miles. What's your name?"

"Catherine, one of the Mahar girls. We live down the road three miles. Why don't you come by sometime? I'll fix you a little lunch."

Catherine Mahar took charge at that first chance meeting and stayed in charge for the next fifty years. She fixed David a little lunch a week later, and from that day forward, he was hooked. Catherine and David were married at St. Columbkill's country church the following spring. She moved out of the Mahar place to the Franklin place with David's father, mother, three brothers and sisters, fifteen Holsteins, twenty-five chickens, six Bantam roosters, eight Hampshire sows, thirteen sheep, one Shetland pony and a team of Belgian dray horses. She started a family and a trend in Belle Creek . . . said the good Lord put her on this earth to raise children and by dern, she was going to do it. That's one reason I had so many aunts, uncles and cousins. I had kinfolk by the bushel because Catherine was determined. She ruled the roost from the first day she stepped onto that Belle Creek sod. She was just an itty-bitty woman, physically, not but five feet tall and one hundred pounds, but Irish women aren't measured only by physical standards. They are measured by what's inside, by what they say and do. She measured up with the best of them, much higher than her five feet. She pulled her hair back in a bun, set her horn-rimmed glasses firmly on her nose, slipped into an apron and took charge. She raised sheep and cows and turkeys and chickens and children. A determined woman that Catherine Mahar-Franklin.

2

The Haustein Ancestry In Red Wing

Joseph Haustein also left the Immigration Center and New York State to investigate the western states. His parents, Franz and Elizabeth, were drawn westward like David's and like the Franklins, the Hausteins didn't travel directly to Minnesota. They stopped in Dayton, Ohio for seven years before pushing onward. Ohio's terrain was excessively flat around Dayton, the top soil shallow and weak, not good for growing crops. Franz was used to the rich soil around his home village of Imst, Austria. He wanted to find similar soil in America. Word around Dayton was that a place called Minnesota was wonderful for farming. Franz loaded the family and belongings in the oxcart and headed west again.

They traveled overland for several weeks before reaching the Mississippi River at Red Wing. When Franz, his wife Elizabeth and son Joseph gazed upon the mighty river from high atop a Wisconsin bluff, they decided this was going to be the place they would find a farm with rich top soil. In Austria, they had lived by a river, although not as sweeping as the Mississippi, so when they reached the crest of the hill on the eastern shore of the Mississippi and looked at the beautiful high bluffs embracing the river, Franz decided to travel no farther. He said to Elizabeth, "This looks like a good place to settle and to raise our family. The bluffs and wooded hills and the river remind me of our little village in Imst. This is where we'll stay."

Young Joseph looked upriver and noticed a ferry barge crossing to the western shore. "Dad, there's a ferry where we can cross with the ox and cart."

"Sure enough, son. We should be able to cross in a couple of hours." By the time the sun set beyond Barne Bluff, Franz Haustein's family and oxcart were parked on the western shore of the Mississippi.

Joseph, only fifteen and inquisitive, strolled down the levee to where folks were passing the time of day. "Hello. What is the name of this town?" Joseph called out.

"Red Wing. They named it after an Indian chief who ruled this land many years ago."

"Red Wing, you say?"

"That's what I said. Your ears plugged up, young man?"

"Does it have other names, like a territory?" Joseph inquired.

"It's called Minnesota. You see all of this water? Let me tell you, young man, we have more water than you can imagine. Why, we have thousands of lakes from here to Canada, and we have lots of farmland, too. By the looks of that cart, I'd say you're farmers. I can see a grain cradle, a three-tine fork, a grain flail and cultivator. If you aren't farmers, you're carting the wrong tools! Anyway, as I was saying, with all this water the Indians who were here a long time before us named it Minnesota . . . means *blue water*. They sure got that right. Then there was this young Indian maiden who laughed a lot. In particular, she laughed when she saw all these lakes, so they named her Laughing Blue Water, but we call her Minnehaha. Get it? Water? Laughing? Well, you don't look real smart there, young fellow, so I'll just jaw on here a bit. You aren't getting tired of listening, are you? Folks say she threw herself over a waterfall about sixty miles north of here, up there in a place called Minneapolis. Longfellow wrote about her and we named the state after her, Minnehaha Minnesota, but only used her last name. So, young man, you are standing in Red Wing, Minnesota, then. Where are you from?"

"Coming from Ohio with my parents, but we spent four weeks on a boat sailing from Austria a few years ago. We're looking for land to farm here in . . . what did you say, Red Wing?"

"You're coming all the way from Austria to live in Minnesota? Now, why would a smart fellow go and do something like that? Come to think of it, a smart fellow wouldn't. You must not be very smart, and by the way, you look real funny in those clothes. What do you call those pants you're wearing?"

"Lederhosen."

"Run that by me again, would you?"

"I said lederhosen. We wore them all the time in Austria."

"Well, I'd say you better get some long pants if you're going to live here else the mosquitoes will carry you away. What's your handle?"

"Handle?"

"Name, son. What's your name?"

"Joseph Haustein."

"That's a funny one. I don't believe I ever heard one like that."

"I'm Joseph. My father over by the oxcart is Franz and that's my mother, Elizabeth. We're Hausteins from Imst, Austria. What is your name?"

"Name's Heaney."

"Do you live in Red Wing?"

"No, sir. I only came in to look at cattle that were barged up the river. I live about fifteen miles south of here out in a township . . . slaughter cattle sometimes. Good farming country. Maybe you and your pa might want to mosey out our way to look at land. Think about it. We've got lots of land what with the government putting blocks up for sale a couple of years ago. Shoot, they have a Land Office here in Red Wing. Tell your pa about it."

"I'll do that. *Auf Wiedersehen,* Heaney."

"Off what?"

"*Auf Wiedersehen* means good-bye. I must be getting back to my parents. We need to find a place to sleep for the night, then look for land tomorrow here in Minnehaha, Minnesota."

"Not Minnehaha, Minnesota, Joseph, just Minnesota. Good luck, Haustein. When you have that farm up and going, bring your father out to the township. I make pretty good sausage, and I'll take you to the Blind Pig for a sarsaparilla, a brew for you dad."

"Blind what?"

"Never mind, just ride on out."

Franz and his family went to the Land Office the next day to sign up for a block of government land. There was little available along the banks of the Mississippi where they had stopped, so they selected land five miles south in Featherstone Township near the Hay Creek. Franz purchased a one hundred sixty-acre tract from the government for two hundred dollars.

In Minnehaha Minnesota (later to be renamed simply Minnesota!), my great-great-grandparents, Franz and Elizabeth Haustein and great-grandfather Joseph began a new life in a peaceful valley down the river from where Minnehaha hurtled herself over the falls. The Hausteins entered Goodhue County in 1860, seventy-six years before me.

3

The Belle Creek Homestead

Catherine and David Franklin started their farm and family in 1882, raising enough crops and children to keep the farm prosperous in the years before the new century arrived. Uncles Jim, Pat and Dave, my father Tom, aunts Anne, Helen and Cecelia soon filled the farm. Seven Irish children with a little English for obstinacy were raised on the rich farm land of southern Minnesota, seven children brought into this world to help feed the livestock, plant corn, harvest wheat, attend Mass, recite novenas and do whatever Catherine said. That was the most important thing—do what Catherine said and do it the way she said, because she ruled the roost with a hard hickory stick. But she was also a kind, loving, spiritual and determined Irish woman who raised her children the way she was raised. Put two Irish families together and you have the Mahars and Franklins, Kate and David.

Grandfather David died in 1925 before I entered Goodhue County in the winter of 1936. He died before I had a chance to play with him or sit on his lap in front of the Christmas tree on the farm, but there were other laps to sit on—Uncle Pat's, Uncle Jim's, Uncle Dave's.

Catherine didn't slow down at all after her husband died. She buried David one day and drove a team of horses for threshing grain the next . . . said she didn't have time to feel sorry for herself . . . said she had too many chickens, cows, sheep and children to feed. But they knew. Dad knew. Years later he told me that after milking the cows he would come in the house and catch Catherine wiping a tear from her eye. "Anything wrong, Mom? You missing Dad?"

"Shush, Tom; go to your room. I have nothing but a little speck in my eye." Catherine was just being Irish.

After years of toiling on the homeplace, the children decided they wanted their own farms to raise cattle, wheat, barley, corn and children. Uncle Jim, the oldest, was the first to leave. He liked farming, so he hopped into a buggy one Saturday afternoon, pointed the Appaloosa toward St. Columbkill's and began looking for a farm to rent. He was ready to start a farm and a family. It wasn't long before he succeeded at both. He found a young lass, Louise, married her, rented eighty acres and began farming, loving and raising children. Jim knew nothing but big families. He commenced raising one himself, and it wasn't long before the place filled up with Cecil, Orville, Eileen, Ray, Gerald and Delores. They raised cattle and chickens, milked cows, partied, played the harmonica and violin on Saturday nights, cussed, guzzled beer and visited Catherine on Sunday afternoons.

Uncle Dave was next to leave the farm. He wasn't excited about farming anyway. Dave meandered around the township doing hired-hand farming for a couple of years until arriving in Goodhue, six miles to the east of the homeplace. Dave found a young McNamara girl, Theresa, along the way and started his family. Dave, however, didn't get into raising a large family like his brothers and sisters. He raised one naming him David in the long lineage of *Davids* emanating from his own father, grandfather and great-grandfather. One child was enough for Uncle Dave and Tres McNamara-Franklin.

Tom (my father) was drafted into the Army during World War I leaving Patrick as the remaining man to work the farm. Anne and Helen both left in 1920 after the war. Cecelia stayed with Pat, the two remaining siblings. Determined like her mother, Cis didn't stay around long either. She had too much spunk to battle, day in and day out with Catherine. They were like two hens fighting in the hen house, both of strong mind and strong will. Each tried to outdo the other; something had to eventually give. Cecelia did what any spunky young Irish woman would do. She found herself a strapping Irish man, one of the O'Neill boys.

She met Victor O'Neill in 1923 on a county road north of St. Columbkill's. For years afterward she said it was a happenstance meeting, but everyone knew that wasn't true. She had been noticing a rugged young man sitting in front of her at Mass for several months. She smiled at him repeatedly, but received nary a glance in return. Cecelia wasn't one to give up easily, so she developed a plan. It was harvest time and she knew the O'Neills would be threshing wheat soon like other families. She decided to drive her buggy past the wheatfield where they would be threshing. As she came abreast of the threshing machine, she got out of the buggy and looked quizzically at the front wheel. Victor meandered over to the fence. "Got a problem there, lady?"

"I think something is broke on my wheel."

"Shit! Don't you know how to fix it?"

"I'm not sure, because I don't know what's wrong."

"Let me take a look at the goddamn thing then," Vic said in exasperation.

He vaulted the barbed wire fence and sauntered toward the buggy intent on fixing it then getting quickly back to threshing. As he approached her buggy, Cecelia saw that he looked considerably different than when in a church pew. He looked like the straw man from the Wizard of Oz—straw in his hair, teeth, overalls, boots. He looked like a walking straw stack. "Shit! I don't see anything wrong with this wheel. What's it doin'?"

"It's squeaking. I'm afraid it will come off."

"Lady, whatever your name is, this goddamn wheel isn't going to come off. All you need to do with the damn thing is put axle grease on it once in awhile. Wait right here; I'll get some from my tractor. What's your name, anyway?"

"My name is Cecelia, but most people call me Cis."

"Cecelia, huh? Well wait here and I'll be back with the grease."

"Wait! What's your name?"

"Victor, but people call me Vic . . ."

Vic returned and gobbed the wheel with grease, "There, that ought to keep that goddamn wheel quiet. You can be on your way now, Cicily."

"It's not Cicily. It's Cecelia and how would you like to take me to Saturday-night's dance at the Belle Creek Hall?"

"What? I don't even know you. Why would I want to take you to a dance?"

"Because I like to dance and Tether's Orchestra is playing and besides, I've seen you lots of times in church and I think you'd like to take me dancing."

"I'll be damned . . . pick you up at seven."

Cecelia got her man. She married Vic, moved up the road a few miles, rented eighty acres and started a family. She had her mother's Irish blood, her father's Irish blood, and now she mixed that with considerably more Irish, the O'Neill's. With that blood-line she raised a large family, too. In the twenties and thirties folks had to have many children sitting beside them when they drove the buggy to church. It was the mark of a healthy woman. Not one or two, mind you, but more like seven, eight, nine or ten. Once Cecelia started bearing children she didn't know how to stop. Vic was a good ol' country boy not knowing how to stop, either. Peggy, Kathleen, Mary Helen, David, Larry, Mike and Colleen sprouted on the O'Neill acres. Victor and Cecelia raised those children on bottom land two miles from where the buggy broke down.

Dad returned from the Western Front in Europe, worked the homeplace with Pat for a brief time, but grew restless with farming. After a brief stint at barber school in St. Paul he decided to purchase a truck to do contract hauling for farmers. That left Uncle Pat and Grandmother Catherine alone on the farm; the same farm that began with great-grandfather David emigrating from Ireland to settle in Belle Creek in 1869 was now down to Catherine and Pat in 1930. Pat did the milking and field work; Catherine cared for the sheep, pigs, chickens, turkeys and flowers. Where had the time and children gone so quickly? But Catherine was content. She had memories. At the end of the day, when her chores were done, she would sit on the porch in her rocking chair watching the setting sun over the cupola, thinking back over the years. She thought about David and how much she missed him and how she cried every night in the privacy of her bedroom and how she never showed her sorrow to anyone, because that wasn't the thing to do around these parts. She thought about how everyone always told her how strong she was and how tired she was of hearing that, and she thought about how she would have liked to tell them she missed David.

Catherine thought about many things during her evening sittings on the front porch. She thought about first meeting David, about raising her children, about Tom being the only child to go off to fight the war and how happy she was when he returned safely, although she didn't show it. These thoughts brought her peace of mind as she rocked slowly on the porch. She thought about the time Tom and Cis carried two cats to the top of the windmill, dropping them to see if they would land on their feet. She chuckled now as she thought of that, but remembered how mad she had been at the time. Two dead cats. Thirty feet from the top of the windmill was too much of a fall. She had wanted to tar and feather them, but didn't . . . simply sent them to bed without supper. She thought about caring for her chickens and turkeys, about David making rope in the machine shed on a hot summer's night. He would amble to the shed smoking a large cigar. There, he would make big ropes from small pieces of twine. He did it to have enough rope for hoisting hay to the mow for the winter months of cattle feeding. She thought about the two houses that burned to the ground on the homeplace, and how they rebuilt them. She thought about the two barns that burned taking several head of cattle and hay with them in towering flames. She wondered how they would survive, but they did. She thought about the Christmas celebrations they hosted on the homeplace every year and how much snow would cover the fields and roads and how difficult it would be for her children and grandchildren to get through the snow. They did, though, because everyone loved her oyster stew, mixed nuts and fruit salads and:

I wonder if they'll come back?

She rocked and thought and prayed her rosary on the front porch of the old homeplace. The sun settled gradually over the barn, just beyond the Nord farm across the meadow. Catherine pulled her shawl tighter as she rocked to the setting sun and the invading night.

4

The Red Wing Homestead

It took an entire day for the Hausteins to reach their land, traveling over rutted Indian trails transposed to meager roads. Their new acreage was beautiful, but wild. Making it into a farm and home would not be easy. There was no cabin on the land, only trees and a meandering creek. Franz and Joseph built a dugout shelter in the side of a hill as a temporary home, then began felling trees for a log cabin. It was difficult work starting a homestead, but they had experienced hard work in Austria, surely Goodhue County would be easier. The men built cabins, lean-tos and fences. They planted, hoed, harvested and grubbed. Elizabeth cooked, washed, made soap, carried water from Hay Creek to the cabin, molded candles and churned butter. Franz and Joseph harvested wheat then transported it by oxcart to Red Wing for shipping on barges. Winters were long and hard, but the farm took shape, and most importantly, they were happy. During some particularly hard winters they lived mostly on bread, maple syrup and potatoes, waiting anxiously for spring when the Mississippi would thaw enough for steamboats to bring fresh food and supplies to Red Wing. Their land was bountiful with wild game—bears, wolves, rabbits, squirrels, elk and deer. Joseph liked to walk through the hills trapping game.

Other immigrants eventually joined them in homesteading the valley. The families shared corn husking, log cabin raisings and threshing bees. They survived epidemics, tornadoes and harsh winters. Gradually, the wooded hills became fields of wheat, the rocky Indian trails became roads, open land became fenced pastures, and the meandering streams were dammed for mill sites.

After eight years much of the land clearing and cabin construction had been completed. Joseph, now twenty-three, began noticing an anxiousness in his heart. He had been living with his parents since coming to America and Featherstone Township, spending every night with them in the log cabin. He wanted to spend evenings with a lady. He found her at Frontenanc on the banks of the Mississippi.

A neighbor had heard that a new load of emigrants from Germany was to be steaming upriver from New Orleans and landing at Frontenac in a couple of weeks. News like that excited the area bachelors, because they were always hoping the new *shipment* would include young ladies for possible courting and marriage. In late May, Joseph and two neighbors rode horses to Frontenac. As they waited along the levee, a steamboat chugged around the bend. Thirty minutes later, twenty-five immigrants landed. Joseph walked toward the gangplank as they disembarked. He was watching them walk down the gangplank lugging heavy trunks when he noticed an especially attractive lady. On other days he had seen fine looking ladies strut down that gangplank to buy refreshments at the Frontenanc General Store, only to reboard the steamboat for the trip upriver to St. Paul. This day and this lady were different. Joseph felt an urge he no longer wanted to control. "G'day, ma'am. Sure is hot, isn't it?"

"Nein sprechen sie Englisch!"

"You don't speak English?" Joseph blurted.

"Nein."

Joseph hadn't been in America long enough to loose his German tongue; he immediately switched, *"G'day, ma'am. Sure is hot, isn't it?"*

"Indeed it is, my good man. Indeed it is," she responded, this time in German.

"You going to be getting some refreshments before you continue your trip to St. Paul?"

"No, my good man; in fact, I'm staying here. I've traveled all the way from Ratshausen, Germany, up the river from New Orleans with these other folks to begin a new life here in . . . what name is this place?"

"It's called Minnehaha Minnesota, but we shorten it to Minnesota. I live eighteen miles from here on a farm. What did you say your name was?"

"I didn't say, but it is Anna."

"Happy to meet you, Anna. I'm Joseph."

"Pleased to meet you, Joseph. Now can you tell me where I might find a sarsaparilla. That steamboat ride was exceedingly hot."

"You bet! There's a general store uptown. Why don't I just walk up there with you and show you the way. Could use a sarsaparilla myself."

"If it is not too much trouble."

Joseph released the anxiousness in his heart. He met Anna, sipped two sarsaparillas and began a courtship ending in marriage one year later. Joseph and Anna married in June of 1870, purchased their own tract of land a few years later in Wells Creek, Florence Township, Goodhue County—seven miles east of the homeplace. They immediately set to work raising a log cabin and a family.

Anna was kind, sensitive and diligent, just the woman Joseph had dreamed about during his lonely nights on the farm. It was a good marriage, one made in Goodhue County, if not heaven.

Children soon arrived because when the two of them worked together, well, it was electric. They increased the population of Wells Creek by five percent, bringing six children into the world—

Casper, Lizzie, Mary, Edward, George and Joseph. Austrian-Minnesotan-Wells Creek Hausteins.

But farming became more difficult as Joseph aged. The years of toiling with the land took their toll on him. After working the land in Wells Creek for a few years, Joseph and Anna moved their family to Red Wing about 1886 in hopes of living an easier life. In town the children attended Catholic school, toiled at odd jobs—unloading steamboats, loading barges, shoveling coal, mowing lawns—courted and married, all except Mary who chose the nunnery instead of a man, and Edward who died at age seven. The children grew up rapidly and became anxious to make it on their own. Casper was no different.

5

Grandfather Casper Haustein

Like his brothers and sisters, Casper was happy to leave the farm, although he did miss hunting the abundant wild game in the woods around his home. He was only fifteen when the family moved into town, but old enough to obtain odd jobs. For the next several years he worked as a roustabout on the levee, delivered milk to homes, and trimmed meat at the Market down by the levee.

On one Saturday morning at the Market, Casper was trimming a side of beef behind the counter when he heard a soft voice murmur, "Please, I would like three pounds of ground beef." He turned to wait on the customer, but was startled at who he saw. Now, someone ordering three pounds of ground beef didn't startle him, but the lady's face certainly did. He was awestruck. "Uh, did you say ground beef, lady?"

"Yes, I would like to buy three pounds."

"Aah, sure, I guess that would be all right. Would you like it wrapped, or would you like to take it like this?"

"I really would prefer having it wrapped."

*What am I saying? Of course she wants it wrapped. What a
dumb thing to say.*

"So, three pounds of ground beef, then . . . that right, ma'am?"

"That is correct, and I would also like six pork chops?"

"Pork chops? You mean chops from pigs?"

"I do believe pork chops come from pigs, do they not?"

"I suppose they do, they sure do, ma'am. I'm going to get you
some right now."

*What's wrong with me? I can't think straight. She is the most
beautiful woman I've ever seen.*

Casper finally collected his thoughts enough to serve the lady
her ground beef and pork chops. He was fidgety but found the
courage to strike up a conversation . . . "Don't believe I've seen you
around Red Wing before, ma'am. Just passing through on the
steamboat?"

"Oh, no, I do not ride the steamboat much. I am from
Faribault, forty miles west. I am visiting my uncle. Maybe you
know him, Peter Spilman?"

"Can't say that I do, ma'am, but then there are some folks I
don't know. Didn't catch your name, though?"

"My name is Margaret Hamm."

"Pleased to meet you Miss Margaret Hamm."

"What is your name?"

"Casper Francis Joseph Haustein."

"I am very pleased to meet you, Casper Francis."

Margaret was indeed visiting her uncle. For several days she
visited the market to buy meat and chat with Casper. After the third
visit he generated the courage to ask Margaret for more than her
name. "Another three pounds of ground beef today, Miss Margaret?"

"No thank you. I do believe I will purchase a chuck roast
today. Uncle Peter loves them with new potatoes, corn and carrots
all steamed together in the same pot, particularly for Sunday
dinner."

"Me too. You know, if you had a little extra roast . . . well, I
was thinking maybe you might want a guest for dinner . . . I mean,
you wouldn't have to ask me, of course, but then, if it wasn't too

much trouble I could maybe come over then and after dinner we could take a walk along the levee to watch the steamboats or something like that but you wouldn't have to you understand."

"I think that would be a lovely idea, Casper. Please to come by at noon?"

In 1893, after two years of trimming meat and courting, Casper Haustein and Margaret Hamm were married in St. Joseph's Church on a small bluff along the Mississippi. Margaret had captured Casper's heart the first day she strode into the Market. It was no wonder, because she was a beautiful woman with a delicate chin and a long, thin, pointed nose accenting her green, oval eyes in the proper proportion. Her skin was fair, delicate and soft. Her ears were tucked back ever so slightly beneath her hair. She carried herself like nobility, although she was only from Faribault with no known nobility in her heritage.

Margaret and Casper rented a small wood-frame house on Fifth Street to begin a family. Casper was a happy man. His father had immigrated from Austria to a new country, state and county in which Casper was born, and now he himself was married. Margaret and Casper raised five children—Lillian, Bertrand, Edward, Frank and Lucille came from the womb of Margaret Hamm-Haustein. Lucille bore four of her own forty years later—Rose Marie, Tommy, Jimmy and Daniel Franklin—but I'm getting ahead of Casper's story . . . .

Casper eventually left his job at the Market to purchase the Trout Brook Grocery, a small neighborhood store. A few years later they also purchased a tiny acreage on Wilkenson Street on a hillside above Colvill Park by the Mississippi. The place had a white clapboard, two-story frame house, a barn, a chicken coop and a woodshed. On ten wooded and hilly acres they grew asparagus, zucchini, sweet corn, tomatoes, peas, onions, lettuce, horseradish, carrots and water cress in their vegetable garden, and they raised two Brown Swiss cows, twenty-five white Plymouth Rock chickens, one Shetland pony, two Rambouillet sheep, three Berkshire sows and an assortment of hounds including a beagle and an English bulldog. At any time of day you could find an assortment of cats lurking in the shadows or the loft. But life on

Wilkenson Street wasn't all bliss. In 1905, after bearing five children, the toll of childbearing began showing on Margaret. She lost the glow in her cheeks, the sparkle in her eyes, the point of her chin. Casper was worried. Margaret Haustein, wife to Casper, mother to five, died.

Casper couldn't stop. He had five children to feed, so he worked even harder on his acreage and at the Trout Brook Grocery. After a couple of years he fell in love and married again . . . married another Hamm from Faribault, Margaret's sister Sybilla. Sybilla and Casper raised four more children, as if five weren't already enough. Jerry, Donnie, Helen and Marie eventually joined the first brood on the farm. Now there were nine Haustein children to go along with the vegetables, cattle, sheep, cats and dogs.

The children worked in the vegetable garden, in the barn, in the house, at the grocery store and on the levee. They attended St. Joseph's Catholic School, had their fingers slapped by the nuns as they learned their A, B, Cs, went to confession, Mass, said their nightly prayers and grew up, all that is, except Eddie who drowned in the Mississippi River. He got cramps swimming one day off the levee. He never came up. Casper had lost Margaret, then Eddie — lost him to the Mississippi, the same river his father had so admired when he first gazed upon it from atop the Wisconsin bluffs. But Casper carried on and the children carried on. They eventually left home, courted and married. The Hausteins had made their presence known in Red Wing.

6

Franklins And Hausteins Meet . . . The Second Time

The Haustein children were natural fishermen, but none could fish like Donald. He was the master angler in Red Wing, a regular Huckelberry Finn. In summer he would rent a flat-bottomed scow not unlike the shanty boats used by Samuel Clemens down-river in Hannibal a century earlier, then cast off with oars to find a backwater slew away from the main channel. He would catch walleyes by the stringer; no one could catch walleyes like Donnie. On a Saturday afternoon in 1930 he floated farther away from the main channel than normal . . . got himself back into underbrush searching for crappies. Walleyes weren't biting anyway, because it was too hot. He rowed toward Collischan's Landing upriver where there would be cooler water, and if he could find a shade tree or on old willow along the river, he might have some luck catching a mess of crappies. He rowed toward a sweeping willow, saw another scow with a couple of fishermen in it, asked if he could fish with them, set his anchor, baited a number ten hook with worms, snapped on a cork bobber, and set back to catch crappies. "Catchin' anything today, fellows?" Donnie whispered through the willow branches.

"Just a couple of small ones. Pretty slow."

"Name's Donnie Haustein."

"Tom Franklin and Bill Ryan here."

"Where you fellows from?"

"Belle Creek. Working farms about fifteen miles from here."

"Farmers from Belle Creek? Shouldn't you be working the fields today?"

"Should . . . fishin's better."

"You got that right!"

While fishing for crappies, Tom Franklin with best friend Bill Ryan, met his future brother-in-law. Ironically, Tom and Bill would marry the same woman someday—Donnie's sister Lucille. It was a scorcher, breezy. The crappies weren't biting.

Donnie's brother Bert wasn't big on fishing. He would fish now and then, if they were biting, but he preferred playing baseball, basketball, any kind of ball. He was wiry, could hit, run and throw. He was fast and mean on the ball field, at least when he wanted to be . . . played third base for the Red Wing River Rats. He could get any grounder between the third base foul line and deep short, scooping the grounder, twisting, twirling and throwing a line drive to the first baseman. You couldn't drive a grounder past Bert Haustein. He could hit, too, a roundhouse curve, a drop, a fastball.

Pitchers didn't slip anything past him. "Lucille. We have a ball-game against the Belle Creek Grainers this afternoon at Hay Creek. Want to go along and have a picnic afterwards?" Bert yelled from his bedroom.

"I don't know. Donnie asked me to go fishing at Collischan's Landing. He said the crappies were beginning to bite again."

"Come on, Lucille, you can catch crappies any old time. Come with me. You'll have a good time."

"Uff da!"

7

Franklins And Hausteins Meet A Third Time

Tom Franklin and Bill Ryan each finished haying late Saturday afternoon on their respective farms, met at the corner of County Roads 9 and No. 7, then drove to the Belle Creek Hall. After putting up hay all day they were ready to relax, dance the shimmy or the hoochie coochie, and have a couple of Grain Belt brews. "You playing ball tomorrow with the Grainers against Red Wing, Bill?"

"Guess so. You going to play?"

"I'm pretty tired now from haying all day, but maybe I'll feel better in the morning. I'd like to beat the River Rats. That Haustein is a braggart and I'd like to help him get his comeuppance!"

"Let's meet at my place, then we'll drive to Hay Creek."

Tom Franklin and Lucille Haustein met at that Sunday afternoon baseball game in Hay Creek. Tom played second base for the Grainers while Lucille watched brother Bert play shortstop for the River Rats. Country Belle Creek versus city slicker Red Wing.

Tom was having a difficult time concentrating on the game, because he noticed this cute girl wearing a print dress and white, high-heeled shoes sitting on a blanket along the first base side. In fact, he committed a couple of fielding errors because of looking at her as the ball slithered toward center field. "What the hell is wrong with you, Franklin?" Pat Rowles, the manager, yelled.

"Caught some dust in my eye. I'll get the next one."

But he didn't. He was still looking toward the first base side trying to catch another glimpse of the girl when another grounder screamed toward him. He booted it, again. "Damn it, Franklin, get your head in the game or I'll have you out of there."

Bert Haustein was next at bat for the River Rats. He drove a hard line drive into center field. He was fast. He rounded first base on the fly and barreled toward Tom covering second base. Bert slid hard sending both Tom and himself hurtling through the dusty infield. Bert reached the base before the ball, before you could say Jack Robinson. It was the third meeting between the Franklins and Hausteins. "Not too shabby a slide there, Red Wing."

"Nice catch yourself, Belle Creek."

"Hey, do you know who that girl is, the one sitting on the blanket behind first base?"

"You mean in the print dress and white shoes?"

"Yes, her."

"That's my sister, Lucille."

"Your sister?"

"Yeah, my sister. You want to make something of it?"

"No, I was just noticing her and . . . could you introduce me after the game?"

"What? Me introduce her to you, a dumb Grainer!"

"Watch it, you river scoundrel."

To this day, I don't know who started the fight. The Hausteins adamantly said it was Tom and the Franklins maintained it was Bert. Suddenly, Tom and Bert swung fists and wrestled to the ground around second base. Both teams converged on them—the entire field erupted into a donnybrook. Now, the Red Wing boys were big, but they miscalculated the ferocity of the Belle Creekers. One fight you didn't want to get mixed up in is one with a bunch of Irish farmers. There wasn't another ball pitched that day. It took half an hour to clear the field of the brannigan. There were broken, bloody noses, cuffed ears and skinned knuckles, but it finally ended. For thirty years afterward, Tom and Bert argued about who started the fight, but they never resolved it; besides, the most important thing happened anyway—Tom met Lucille, married her and raised Rose Marie, Tommy, Jimmy and Daniel. Tom forgave Bert, Bert forgave Tom and the Franklins and Hausteins united and lived happily every after . . . for the most part.

Great-grandfathers David Franklin and Joseph Haustein had each left their homelands on the same day in 1853 and arrived in New York City four weeks later. Both eventually began new families and new lives in Goodhue County. The two families were united on a rocky, sun-scorched cow pasture of a baseball diamond alongside a meandering creek. Both David and Joseph raised large families, their children, in-turn, raising many more, all above average. Their ancestors had done it in Ireland and Austria; they did it in Minnesota. Grandparents Casper, Margaret and Sybilla Haustein raised nine children; grandparents David and Catherine Franklin raised seven children, eighteen Holsteins, five Guernseys, and seven turkeys. Those children, in-turn, raised large families, so large that I have in the vicinity of forty-five first cousins . . . can't count them all, can't remember them all.

Chapter 10

Baseball

Sunday Afternoon at the Ball Diamond

T HE MAZEPPA BASEBALL TEAM COULDN'T LOCATE the ball diamond. They saw the water tower, the white grain silo, corn and wheatfields besieging the village, barley stocks swaying gently in the warm breeze, yet they weren't able to find Goodhue's field. They resorted to asking an old-timer . . . "Head up the street, hang a Ralph at Emily Parker's, go two blocks, hang a Louie at Bill O'Reilly's place, drive two blocks, hang a Ralph at the big elm tree, head west toward Elmer Bremer's place. So, the ball diamond is out there on the edge of town, then. Can't miss it."

____1

The Town Team

Edges weren't difficult to find, there being only four. The village was an oasis among golden fields of grain, a watering hole in the illusionary grain-field desert. On endless Sunday afternoons, when the home team wasn't playing baseball, I could gaze in any direction from my tree house and imagine a swelling sea in the shimmering wheatfields that rolled like waves across the prairie. But within that sea of grain was our oasis.

To some folks the diamond was only a rock-strewn field, but to my friends and me it was a *sparkling* diamond. Baseball was one of the most important things in our lives, if not *the* most important. We didn't have tennis courts and didn't play golf because it was considered an expensive, frivolous pastime, certainly not a respectable sport nor within our means. Parents didn't want us spending money for golf clubs and green fees. They worked long, hard days earning only enough money to put food on the table, buy second-hand clothes for our backs, slip a dollar in Sunday's envelope, shake and shimmy at Gorman's Dreamland Ballroom to the music of Jules Herman or Fez Fitch and the Polka Dots on Saturday night, or walk to the ball diamond on a drowsy, butterfly-filled Sunday afternoon to watch the town team versus Mazeppa.

About 1946 I began traipsing nightly to that patch of dirt with Tom to watch the town team practice hitting and fielding. Tom usually beat me, being two years older and faster. At ten, two years is like twenty-five to an older brother. He couldn't wait for his tag-along younger brother, much less be seen in his company. He tolerated me. Tom played baseball with older fellows—George O'Reilly, Lyle Rusch, Harold Lensch, Terry Shelstad, Dale and Darrell Jonas—which made me seem even younger. As I brought up the rear, the town team would already be practicing just beyond Blanche Barry's back yard. Blanche didn't get home run balls in her yard, but she acquired many foul tips that eluded the chicken-wire backstop. I don't believe I ever saw that backstop actually stop a ball. Foul tips either slithered through one of a hundred holes or skittered underneath like a wounded chicken. I watched our boys of summer practicing during the week, but I was also at the diamond Sunday afternoons when a Mazeppa batter would lift a long drive to deep right field, our fielder treading backward until finally losing the soaring ball in the cornfield. Home run!

When Dad was playing baseball against the Red Wing River Rats that day he met Mother, the Belle Creekers were called The Grainers, but in the forties the Goodhue town team didn't have a name or a mascot. They were still my heroes. Billy Schulz and his side-winding brother Elroy, Vaughn David Bien, Burt Eppen, Harold Lensch, Joe Boxrud, Terry Shelstad and Lefty O'Reilly were on the team. The four Lodermeier brothers appeared one day seemingly out of nowhere. They arrived after journeying across a wilderness to the east. Wisconsin. They could all play baseball, being tough and ready fellows with strong hands, bulging shoulders, but warm hearts. Leonard, Jerry, Norb and Ed were good players and good to me. They let me fetch their bats, chase foul balls, snag grounders, chew Beech Nut and spit on their gloves.

Practice consisted mostly of batting and fielding, but if the infield wasn't muddy, they perfected double plays and cutoffs and run-downs. Occasionally, someone would drag the diamond with his Farmall so the infielders would have a reasonable chance of fielding the hard grounders that shot off opposing bats.

Joyce Shelstad was the manager, or I should say, usually the manager. He owned and operated Shelstad's Cafe but baseball was his real love. He knew the game well and even managed me when I played later in the fifties.

On Sunday game days, I couldn't wait for Father to finish the *Sanctus,* the *Agnus Dei,* his long, boring sermon and to read yet another letter from the bishop asking for money to support some far-off mission I had never heard of. I couldn't wait to finish dinner (Sunday roast beef, Monday hash), and rush to the diamond for the game. Wiping ketchup and gravy from my mouth, I would rush out of the house with bat, ball and cap, dart through our back yard through the pine trees, around the high school, through Blanche's yard, hurdle her fence to the baseball field and slide into home plate. The crowd would already be gathering, because baseball was the most popular entertainment, after free movies that is. Goodhue's population was four hundred fifty, but on a Sunday afternoon there would be that many fans and more sitting on rickety bleachers around the first and third base sides, and picnicking with chicken sandwiches down the left field foul line. Many chicken dinners were toppled during those years by a left fielder chasing a foul ball into the picnicking fans. They didn't care. They were watching husbands, brothers, and friends play baseball.

2

Babe Schulz

When not at the local diamond, I listened to WCCO out of Minneapolis as Mickey Mantle drove a long ball beyond the Babe Ruth monument in Yankee Stadium's cavernous center field. I could envision the soaring horsehide and Mickey racing around the bases. He was my Major League hero, but was way off in New York. Where was New York, anyway? Mantle was fast and could hit something terrible. The word around town was that he could be down to first base in 3.3 seconds when he batted from the left side of the plate. That's fast. Vaughn David Bien was speedy, but not that fast. I would have loved to see Mantle play, yet I didn't need to because I could transport myself to Yankee Stadium through the magic of radio and my imagination.

The Yankees also had Roger Maris who during my high

school years was trying desperately to break Babe Ruth's single season home run record. Fellows tended to forget about Mantle as Maris edged closer to Ruth's record, yet Mantle had almost as many home runs. Then Maris finally broke Ruth's home run record of sixty in a single season. "Way to go, Maris."

"Heckuva deal!"

"Not too shabby!"

But I still liked Mickey best. I never knew what to think about Maris. He broke the great Babe's record. Were home run, hitting and pitching records made only to be broken by some smart aleck upstart? Hard stuff for a boy to understand.

We had our own Babe—Elroy "Babe" Schulz. El could hit the ball out of sight. Now, some local cynics said that wasn't too difficult considering the close horizons of the village; nevertheless, he sure could smack a baseball. He was a big man towering over smaller guys—six foot three inches, tough, a mean two hundred thirty pounds. On his long stride to the plate, big stick in hand, he struck fear in the hearts of every would-be baseball player in the county. He batted right-handed and could drive a screaming ball over third base, into left field, across the ditch, over the gravel road and into Elmer Bremer's beanfield where it wouldn't be found until the beans were harvested in the fall. Elroy did this so many times it didn't surprise us, but visiting teams were amazed.

On the third Sunday of July 1949 he hit one. As the ball arced over the mid-day sun, picnickers along the left field foul line shuddered, chicken legs suspended in their mouths, eyes following the horsehide across hazy skies. Mazeppa's left fielder stumbled backward until he reached the ditch in front of the gravel road. His left leg gave way, then he hit the bank on the far side of the ditch, reeling one hundred eighty degrees, sprawling onto the gravel road. He slid across the road skinning his face and arms while scooping up a mouth full of sand and grit. As he looked up he saw the ball sailing headlong over his head into the beanfield: *Who is this guy?* We knew who he was. Babe Schulz.

Elroy was one of the few players who could strike fear in the hearts of those wily Mazeppians. He used a thirty-six-inch bat. A bat of that length and heft was dreadfully convincing. I don't know if he needed a thirty-six-incher or if he just knew that size was the most intimidating to teams from Zumbrota, Wabasha, Mazeppa and Oronoco. He could tear the horsehide off the ball with one mighty swing. When he connected, he connected big; when he missed, he missed big. He was a white-southeastern-Minnesota Reggie Jackson swinging for the fields—corn fields, wheat fields, bean fields. There was no joy when Big El struck out.

It was a scorcher that day the Mazeppa team finally found the ball diamond. Ninety-five degrees, sun beating down unmercifully, and the team's uniforms made from heavy wool, probably some of the same wool we stomped at Heaney's. Some players even wore a sweatshirt underneath their wool shirt to enhance sweating, a local baseball fallacy, "The more you sweat the better baseball player you will become. Put on more clothes, boys. Sweat!" The team would have preferred the shade of Blanche's back yard, but there was Mazeppa to beat, always Mazeppa.

In the seventh inning, Billy Schulz drove a ball to deep right field, rounded first base and slid into second. He had to stay in the game because he was the only pitcher we had left, and there were three more innings to play. From the bench, "Keep that arm warm, Pitch!" From the bleachers, "Don't cool down, Pitch!" From the backstop, "Put on your jacket, Pitch!"

Joyce looked down at me sitting by the bat rack. "Take this jacket out to the Pitch, kid." I was startled, stars in my eyes, but I grabbed the warmup jacket and ran across the third base foul line kicking up a cloud of white lime as I rushed toward second with the jacket.

"Put it on, Pitch. Keep your arm warm. Nice double, Pitch."

"Thanks, kid."

They struggled back and forth throughout the sweltering afternoon. Swirls of dirt twisted like small tornadoes across the infield blurring the sight of the infielders. Our team played hard to win. Winning was very important for them, and me. Billy Schulz versus Mazeppa. Lefty O'Reilly versus Zumbrota. El Schulz versus Wabasha. The boys of summer. Win one for Jimmy.

They ran, slid, hit, caught, stretched as far as they could to make great dives for double plays. Billy struck out seven of the remaining nine opposing batters. Harold drilled a line drive to deep right. Hot, dry, "Damn, I'm thirsty. Let's get this over," Billy shouted as they left the bench for the ninth inning.

Mazeppa ties in the bottom of the ninth. Extra innings.

Top of the tenth, Bien doubles. Lodermeier (one of the four) singles in the winning run! Goodhue prevails. We've won!

A tattered ball, hide torn off is driven deep into Bremer's beanfield. A case of Grain Belt beer is tapped by the boys of summer in the shade of the elm tree along left field. A boy's heroes had won to play another day.

3

Corkball By The Apple Tree

Our town team heroes inspired me to develop my own baseball skills, but there were seldom enough fellows around to get up a full-fledged game, so we reverted to the next best game. Corkball.

> *It's a long, long drive to right field. Will it stay fair? It's headed toward Ole's house. Will it hit and be foul, or will it miss and be a home run? It's going . . . going . . . gone!*

We played corkball by the hour, by the day, by the week, by the summer. New York boys played stickball in the canyoned streets of the Bronx, but Goodhue boys played corkball on the prairie. I don't know to this day who invented the game, whether it was George O'Reilly, Harold Lensch, Terry Shelstad or someone from out of town, but this is how we played the game.

It was a simulated game needing only a pitcher, a batter, a Louisville Slugger and a couple of Jesse's fishing corks—one to play with and one for a spare. We didn't need much space either. We would set up a miniature diamond by measuring twenty feet to first base (place a coal cinder), twenty feet to second (place a cinder), twenty feet to third (another cinder), and then designate the corner of Haga's house as the right field foul line, the corner of our house as the left field foul line. The apple tree would be the backstop, and the street would be home run territory. Jack O'Reilly and Jimmy Franklin became Mickey Mantle and Warren Spahn on that field. The Boston Braves were playing the New York Yankees in the World Series . . .

> *Top of the seventh inning here in Yankee Stadium. The Yankees are down by one run because Spahn is pitching well today. He has a good fastball, and I've never seen a better curveball in my life. He started that last curveball toward first base, but it came across the plate at the last second. He's got a one-hitter going, and that was a measly little Texas Leaguer by Billy Martin back in the third inning, but now he's facing Mickey Mantle, and although Mantle has already fanned twice today, it's not likely even the great Warren Spahn can strike him out three times in a row.*

Dig in now, Jimmy (aka Mickey Mantle). You can get a hit off the ol' southpaw. Don't swing early. You know he'll throw that big roundhouse that floats in from first base. Just wait and be patient.

Jack (aka Warren Spahn) crouched low on the mound, tugged his cap, pulled up his britches and squinted toward his catcher (the apple tree). He shrugged off the first sign, *Must have been a fastball*, shrugged off the second sign, *Must have been a screwball*, and nodded for the third sign, *Must be a curveball*. Jack began his big, sweeping windup. Through the creases of his fingers I could see the corkball. It seemed as if he had thrown it straight at Ole's house instead of to home plate, but you could do that with a corkball. (A corkball hurler could throw peculiar stuff. If they had a little wind working for them, guys could make that cork dance. They could throw huge Warren Spahn-like curves. They could throw "drops" that would drop ninety degrees twelve inches in front of the batter. A pitch like that left the batter wondering where the ball went. And they could throw screwballs that curved away from a left-handed batter.) Jack's pitch acted like an Australian outback boomerang. It headed toward Ole's, came around the evergreen tree in a big arc, slipped through a limb of the apple tree and fluttered toward the plate.

Be patient, Jim. Don't swing early.

I waited an eternity for it. I was in a state of animated suspension. But at last it was only three feet in front of me. I gripped harder just like Mickey and Big El. I spat Beechnut chew at the plate like Billy Martin and Norb Lodermeier. The bat and cork met, clean and square sending that corkball sailing down the right field line. It was flying foul, toward the house when a gust of wind suddenly blew it fair and into the street for a home run.

Yankees 1, Braves 0.

Getting up a game was easy. If Harold Lensch shuffled by we would let him in the game for an inning or two. If Davie Franklin sauntered by we would play two against two, but it was usually Tom, George, Lee or Jack playing. Bob and Larry weren't interested in corkball.

We argued a lot, though, because we didn't run the bases or even catch the corkball. If we drove it directly toward first base it was assumed the first baseman could make the play, and if we hit one in the hole, we could get a hit unless the other team had a fantastic shortstop. "It's a drive through the hole."

"Hey, no way, my shortstop had it clean."

"What do you mean, had it? He could never have gotten to that ball; it was belted too hard and on the line."

"Wasn't either."

"Was too."

Eventually we would make a decision and the game would continue past dark, in the street under the street light. It was a good way to pass the summer hours; besides, we were developing skills for real baseball.

Although I became increasingly interested in softball and baseball, I didn't give up corkball. If the afternoon was slow and drowsy, I would call up Lee or Jack and get a quick game going.

Goodhue High School fielded a baseball team and I sure wanted to play on it when I became a freshman; consequently, I began playing more softball and baseball during the summers of '48 and '49. There was a vacant lot behind Ole's house, just right for a neighborhood diamond. I thought it would be more realistic if we had dusty base paths like the major leagues, so I carried several buckets of cinders from our coal-burning furnace to the field and sprinkled them on the base paths. Then when we slid into second base like the Yankees and Braves, dust would spiral skyward. It seemed like a good idea at the time, but practically, it didn't work. Those cinders were rough, scraping our knees, elbows and hands. The fellows didn't think much of my idea. I scooped up the cinders, carried them away and returned the base paths to their natural dirt state. Everyone was happy again, even without dust.

I couldn't always get a game going, but I could usually play catch with someone or alone. I carried my glove and ball with me everywhere, so I could work on a curve- or screwball at anytime. But I wasn't a Bob Feller, the Iowa farm boy who developed pitch–ing accuracy by throwing into a fruit basket nailed to the side of the barn. I tried that but early on knew I wasn't destined to be a pitcher.

Mother was patient with me as I transformed our lawn into a ball field and the house into a stadium. She had the patience of Job, because hour after hour I bounced a baseball against the second story of our house to catch it as if I were in Yankee Stadium taking a home run away from Willie Mays. It must have made a horren-dous noise inside, but she seldom complained. She never told me to stop, until one day . . .

There were two front bedroom windows on the second story with fifteen feet of clapboard siding between them on which I threw the ball. I mentioned earlier that I wasn't a Bob Feller? It wasn't usually that difficult to throw the ball between the win-dows, but on a Friday in June of 1949, I had trouble. My arm wasn't accurate that day. It was June 6 that I struck out. Here's how it happened . . . .

About ten o'clock I took my first strike. Instead of throwing the baseball between the windows, it slithered off my index finger and soared straight through Rose's bedroom window. Strike one! Mother stormed through the screen door, "Heaven help me, what on earth have you done now?"

"Well, you see, Mom, it slipped and . . ."

"Well, don't break any more windows today. Lord knows how we'll be able to pay for a new window."

It set me back for awhile. I shimmied up the apple tree for a Jonathan, climbed into my tree house to eat it, strolled around the softball field kicking up dust around home plate, but there wasn't anyone around. I was bored, hot and thirsty. It was so hot that talking slowed to a halt in the village. You know it was hot when villagers didn't want to talk. I set my ball and glove on the porch and walked downtown to the Shell Station. "How ya doin' today, Luverne?"

"Sonofabitchin' hot!"

"Giving that piece of junk a valve job?"

"Yup."

I had never heard Luverne say *yup*. He was always good for many more words, words that I sort of liked and didn't hear at my house. Salty words. Tasty words. Words you could get your teeth into. Words that twisted your tongue when you tried them. Confession-telling words. I would try them as I kicked an empty Hamm's Beer can through the alley behind the station . . . "SonofaBITCH! . . . SonOFabitch! . . . SonofAbitch! . . . SONofabitch!" If I timed it right I could pronounce a word just as I kicked the can so Florence Taylor wouldn't hear me from across the alley at her Eat Shop. I didn't want her telling my mom what she might have heard . . . "Shit! . . . SHEit! . . . SheeIT! . . . Shit! . . . Shit!"

Then there was the F word. It was harder to say because it was considerably stronger. I didn't know why, but I had noticed Luverne using it only when he was mad like when he couldn't get a piston back into the block of a Ford engine or when the wrench would slip skinning his knuckles; then the F word certainly came out . . . "F . . . ! . . . Goddamn this sonofabitch! . . . F . . . !" When that happened you could hear him for blocks. You knew he wasn't having a good day.

Mother didn't use those words, although she came real close later that day, and Dad didn't use them; I picked up my early salty-word training from Luverne. I tried "sonofabitch" in the alley, but I had to walk to the outskirts behind the baseball diamond to try the F word. I would walk behind the backstop, or maybe into the third row of corn . . . "F . . . ! . . . F . . . ! . . . F . . . !" I practiced it, because I didn't know when I might need to use it. I wanted to be prepared.

But all I got out of Luverne today was a clipped *yup*, so I tried my luck elsewhere. I sauntered to Sidney's where I found him nailing a pair of new heels on Cy Benda's work boots. "Hey, Sidney, how you doing today?"

"Hot."

That was it. That's all. "Well, I'll be seeing you then, so long."

"Whatever."

I skipped over to the Blacksmith Shop to search for some guys talkin'. Conditions were even worse there, because in addition to a blistering sun beating on the tin roof, Bill was creating more heat in his forge. "Hi Bill. Making horseshoes?"

"Yup."

Clink, clank, clink, clank. The only sound was the tap of his hammer against the anvil as he pounded red-hot metal into a horseshoe. Erv Richter watched from a keg of nails. Tommy Schinnert watched from a wagon tongue. Norris Husbyn supervised from a wagon seat. Nobody talking. "Well, I guess I'll be going, then. See you fellows," I hollered on my way out the door.

"Whatever."

There was no talking this day. I walked back home to my glove and baseball. That was a mistake.

I was soon back to my game of bouncing the ball off the second story wall. Things were going well. I had the entire outfield covered when, suddenly, I was distracted by Mrs. Hennings' bulldog as they walked by. I was about to throw the ball when that dog barked and nipped at my heel. I turned to kick the dog off just as the baseball left my hand only it wasn't going in the right direction. "Oh, no, that F . . . ! . . . dog!" I shrugged it off, turned and saw the ball heading toward my bedroom window, on line. If I had tried to hit the window I couldn't have, but this throw was straight as an arrow, a clothesline throw all the way from Yankee Stadium's center field Babe Ruth monument to home plate. It was fast, strong and accurate. It crashed through the window, rolled through the door and bounced down the stairway stopping at Mother's feet in the kitchen. Strike two! She exploded through the screen door. "Jesus, Mary, and Joseph, now what have you gone and done?"

"Well, you see, I was playing center field and this dog came onto the field and just as I was ready to throw the runner out at home plate, this dog . . ."

"I don't want to hear another word. Put your glove away and don't touch it for the rest of the day. Lord, have mercy! I don't know how we're going to pay for two broken windows."

About four o'clock Tom and George sauntered into the yard. I had been sulking for a couple of hours, so when I saw them, my spirits rose.

Maybe we can get a game going, but Mother told me to put my glove away and not touch it for the rest of the day.

"What's happening, Jimmy?" George yelled.

"Not much, just sittin' around."

"Want to play some catch?"

"Naw, I don't think so. I'm kind of tired."

"Oh, come on, get your glove and the three of us can play catch."

"Well, I guess I could play for a few minutes."

It was a mistake. I should have obeyed Mother and left my glove and ball under the bed. I had already made two mistakes today—the count was two strikes and no balls—but I wasn't ready for strike three, no one was.

I don't know if Tom and George had heard about the two broken windows earlier in the day. If they had, they might have set me up; anyway, we started playing catch. Tom stood by the apple tree, George stood in front of the porch which was in front of the living room bay window and I stood on the sidewalk. We formed a triangle. George threw to Tom by the apple tree. Tom threw to me on the sidewalk. I threw to George in front of the porch in front of the bay window. They should have known better, because they were older. They should have realized that triangle-throwing arrangement was a disaster waiting to happen. They placed me in the wrong position; I should have been by the apple tree throwing toward the street so that if the throw was wild it could have rolled innocently into the street. But we were having fun—George to Tom, Tom to Jim, Jim to George. Again, around the triangle. It was like throwing from right field to center field to left field to right field in Yankee Stadium. George to Tom. Tom to Jim. Jim to . . . disaster struck! To this day I don't know how it happened, but the ball went awry. I don't know if I had too much spit on the ball or if I was holding the seams wrong or if I had a poor grip. Jim to George short-circuited. George never caught the baseball. It sailed over his head, over the evergreen bush, into the porch on a beeline toward the bay window—the stained glass window behind which Mother placed her house plants and figurines. I covered my eyes with my glove. I couldn't stand to watch, but I heard it. The crash was deafening. Strike three!

I had never seen that expression on Mother's face before. I had seen her angry when the roast beef burned, or when Tom and I didn't mow the lawn on time, but I hadn't seen this particular expression. She stood on the porch for the longest time, not saying a word. Tom, under the apple tree, was doing all he could to keep from laughing. George was holding his side from laughing so much. I think she was saying prayers for me, because she was looking at the heavens. Then she turned and marched into the house. Tom and George ran to tell Dad what had happened. Had I been Luverne Haas' son I would have heard some choice words, but Dad was quiet; he wasn't prone to using salty words. I didn't follow them. I reasoned I would be better off staying right where I was. Dad's only comment was, "What the hell is wrong with that kid?" Oh, it was tough being a boy, sometimes.

Chapter 11

Music Pioneers

Goodhue Community Concert Band, 1926

CHARLES WOOD WAS THE PIED PIPER OF MUSIC during my school years in the forties and fifties; however, he was preceded by two prominent local music pioneers. Long before Wood ambled into town, Ben Gorman and Marldine Richter had provided music for the village in the twenties and thirties.

___1

Ben Gorman & Marldine Richter

I began my musical career—one I was to follow professionally for thirty years—in the school gymnasium that September evening of 1947. But I wasn't beginning my journey alone. The spirits of Ben and Marldine guided my quest. Long after they were gone, I could still walk downtown on a summer's night and by listening carefully, hear those sweet, melancholy melodies emanating from the old Dreamland Ballroom building—Ben Gorman's mellifluous C Melody Sax floated across the street to the curb in front of Eddie's Drugstore where I sat. Old-timers sauntering by told me about Ben's music. They said he could render a fine rendition, playing his heart out on *The Waltz You Saved For Me*. They said there wouldn't be a dry eye in the ballroom. I played my own waltz several years later.

Mother and Dad took me downtown on Saturday nights to hear Marldine Richter play clarinet and conduct the Goodhue Concert Band—upper street the first and third Saturdays of the month, lower street the second and fourth—where the band's music made an early impression on me. We sat on blankets and listened to Sousa, Pryor, Kriatori, King and maybe even a von Suppé overture. Marldine conducted and played clarinet at the same time! I had seen cornet players with the Barnum and Bailey Circus Band in Red Wing doing that, but never a clarinetist. With only three valves to press, cornetists could easily play one-handed while conducting with the other, but clarinetists taking one hand off experienced disaster. But Marldine could do it because of a special device.

He was marginally acquainted with John Yungers, Senior, the inventor *par excellence* in the village. Marldine had an idea; he went to see John. He told him he wanted to be able to play the full range of the clarinet with his left hand while leaving his right hand free to conduct. To-date, he could only play five notes on the upper section. John didn't know a damn thing about music, but he loved solving mechanical problems, like how to make a two-handed clarinet player into a one-handed player.

John designed a special mechanism that Marldine could operate with his left pinkie finger. An additional foot pedal device permitted Marldine to operate keys he normally played with his right hand. The Rube Goldberg contraption, and you would surely have to call it that, worked fine. Marldine could now play anything one-handed that he normally played two-handed. There was only one problem. The contraption was heavy. John had used heavy metal long before *heavy metal* meant anything in the musical world. He had used plate iron for the foot pedal device; it weighed over one hundred pounds. Marldine could use it for Saturday concerts in town, but it was too heavy to tote out of town. It was a one-of-a-kind, John Yunger's, one-handed-clarinet-player device.

Marldine directed the town band for many years, an ensemble of bakers, butchers, farmers, bartenders, housewives and merchants, folks who unpacked their tarnished Conn silver cornet or Pan American clarinet a couple times per week to play Sousa's *Stars and Stripes* or the *Washington Post* march. He directed the village band until the school board encouraged him in 1936 to start a school band. He did. I joined that band eleven years later after Marldine had retired and Charles Wood whistled into town.

In addition to Ben and Marldine, other musicians, bands and orchestras contributed to the village's musical environment. Burgs from Belvidere to White Rock supported various music groups. Cornet bands, string bands and saxophone orchestras played at dives and dance halls from the Mississippi to Zumbro rivers. Our parents and grandparents danced to the Wilcox Orchestra and Rehder's Orchestra at Anderson's Opera House on lower street. Later generations danced to Ben's saxophone and orchestra at Gorman's Dreamland Ballroom on upper street.

Dancing was a popular pastime during the twenties, thirties and forties. High steppers would dance all night doing the Big Apple, the Black Bottom, the Hoochie Coochie, the Shake, the Shimmy, the Cakewalk, the Charleston, the Lindy Hop, the polka, the mazurka, the waltz, tripping the light fantastic cheek to cheek and belly to belly. Territory bands played anyplace they could. A pianist, a C Melody saxophonist, a cornetist, an accordionist, a tubaist, maybe a violinist and guitarist made up a band for swing, old-time or square dances. They might have appeared at Anderson's Saturday night, White Rock Town Hall Sunday night, Gorman's Dreamland Ballroom Monday night, then moved on to Wastedo, Vasa, Bellechester, Zumbrota, Oak Center or Oronoco.

I listened for those music ghosts of nights past whenever I could. Mom and Dad talked about the dances they had attended as young adults, so I knew there had been good orchestras barnstorming the area. They talked about dancing to Tether's Orchestra in 1915 to *Alice Blue Gown, Girl Of My Dreams, You're A Million Miles From Nowhere When You're One Little Mile From Home,* and *Shine On Harvest Moon*. They danced to the Bennett-Greten band. They told me stories about bands traveling in horse-drawn carriages when Grandfather and Grandmother Franklin danced to Rehder's Orchestra at the Belle Creek Hall in 1890 to *Poor Butterfly, Royal Garden Blues* and *Oh! How I Hate To Get Up In The Morning*. The orchestra had used two reeds, two violins, and a piano. Dad said Catherine and David had also danced to Martin's Orchestra and Halstad's Orchestra around the turn of the century to *The Whippoorwill, Mighty Lak' A Rose* and *Won't You Waltz 'Home Sweet Home' With Me For Old Times Sake?* Dad told me about other bands and orchestras that traveled through southern Minnesota when he and Mother were courting in the twenties. They danced the Shimmy and the Hoochie Coochie to *After You've Gone, Alexander's Ragtime Band,* and their all-time favorite, *Sorry, I Ain't Got It You Could Have It If I Had It Blues!*

I wanted to hear those bands, too; I did . . . sort of. I would retrieve my clarinet, walk downtown about dusk tooting a few notes as I rounded the Corner Bar, sit on the curb across the street from Marshall-Wells Hardware (formerly the Dreamland Ballroom), hold my clarinet gently, sit quietly and soon *hear* Halstad's Orchestra. Such a sweet band. They had the Guy Lombardo sound before Guy was around. I heard them play *The Waltz You Saved For Me*, *Anniversary Waltz*, *Apple Blossom Time*, *By The Light Of The Silvery Moon*, *La Paloma*, and *The Rose of Tralee*. Before long I would be playing along with those orchestras of times past. I didn't know the tunes very well, but I could figure them out. My fingers seemed to find the right keys; besides, I didn't have to fuss with John Yunger's contraption. I listened and dreamed and played. One evening Red Ryan staggered by . . ."Hey, kid, you know *Melancholy Baby?*"

"Sure, Red, I can play it. Wanna hear it?"

"Naw, just wonderin' if you could play it!"

Red wobbled to the other end of the street to find another bar, but I played *Melancholy Baby* for myself . . .

Come to me, my Melancholy Baby,
Cuddle up and don't be blue.
All your fears are foolish fancies maybe,
You know, dear, I'm in love with you.

I could play anything, at least I could make up anything. Sometimes I lost track of time sitting on the curb in front of Eddie's gazing across the street where Dreamland used to be . . . listening . . . imagining. Townsfolk became accustomed to seeing me with my clarinet . . . "How you doing tonight, Jimmy?"

"Could be worse, Erv."

"What band are you listening to tonight."

"Oh, Martin's Orchestra is playing. They're a good group, you know."

"Yeah, I danced to 'em as a kid. Want to play me a song?"

"Darn tootin', Erv, what would you like to hear?"

"That Old Gang Of Mine."

I would begin playing . . .

Gee, but I'd give the world to see,
That Old Gang Of Mine,

I can't forget the old quartette,
That sang 'Sweet Adeline,'

Erv sat beside me on the curb singing, then wiping his eyes. He would lift a pint of Seagram's Seven out of his back pocket, take a swig, wipe his mouth on his shirt sleeve . . .

Good-bye forever, old fellows and gals,
Good-bye for ever, old . . . sweet . . . hearts . . . and . . . pals
God Ble . . .

He would forget the words and begin dozing off as I played his song softly in the shadowy, moonlit evening.

Gee but I'd give the world to see,
That Old Gang Of Mine.

Erv liked *That Old Gang Of Mine* . . . made him sad for his long lost sportin' buddies. He like waltzes, too, especially *I'll See You Again.* He asked me to play *Melancholy Baby* often, but he never heard the end of it. As I played the second chorus, he would slump to his elbow until settling on the sidewalk like ol' Buck, feet in the gutter, head nuzzled against my leg, arm cradling the Seagram's. After he was asleep, I would disassemble my clarinet, then walk home leaving him with his favorite melody lingering in his head. Tomorrow night would be the same . . . "Hi, Jimmy. Do you know *Melancholy Baby?*"

"Sure, Erv. Would you like me to play it for you?"

"Yeah, that'd be nice."

As I grew older, I became anxious to play in a real band. I could still *play* with my ghost bands, but I was ready for a band with live musicians. Jimmy Ryan changed that.

_____2

Jimmy Ryan's All-Star Orchestra

I wouldn't call Jimmy Ryan a music pioneer, because he appeared on the village scene much too late to qualify for that, but he did saunter by one evening—no pots and pans nor dangling knives this time—whistling *In The Mood* as I finished my second rendition of *Melancholy Baby.* "Hi, Franklin. Say, I'm organizing a dance band and need a clarinet player. How'd you like to join me?"

"Join you? Boy, would I. You bet I'd like to play!"

"We're having our first rehearsal Friday night at my house. Why don't you ask your mother if you can come?"

"I'll be there. Mother will let me play. You can count on that."

I didn't think Friday night would ever arrive. I practiced scales and arpeggios nonstop for two days in anticipation of my first dance band rehearsal. But I was also nervous, because Jimmy and his music friends were older than me, all in high school while I was only in seventh grade. I had confidence, though. I had been playing on the streets, playing for Grandmother Franklin and Grandfather Haustein, and playing *Melancholy Baby* for Erv . . . I would hold my own.

I strolled into Jimmy's house to see saxophonists, trombonists, cornetists, a piano plunker and guitarist warming up in the living room. He had organized the rehearsal because he wanted a band, too. He even had a name: The Jimmy Ryan Goodhue All-Star Orchestra: Sweetest Music You'd Ever Want To hear In Goodhue County. I thought it was a good name, but didn't see how he would get all that printed on his music stands. "Sit over here with the saxes, Jimmy."

"You bet." I sat and took my clarinet out of the case. Jimmy frowned, "What's that Seagram's Seven label doing in your case?"

"Oh, that must be Erv's. You see, he likes *Melancholy Baby*, and I play for him and . . . well . . . it belongs to Erv."

Jimmy's orchestra used four saxophones: Janie Yungers on tenor, Mary Lou Majerus on alto, Lyle Rusch on tenor, and Jimmy himself on alto. I was to play lead clarinet. Mary Ann McHugh and Dave Hutcheson were on trombone, Kenny Hodson on lead cornet, Jimmy Lohman second, Glenn "Sunkist Orange" Dankers third. Sister Rose played piano, brother Tom drums, sort of.

Lyle passed out the first arrangement—Glenn Miller's *Moonlight Serenade*. I knew it. Jimmy counted off. "One, two, one, two, ready, play . . ." I don't know if Glenn Miller began that way or not, but those first notes from the All-Star Orchestra were excruciating, because the parts were all mixed up. The B-flat tenors were playing the E-flat alto music. I was playing an E-flat baritone sax part on my B-flat clarinet. We were playing in three different keys simultaneously. Jimmy realized the problem, redistributed the parts, counted off again and the Jimmy Ryan Goodhue All-Star Orchestra was born. The saxes played the introduction, then I brought in my clarinet part over their harmonies. It was beautiful. I was in heaven. I loved the texture of the saxes, the brooding trombones, the punctuating cornets and the tinkling of Rose's piano. I wanted my own orchestra some day—The Jimmy Franklin Greater Goodhue All-Star Orchestra.

We played *Moonlight Serenade*, *Tuxedo Junction* and *Let's Dance* then attempted *One O'clock Jump* before it was time to quit. "Thanks for coming, Jimmy, you don't sound half bad for a seventh grader."

"Thanks. I've got to go now. Have to stop at Eddie's Drugstore to buy aspirin for Mother."

"We'll practice again next Friday night."

Mother didn't need aspirin, but I knew Erv would be waiting for me.

"Jimmy! Where you been tonight?"

"We had an orchestra practice tonight, Erv. Just finished."

"That's nice. You want to play that waltz for me?"

"Sure."

I'll See You Again . . .

"How about *Melancholy Baby?*"
"You bet."
"Just the first part, though, 'cause I never remember the second."

Come to me, my Melancholy Baby,
Cuddle up and don't be blue.
All your fears are foolish fancies maybe,
You know, dear, I'm in love with you.

Every cloud must have a . . . sil . . . ver . . . li . . . ing,
Wait . . . un . . . til . . .

Jimmy's orchestra prepared ten arrangements, enough to play for the Featherstone Future Farmers of America Banquet, the Goodhue County Breeder's Association Annual Meeting, the Lutheran Church's Four Square Ladies Bridge Club, and the White Rock Co-op Dairy Fourth of July picnic. We were a hit everywhere we played, although the Breeder's Association said we didn't sound quite like Glenn Miller. But the orchestra disbanded after playing for the Co-op Dairy picnic, because too many musicians had conflicting summer jobs.

Several years later, I played in old-time bands. Polka bands were very popular, because many pioneers who had settled in the county were from the old country and they certainly liked their polkas, waltzes, schottisches and mazurkas. I could play the *Clarinet Polka, The Waltz You Save For Me, The Blue Skirt Waltz* and other old-time tunes, but I liked modern swing music better.

By the time I graduated in '54, I had played clarinet in Jimmy Ryan's All-Star Orchestra, the Kufus Brothers old-time band, and Charles Wood's High School Concert Band. The Concert Band numbered fifty and we had played Dvorak's *New World Symphony*,

Moussorgsky's *Great Gate of Kiev,* and von Suppé's *Light Cavalry Overture.* "Bets" Lundie, Chuck Thomforde, Bob O'Reilly and I competed for the first clarinet chair for four years.

GHS didn't have a jazz band in the fifties, Jimmy Ryan had graduated and gone off to St. Thomas College, so I had to make do listening to Saturday night radio broadcasts and to the bands I could hear at the Skyline and Oak Center ballrooms. Gorman's Dreamland Ballroom with its sparkling crystal ball had long since ceased operation, but I could still *feel* the rhythms, *hear* the melodies of the bands that had played there in the twenties, thirties and forties as I sat on the curb on a moonlit summer evening.

Every cloud must have a silver lining,
Wait until the sun shines through.
Smile, my honey dear, while I kiss away each tear,
Or else I shall be melancholy too.

Chapter 12

At Home

The Family, 1939

"**Y**OUR FOOT IS OVER THE LINE ON MY SIDE."
"No, it isn't. It's on my side of the bed. I'm not over the line."
Sleeping two in a bed was difficult at times, but other times it had its advantages like during January's icebox when bone-chilling winds crossed County Road Number 9 bringing sleet and

minus twenty-two degree temperatures from Alaska to our house where Tom and I slept in an unheated upstairs bedroom. But if the temperature was high on a summer evening, two in a bed wasn't good . . .

"Stay on your side of the bed; quit crossing the line."

"I wasn't on your side. Who would want to be, anyway?"

With all the fighting between us about the line, I don't know why Mother didn't paint a line down the middle of the sheet, then we wouldn't have fought so much. She didn't. We did.

We shared a bedroom and a bed until Rose Marie graduated from high school, left home and left Goodhue for the Siberian city of Duluth to begin nurses' training. After her departure, we no longer fought about the line, because she hadn't passed the Elevator on her sojourn north before I moved into her bedroom.

_____1

Two In A Bed

We grew up on the tails of the Great Depression and FDR's reign in the White House. Life was a struggle for most parents, but the children had never known anything different. We didn't complain. We hadn't known the Roaring Twenties when Mother and Dad Charleston'd their way across the county. We had a house, food on the table, a bed, heat . . . well, some heat.

Our house was a typical white, two-story wood-frame Midwestern house like thousands dotting the prairie, a basic house with small kitchen, dining room, living room and one bedroom downstairs, two up. No toilet. No bathtub. No upstairs heat. Inside toilets and second-story heat were unheard of in 1940.

A Jungers Heatrola heated the living room and dining room just fine, even when the thermometer dipped below freezing and dagger-like icicles bent the eaves and downspouts, but little heat ascended the stairwell.

Every fall Dad followed his ritual of winterizing the house. On a Saturday morning he would begin the task while simultaneously recruiting Tom and me to help. He might get a few minutes of work out of us, but if we complained excessively, he would simply do it himself. That was Dad, a quiet, good-natured man who seldom raised a ruckus with us. But we helped, usually, to winterize before those nor'westerlies attacked the village.

Dad was a general trucker for area farmers, so he had access to straw bales. He would buy them from Pat Rowles or Francis Ryan then circumvent the house with bales at basement level, the straw providing insulation for the coming long, bleak winter. He would weather-strip window sills and place storm windows on every window. He did his best to protect us from the relentless winds, but even with his most valiant efforts, it was still freezing upstairs.

During the day Mother kept the upstairs door closed to contain the heat downstairs. A half hour before bedtime she opened it to let heat rise to the bedrooms—kids' bedrooms. Mother and Dad slept downstairs by the Heatrola. Her theory was good; however, little heat actually rose to the top of the stairs and into our bedrooms. But times were hard and, "Money doesn't grow on trees," and "I would have sent you a letter, but I didn't have three cents for a stamp," and "We can't put a Heatrola upstairs just for you kids." So, we slept in thirty-degree rooms, the honeypot ice by morning. Sleeping two in a bed was all right in January and February.

We would put on flannel pajamas downstairs by the Heatrola, kneel by the sofa to say our nightly prayers, then bound the stairs as fast as we could taking a flying leap into bed without ever touching the frozen floor. Well, we tried to fly directly into bed, but it was an effort. Mother had placed a ton of quilts and horse blankets on the bed, ten inches deep. No wonder we were skinny. They squeezed the fat right off our bones. It took five minutes to get under the covers, another five to crawl out in the morning, but on a stick-your-tongue-on-a-metal-sled-handle night those quilts were appreciated. We didn't complain about the line down the middle of the bed when it was below zero outside, either. In fact, on a night like that, both Tom and I moved closer to the line. We stretched our knees and arms to get as close to the other guy as possible without actually touching.

Two in a bed during the summer was different, however. When Old Man Winter finally released his deathly grip permitting the sun to return, our sleeping habits returned to normal. Summers were hot, sticky and steamy. The one thing I didn't want to do was to get too close to another body. In fact, the line wasn't much of a factor, because we moved far away from each other. During July and August we had so much room in that bed there was even space for another person. That frequently happened.

Southern Minnesota experiences fierce summer storms which generate powerful rain, thunder and lightening. The thunder begins rolling through thunderheads to the west around Northfield. It growls and tumbles toward Goodhue, lightning bolts cracking out of the gray clouds so loudly that within a half second Rose would be out of her room and in bed with Tom and me. Bang! Crack! Zap! Suddenly, three kids in a bed where moments before there had only been two.

Summer evenings weren't always that stormy, though. We frequently received gentle rains. Without those showers our grandparents would have kept moving westward until they found the land and the rains they were looking for. That's why they stopped in Minnesota. Folks welcomed rain with open arms. Children let it lull them to sleep. A tin roof covered the front porch outside our bedroom window. Rain fell gently on it creating a persistent rhythm, a symphony of pitter-patter caressing the roof. I could see the swaying street light from my bed; as I listened to the rain, I would fall peacefully asleep.

2

Purina Mills Shirts

In spite of stick-to-the-sheets August nights and no bedroom heat, the Franklins shared a good family life. Mother and Dad struggled with the effects of The Depression, but the family was secure. We had shoes on our feet, clothes on our back and even though they weren't fancy, they were as good as what other children wore. There weren't any "Joneses" to keep up with, anyway.

A clothing fad passed through town in the summer of '46. The Goodhue Elevator was receiving feed in fancy sacks, not the typical gunny sacks with rough, coarse weaving; rather, pretty sacks with soft weaving and decorated with colorful chrysanthemum, geranium and hyacinth prints. Some even had *Purina Mills* printed on them. It wasn't long before someone got the idea that they would make nice shirts or blouses. The Elevator suddenly experienced a run on feed sacks. John Angus couldn't keep enough on hand to meet the demand of the mothers who began sewing shirts and blouses.

Mother sewed ours after the family had finished supper, after she had fought with Tom and I to wash and dry the dishes. Most village mothers sewed, darned and patched shirts, pants and socks to save money. They patched until there were patches upon patches, throwing nothing away. I purchased a pair of yellow sweat pants for high school basketball practice a few years later; she patched them even into my college years. Every time I ripped them, she got her needle and thread out to sew another patch. Eventually, there wasn't a spot without a patch. In some places they were three deep, vivid patch-work colors. They're hanging on my studio wall today as a tribute to Mother, her needle and thread.

On a typical evening Mother sewed, Dad read the *Republican*

Eagle or *Reader's Digest* and the children tried desperately to finish washing and drying the dishes. I don't know why we couldn't have simply accepted the task. We knew it was our job to clean the table and do the dishes, but we fought it nightly as if just maybe this one night we would get out of it. "We'll get it done, Mother. Tom isn't doing a good job of washing. There's yuck all over the forks."

"Shut up you little turd. I'll beat the shit out of you when we get outside. I'll kick you out of bed tonight when you're sleeping," Tom hissed under his breath.

Washing, drying and putting the dishes away, fighting, punching and snapping the drying towel on Tom's butt. Eventually we would finish and a calmness would settle over the house.

3

The Work Ethic:
So, Make Something Of Yourself, Then

Washing and drying dishes notwithstanding, we were raised with a strong work ethic. Parents told us day after day that we could do anything if we set our minds to it, if we worked hard enough. If eight hours didn't accomplish the task, then surely ten would. If ten hours didn't get the job done, then twelve would. Work long. Work hard. Parents valued hard work and those values were, in-turn, instilled in us, infused from the day we were born. No, you didn't want to be lazy in Goodhue. *Lazy* was the worst of sins. "Jimmy, it's time to get up."

"Oh, Mom, I'm tired. I want to sleep for a another hour."

"No siree, young man. So, get up and make something of yourself, then!"

We certainly had to, ". . . get up and make something of ourselves." If we didn't, we were no-good bums.

"Get out of bed now, you no-good bum."

I learned early to accept work. I saw its benefits, particularly when Saturday night came and I had a couple of dollars in my pocket for a malt, fries, and hamburger at Swenson's Cafe; even so, developing a work ethic was difficult to achieve. Children don't enter this world with a well-developed work ethic. They need to develop it, and most don't want to work at it. But we received considerable encouragement from parents and villagers. Dad came off the farm as did many other dads, and when your father had been a farmer it meant he was accustomed to working thirty-six hours a day! He had trudged forty-five miles, one-way, to a one-room schoolhouse. He had walked through twenty-two feet of snow without boots. And when he hiked back home through deep snow he still had two hundred cows to milk and a thousand chickens to feed! He didn't sit to read a book or think. My grandparents surely didn't tolerate that. Walk to school. Do the chores. Feed the chickens. Milk the cows. Work.

Hard work was the tenor of the times. Farm work was hard, dirty and endless; it became an important value system in their lives. If they hadn't toiled every hour of the day they wouldn't have finished their chores—the Holsteins wouldn't have been milked, the chickens wouldn't have been fed, the eggs wouldn't have been collected, the alfalfa wouldn't have been baled and stacked in the hay mow, the sheep wouldn't have been sheared. That would have meant no milk, no eggs, no wool, no beef . . . no money.

The work ethic wasn't confined to farmers. It was also evident in the villagers, because the village was made up of people who depended upon those farmers. And the ethic was transferred from generation to generation. Lazy children were run out of town as surely as the bums and tramps were during The Depression, "Here's a slice of bread and a glass of milk, and now you be gettin' the first freight out of town. This here's a workin' town. We don't have room for lazy bums around here."

I wriggled out of the sack daily to, ". . . make something of myself." Mom's theory was that if I worked eight or ten hours, I would surely come out all right in the end, wherever the end was. I tried to believe in work; it's just that it was hard getting excited about it. At twelve a boy isn't as excited about working as his dad and mom are. He has a roof over his head, the rent is paid, there is roast beef on the table; he doesn't have the same concern for money—things weren't so bad. But I worked whether I wanted to or not. If Dad toiled in the fields from sunup to sundown as a boy, and if Mother labored from sunup to sundown cooking and baking and cleaning and canning, then I could be expected to do the same.

4

Vegetable Garden

Mother and Dad worked in our vegetable garden after supper during spring and summer evenings. Most families planted gardens to help make ends meet, big gardens, not little vegetable patches seen today. Our garden was a cornucopia of sweet corn, tomatoes, rutabagas, green beans, cucumbers, turnips, rhubarb, peas, celery, string beans, carrots, butter beans, Irish potatoes, sweet potatoes, white potatoes, eggplant, cabbage, watermelons, muskmelons, cantaloupes, horseradish, summer squash, leaf lettuce, asparagus, radishes, beets, strawberries and zucchini. My mouth waters just thinking about it. And gardens weren't for show; they were for sustenance itself. Vegetable gardens were as important to townsfolk livelihoods as wheat and barley fields were to farmers. Walking the streets and alleys on any summer's eve, one would see parents, not children, hoeing, weeding, planting, pruning and cultivating their crop. Garden work was for parents. We played ball, but we liked the fresh vegetables the garden released.

Later, after popping a bowl of popcorn and fixing lemonade, we would sit in front of the Setchell-Carlson listening to our favorite shows—*Ma Perkins, The Lone Ranger, The Shadow*. Radio developed our imaginations . . .

When we last left you, Willie was out in the yard cutting two-by-fours and Schuffle was loading bags of cement on the truck. Ma was in the office . . .

We could travel the world through the magic of radio, to the town where Ma, Willie and Schuffle lived, or to the Texas panhandle to ride with the Lone Ranger as he tracked down a desperado.

Many evenings we played cards and board games: Checkers, Canasta, Monopoly, Whist, Euchre, Hearts, Old Maid, Gin Rummy and Michigan Rummy. Playing cards was a popular pastime for everyone. Bridge and Five Hundred took the place of movies and restaurants for Mother and Dad.

The post-Depression World War II years was a time before sleek Fords and Frigidaires. The Franklin family didn't own a refrigerator—never got the sleek Ford—until after the war; instead, we depended on the ice man who drove to town twice a week to make deliveries. Ice day was an exciting day for my pals and me, particularly on a blistering summer afternoon when both the temperature and humidity hovered above ninety. We ran after the truck catching chunks of ice as the ice man made his deliveries. He lugged fifty-pound blocks of silvery, cold, steamy ice on his shoulders, distributing enough ice to last several days. But after the war, refrigerators and pop-up toasters became available signaling the demise of the ice man.

We purchased our first refrigerator and pop-up toaster from Eppen's Electric Shop in 1946—the refrigerator didn't use ice and the toaster flipped the toast into the air—fancy. It's amazing we could get excited about a pop-up toaster, but we had been toasting our bread in an antique toaster, turning the bread manually. Refrigerators and pop-up toasters; things dreams were made of.

5

Saturday Night Baths

Evenings before the war, when we were toddlers, the routine changed on Saturdays. We didn't have "indoor plumbing" in the late thirties; our bath was a galvanized tub, our toilet an outhouse.

Dad toted out a fifteen-gallon galvanized tub about six o'clock on a Saturday night. He would build a wood fire in the kitchen stove to heat water, then when hot, ruba duba dub three toddlers in a tub. All three of us fit into that tub when we were two and three years old, but it wasn't long before we lacked ample space. Rose got fussy about bathing with Tom and me, anyway. We were eventually abandoned. It wasn't long before each took a bath alone, but that created a challenge to see who would bathe first. If you were first you had clean water. If you were second the water was dingy, if third the bath water was mud, particularly if you followed Tom. He had a way of finding every mud hole in town. If I followed him I would have more dirt on me when I got out than when I got in. Once Tom and I encouraged Mother and Dad to get in, but they didn't accept our offer. Mother became red-faced; Dad walked silently out of the kitchen.

The outhouse was a freestanding structure fifty yards from the backdoor, and although it was easy enough to use during the summer, it took considerable courage in the dead of February, stout-of-heart determination to leave the warmth of the kitchen and traipse that fifty yards. But a boy could only wait so long. But even after I traversed the tundra there was still that sitting down to do. If I only had to take a leak I could do that right outside the back door behind the lilac tree. A boy doesn't just piss in one spot, you know. No, sir, he becomes an artist. I created circles, squares, animals and yellow ice sculptures that remained until April's thaw. And I wasn't the only one sculpting. George, Jack, Bob and Larry were artists, too.

Of course there were times I needed to tramp all the way to the outhouse. That took fortitude. Sitting on a cold outhouse seat at ten below zero took grit. I needed even more courage to use the Ward's Catalog for paper. Toilet paper was expensive and the Village Council was saving newspaper print for the war effort; we were left with cold, freeze-your-butt-off-shiny-papered Ward's Catalogs.

6

Mother's Maytag Wash Day

Saturday night was bath night, Monday was washday. Each day of the week was relegated to a special job. Village mothers somehow agreed that Monday was to be washday. They owned few household conveniences, so bathing the kids and washing clothes were major undertakings, one-day-per-week tasks. Mother owned a Maytag ringer washing machine like most moms. She would rise at the crack of dawn to heat water and collect dirty clothes. Throughout the day, she toiled at the Maytag. "How are you doing, Mother?"

"Good morning, Jimmy. It's washday, you know. Did you bring your dirty clothes downstairs?"

"Not yet, but I'll do it after I eat my Wheaties and toast."

"You'll do it right now, young man or I'll toast you!"

She slaved all day at the Maytag, repeatedly filling and emptying the washer tub until all the clothes, sheets and towels were clean. She ran the clothes through the ringer, then hung them on the outside clothesline for drying—pants, long Johns, shorts, socks, dresses and towels. The entire village was hung up. She washed everything in sight with Oxydol and bleach and eliminated every spot of dirt from our clothes.

She had worn herself out by six o'clock, exhausted after washing, drying and fixing supper. After Tom and I had once again resisted the dishes, she would collapse in a chair, let out a big sigh and utter Uff *da!* That phrase said it all for her. If she couldn't have said *Uff da!* she would never have made it through life. In fact, she could put up with almost anything as long as she could say it. It was better that even a well-placed "Jesus, Mary and Joseph help me!" Don't ever ask what it means because it's untranslatable. *Uff da!*

means *Uff da!* "Mom what does that phrase mean that you always use?"

"What is that, Jimmy?"

"Uff da!"

"It just means *Uff da!*"

"But I don't understand. It doesn't make any sense to me."

"It's Norwegian. They use it all the time."

"Could I use it in school when the teacher asks me a question I don't know?"

"Jimmy, what's three times seven?"

"Uff da! Miss . . ,"

"I don't think that would work very well."

"Maybe I could use it in confession then with Fr. Smith."

"Bless me Father for I have sinned. Since my last confession, I Uff da'd *three times and I* Uff da'd *six times."*

"Jimmy, is that you? What's all this Uff da *stuff?"*

"Well, Father, my mother said I could use the word anytime I needed it, so I thought I might use it in the confessional."

"I'll Uff da *you, young man. Now I don't know what kind of a sin* Uff da *is, or whether it's even a sin at all. I never heard of committing* Uff da *three times, and besides, I don't know what kind of penance to give you. Stick to the sins, kid. I want to know how many impure thoughts you had, and how many times you disobeyed your mother and father, how many dirty pictures you looked at. Forget this* Uff da *shit when you come to confession!"*

It didn't work in the confessional.

Our mothers had an interesting way of speaking to us, even without a pet phrase like *Uff da!* Their language was direct though lacking a certain logic, but we received the message, nevertheless. If we didn't do a task fast enough or good enough, we heard the same phrases:

"If you don't clean your room now, I'll clean you!"

"If you don't make your bed right away, I'll make you!"

"If you kids don't quit fighting right now, I'll fight you!"

Those phrases never made sense to me, but I knew she meant business. Maybe it wasn't even the words. Maybe it was the way she spoke, plus the back of her hand on my head if I picked my nose in church, or if I didn't say "please and thank you" at the neighbor's house. When I got home I would probably get more.

Mothers need special words and phrases to get their children to do things. It takes so much effort to get children to function on a regular basis that mothers reduce the English language to workable phrase they can say without thinking, because if they had to think and use logic every time they dealt with children they would be in the grave long before their time. Dads don't deal with it, "Go ask your mother."

"Rise and shine,"

"Get out of bed and make something of yourself."

"You can't make hay lying in bed."

"The early bird gets the worm."

"*Uff da!*"

____7

Dad's Milk Route

Dad didn't use pet phrases; actually, he didn't talk much at anytime. He was a quiet, gentle man—a farmer, a trucker, a janitor, a pipe smoker, a fisherman. "Dad, can I go with you in the morning on your milk route?"

"Four o'clock is awfully early for you to get up. Are you sure you want to go with me?"

"You betcha!" I would feel a gentle tap on my shoulder in the wee hours of the morning; it would be Dad. Rising at four o'clock wasn't easy, but once out of bed, a bowl of Wheaties in my stomach, I enjoyed riding as he drove his red International truck through the rural townships collecting milk from farmers.

In the early hours, we drove from farm to farm across fertile farmlands picking up full milk cans, leaving empties, petting dogs, chasing cats, and talking about weather and crops with Pat Rowles,

Francis Ryan, Ernest Gorman, "Bookie" Bucholtz and David
Gadient. Dad wasn't a big talker, though. Oh, he would periodically get into some good conversations with farmers, but when he sat
behind the wheel of the International he didn't say much. But that
was all right with me, particularly at five o'clock. I enjoyed riding,
looking out the window and watching fields of new corn, soy
beans, wheat and barley pass by. I would see herds of milk cows
trudging back to their pastures in single file after their morning
milking. I watched the breaking sun sneak over a feed silo, and I
heard meadowlarks singing along the fence posts. I didn't need to
talk. Just being in the International and having my own lunch
bucket was good enough for me.

The route was hard work for Dad, but easy for me. The grass
would be so wet with dew that as we walked to the milk house our
shoes became covered with water. The fields glistened with dew as
the sun rose gradually into the eastern sky. Dad was in the milk
business before bulk tanks, so he had to lift every eighty-pound can
up onto the truck bed. 'Big milkers,' as Dad and I called them,
would have twenty to thirty full cans. He loaded them, unloaded
empties for tomorrow's milking, then headed for the next farm
with a wave and a honk, barking dogs chasing us out the driveway.

If we didn't get stuck in a muddy farmyard or if the truck
didn't break down, we would unload by one o'clock leaving
enough time for fishing. Dad went fishing whenever he had the
opportunity, which wasn't often. But if he didn't have a job hauling
grain, or hauling livestock to the slaughter house in South Saint
Paul, we would drive to Red Wing, wind the back roads to
Collischan's Landing, rent a boat, motor up a slew to our favorite
spot by the sweeping willow—great place to catch crappies—
maneuver the boat in close, drop the anchor, bait our lines, then
settle back for a lazy afternoon of fishing. He sat in the rear and I
sat up front watching the red and white bobbers dipping gently in
the calm river, hour after hour, hoping it would suddenly go down
. . . getting drowsy in the summer heat . . ."Dad. I got a bite!"

"Just let it take her, Jimmy. Don't yank it too fast."

"He took her all the way down. Can I yank on the line now?"

"Give her a good one!"

It was a beauty, a crappie with blue and white stripes down its side. It was big and it was my fish and I would take it home to show Mother and we could clean it for supper. We sat in the flat-bottomed scow watching the darting bobbers, catching some fish and losing others, getting sleepy. By the end of the day we would have done all right, catching enough for supper, but if we didn't, it was still a good day with Dad.

There was another time Dad and I were in a boat that didn't go as well and could have turned into a disaster. He had volunteered to be a chaperone for the Boy Scouts annual outing to the Boy Scout Camp near Lake Pepin, a Mississippi River lake three miles across and ten miles long. The camp leaders decided to paddle several miles down the lake by canoe for an overnight camping trip near the Terrace Supper Club. We loaded tents and supplies into five canoes and headed out like Joliet and Marquette. Dad and I paddled a canoe with our supplies stashed in the middle. The wind came up suddenly creating white caps two feet high. The five canoes stayed close to shore to avoid the white caps, but the situation grew increasingly precarious. Neither of us were experienced. We could handle a flat-bottomed fishing boat at Collischan's, but maneuvering a canoe on Lake Pepin was completely different. We couldn't get that canoe to go where we wanted. Dad paddled from the front and I steered from the back. That was a mistake because he outweighed me by seventy-five pounds; consequently, the rear end rode high in the water. I couldn't steer worth a damn. Even in calmer waters we spent more time going in circles than forward. Fortunately, we hugged the shoreline, thereby avoiding capsizing, eventually arriving safely at the campsite. Mother almost had a heart attack when we told her about the episode later. I didn't know that Dad couldn't swim, and he wasn't even wearing a water safety jacket. We were being held in the hands of the Lord that day.

Dad loved his International truck and Model A car. He took care of them as if they were the most priceless vehicles in the county. He wouldn't leave home on a Sunday outing without wiping the dust off the car with a soft cloth. When finished, it shined like black gold. The Model A was a four door with a spare tire mounted on the right side running board and a humpback trunk in the rear. It had a windshield that swung forward for "air conditioning," wire-spoked wheels, upholstered seats and a horn . . . AOOGHA! AOOGHA! I thought it was a great car.

Dad's primary male social outlet was being a volunteer fireman for the village. Men didn't have time or money to play golf or tennis, because there was always too much work, although they did find time to fish and hunt. Being a volunteer fireman gave them an opportunity to get out of the house to be with the guys, all under the guise of practicing firefighting. They met at the firehouse to work on the fire truck and hoses, and to practice fire fighting, but it was mostly a men's social club. Infrequently, there would be a fire in a hay barn and the firemen would have to earn their keep. Casey Ryan, Bert Majerus, Francis Majerus, Fred Luhman, Bill Mans, John Angus, Art Lohman, Ray Banidt, Clarence Lunde, Art Haas, Dennis Heaney, Cy Buck, Les Banidt, Fred Rusch, Henry Befort, Reinhold Schulz, Luverne Haas, Francis Moran and Jim Ryan got together the first Monday of each month to be firemen and drink Grain Belt.

In 1947 Dad sold his milk route to Toby Buck to replace Louis Schinnert as janitor and bus driver at the school. In addition to maintaining the school building, he transported country students to and from school each day. Because of his bus-driving duties, Tom and I acquired jobs. Every day after school we assisted dad by cleaning the classrooms. I was assigned the first, second, third, fourth, fifth and sixth grade rooms while Tom cleaned seven, eight and the high school rooms upstairs. We swept floors, emptied waste baskets, washed blackboards, swept hallways, and carried the waste paper to the incinerator. We didn't get paid, but children were expected to work without pay, because we had a place to sleep, food to eat and clothes to wear. Dad was good at handing out nickels, though. He kept me in Hershey bars and ice cream cones.

8

Cis and Vic O'Neill's Eighty Acres

Sunday's were for attending church and visiting relatives. We frequently hopped into the Model A for a drive to Belle Creek or Red Wing to visit an aunt or uncle and their families. We would drive out County Road No. 9, turn right past St. Columbkills until reaching Cis and Vic's place. Those two raised seven children in a little house on a postage stamp farm—Peggy, Kathleen, Mary Helen, David, Larry, Michael, Colleen—and frequently hosted Sunday afternoon picnics. Men sat on blankets in the yard telling stories, chatting about crops, drinking beer and spitting while women prepared the dinner. Children played softball, played in Vic's hay mow, climbed his Allis Chalmers, and played tag around the outhouse.

Chicken, roast beef, ham, rolls, corn and coleslaw were served about one o'clock, then the remainder of the afternoon was spent talking, frolicking and playing games until it was time to eat again—leftovers. But before that evening meal, Vic milked his dairy herd, an enlightening experience for the children.

Vic could cuss as much as Luverne. If there had been a cussing contest between them, it would have been a toss up, because they could both expound something fierce. Luverne when fixing a carburetor, Vic when trying to get a Holstein into a stall could both expound with a string of expletives that would burn the ears off a nun. Vic kicked, slapped and swore at those Holsteins all the way through the milking. While pulling on a cow's teats, he would get knocked off the stool by a cow, simultaneously knocking the milk into the gutter. I saw it many times. He would stammer, cuss and rap the cow on the ass saying it would be hamburger before morning. But those cows didn't listen to Vic. Nobody listened to

Vic. He hollered at his sons to get their rears in gear, to get the milking done, but they didn't listen, either. Only Vic listened to Vic. The boys just did their work at their own pace.

The only thing better than watching Vic milk was watching him start the Allis Chalmers tractor. He owned that tractor for twenty-five years, and it provided him with twenty-five years of bitter pills. It was just a one-horse tractor, but when it started, it was good enough for Vic on his tiny farm. With only eighty acres to till, he didn't need a big International tractor like his neighbors—the Ryans, the O'Connors, the Gormans, the McNamaras. He got along just fine with the Allis Chalmers; that is, when it started. He didn't have a shed for the tractor, so it stood out in the rain, hail, sleet and snow with a rusted Hills Brothers' coffee can covering the exhaust pipe to keep the elements out. It was a good runner, but it wasn't a good starter. Vic went through the same starting procedure every time. He pulled the choke, depressed the gas handle three times, turned the key and cussed . . . "You'd better damn well start this time, you sonofabitchin' machine!"

Rrrrr . . . Rrrrrrrr . . . Rrrrrrrrrrrr.

Nothing.

Rrrrrrrr . . . Rrrrrrrr . . . Rrrrrr.

Nothing.

"Larry, get out in front and give the damn thing a good crank. This goddamn tractor is fartin' up again. Give her a good crank, you hear!"

Rrrrrrrrrrrrr. Rrrrrrrrrrrrrrrrr.

Nothing. Not even a spark.

"Shit! If I never buy another Allis Chalmers in my life it will be too soon. I'm going to trade this sonofabitch in for a couple of good Belgian drays."

Choke. Gas. Crank! He would spend all morning on it. Take the carburetor off, clean the fuel line. Swear, holler . . . "Crank her harder there, Larry. Put some muscle behind it."

"Hey, Dad, I'm cranking as hard as I can."

"Goddamn it, crank her harder then."

Chug-a-chug . . . a-chug.

"Crank harder now, Larry. By God, I think the sonofabitchin' thing is going to start!" It finally would after two hours, enough time to waste the morning, but Vic, Larry, Dave and Mike went through the same process every time. Goddamn cows . . . sonofabitchin' tractor.

9

Wakes

When the Grim Reaper roared into the village, Protestant corpses were laid-out in Ole Haga's Funeral Home on upper street. When Catholics died their corpses were taken back home for a proper wake. Catholic wakes were a unique experience, and with my sixteen aunts and uncles, somebody had either just died or was in the process. Wakes were festive gatherings, though, times when family, relatives, and friends gathered to pay their last respects. Real grieving came after the funeral when the multitude left, but even then there were friends and relatives down the road to talk with, to share a cup of coffee with, to share hot apple pie.

The process began as soon as word was received that a friend had *passed away*. A multitude immediately descended upon the home like a swarm of locusts settling on a cornfield. Everyone knew what to do. The deceased's spouse—frequently a woman because of all the male heart attacks—was swept off her feet, not permitted to do anything. Folks transformed the house into a properly waked home—the house cleaned, the lawn mowed, the cows milked—the home of one who had gone on to a greater reward. And the food factory began immediately.

The corpse was brought home and placed in the living room where all could pay their last respects, because that wasn't simply a cadaver in the casket. It was Helen or Tom or Bill or Jim or Vic or Marie or Anne, an aunt, uncle, dad, friend. They didn't belong in Ole's cold Funeral Parlor downtown with no one around to keep them company throughout the night. They belonged at home with friends, and even though they couldn't talk to us, we could talk about them. The adults did most of the talking while the children played outside in the barn or on a haystack, only occasionally going into the parlor. It was hard for children to relax around a corpse, so we gingerly paid our respects, then discretely left the parlor.

Mourners talked, laughed, cried and prayed into the wee hours of the morning drinking coffee by the gallon and Grain Belt by the case. The deceased was never as big in life as in death. Oh, the stories they would tell. They told about the time Tom and Cis climbed twenty-nine steps to the top of the windmill on the home place to drop two cats wanting to see if they could land on their feet from thirty feet. They told the story about Vic driving his team from the wrong side of the hilly hayfield, eventually tipping the load. They told how Bill took a corner too fast in his Model T out on County No. 7 rolling into the ditch but escaping with only a scraped knee.

Considerable food was consumed: roast beef, chicken, ham, coleslaw, pie, cake and coffee. Every woman in the township who was even remotely related to the deceased baked her best hotdish. Even if she didn't know the deceased's family well enough to stay for the rosary, she brought her dish, because she never knew when one of her own would die and be needing a wake.

About eight o'clock, Father Smith would drop by to lead the mourners in the rosary for the repose of the deceased's soul. Father would enter blessing everyone in his path, proceed to the casket and begin the rosary . . ."In the name of the Father, and of the Son, and of the Holy Ghost . . ."

"I believe in God, the Father Almighty . . ."

"Our Father, who art in heaven . . ."

"Hail Mary . . ."

"Glory be to the Father, and to the Son . . ."

"The five Sorrowful Mysteries, The Agony in the Garden . ."

"Our Father . . ."

"Hail Mary . . ."

"May his soul and the souls of all the faithful departed, through the mercy of God, rest in peace, Amen."

Rosaries were long. I had to kneel for five decades and kneel straight lest I get whomped on the back of my head by Mother. But the good news was that by saying those fifty Hail Marys we could get off our knees knowing the deceased had a good chance of circumventing purgatory and getting to at least level one in heaven. If we had stopped at forty-eight he might have had to spend six months in purgatory.

Friends stayed up throughout night attending the deceased. That's why the wake was held in the home in the first place. If folks weren't going to sit with the body, it might as well have been taken to Ole's. The deceased didn't leave this world alone. No, sir. They left in the company of friends and relatives. It was good partying. It was good parting.

_____10

Acolyte Agony

Many boys served as altar boys in the forties, and even with occasional impure thoughts, I became one in a lineage that had begun centuries before. Altar boys were invented by a forgotten sixth century pope to help him carry the wine and water from his Vatican apartment to St. Peter's Basilica. One Sunday, as the pope was walking toward St. Peter's to say Mass carrying his own wine and water in porcelain cruets, he encounter a young street urchin nonchalantly kicking a rock through the cobblestone streets of Rome. He inquired of the boy whether he would help carry the cruets to St. Peter's, then he added, "Why don't you stay during Mass to assist me?" The urchin answered, "I don't have anything else to do right now; I guess I could."

I began as an altar boy in 1944. If a boy were good at the job, didn't falter excessively and could pour water and wine without spilling it down the front of his surplice, he could be an acolyte for life. I was adept at most liturgical tasks; consequently, I continued serving Mass even into my college years even though I recited Latin prayers without knowing what they meant. We never had Latin lessons, and no one translated the language for us. Instead, we were simply expected to know what those foreign words meant, expected to have the faith, "Don't question it, young man, just believe."

And believe we did. Remember, Catholics had faith, the poor Lutherans didn't—recite the Latin, carry the water and wine, move the missal from the left side of the altar to the right, pray to God you don't trip over your surplice and make a fool of yourself, pray to God you don't spill any water or wine so you don't have to face the wrath of Father Smith after Mass. For the unfortunate, Father's wrath was administered as we stood at attention in the sacristy behind the altar being dressed down by a drill sergeant masquerading as a priest, a drill sergeant wondering why we couldn't do anything right.

On second thought, I'll bet that's why altar boys were invented by that sixth-century pope, so priests could holler at and intimidate them. God didn't need altar boys. Priests served God just fine. Where was Hubert Humphrey when I needed him? If Hubert had been pope he wouldn't have allowed priests to holler at altar boys when they recited a *mea culpa* instead of an *amen*. Yes, Hubert would have been a fine pope.

Holy Week was a particularly difficult liturgical season to be an altar boy, because that was when we reluctantly trudged down a dusty, washboard country road to St. Columbkills in Belle Creek—an ancient, forlorn stone church surrounded by six-foot-high Dekalb corn, soybeans, wheat, and every dead Catholic from Goodhue and Belle Creek who had died since 1860—to assist Father on Holy Thursday, Good Friday and Holy Saturday while our friends played baseball back in town. Serving Easter Sunday Mass was tiring enough, but Holy Week services were excruciating. It was the season when Father performed many priestly chores for the remainder of the church year: praying for the poor souls in purgatory and the babies in limbo, blessing the holy water. All the holy water for the entire year was blessed on Holy Thursday, and it was the altar boys' job to lug gallons of water to the church for the ceremony. Little fellows, nine- and ten-years of age weren't strong enough to carry that much water, but we did. We collected buckets of well water then placed it in the sacristy until it was time for the annual water-blessing ritual. Huffing and puffing while trying to remain holy, we lugged water to the vestibule where Father blessed it for the congregation. Those farmers and towns-folk who were able to attend the morning services brought water containers to church and took home enough holy water to sprinkle the house, the barn, the chicken coop, the Model A, the John Deere, the kids and anything else around the farm that stood, moved, squawked or mooed, because they knew that with enough holy water sprinkled around the home place the family, crops and farm stock were good for another year. We created a reservoir of water large enough to keep both St. Columbkills and Holy Trinity free from the devil and the Lutherans for another year.

I don't know why Holy Thursday services needed to be three hours. Pope Hubert certainly would have reduced that time. It was difficult for altar boys to be pious three minutes, let alone three hours. Father gave thanks for everyone and everything—last year's crops and blessings, the new babies in the parish and blessings for pregnant mothers during the coming year. We said rosaries and began novenas for couples contemplating marriage, and we prayed endlessly for the dead. The dead of St. Columbkill's and Holy Trinity were buried in the cemetery across the gravel road by the beanfield. The dearly departed souls of the two parishes had so many prayers said for them over the years that there wasn't a soul left in purgatory. They were in heaven and few, if any, even had to genuflect in purgatory. I believe those two parishes set a heavenly record for the fewest dead babies in limbo or adults in purgatory. God didn't need purgatory for those two parishes.

Holy Thursday services persisted until noon, and you could find no happier group of altar boys when they finally ended, but not Father Smith. You see, priests get paid to pray. They receive money directly from the pope—five cents for every Hail Mary, ten cents for an Our Father—but altar boys don't. For a priest, that adds up to considerable income in a year's time. Priests get a check from the Vatican every December 31, just like clockwork. But boys don't take up altaring as a profession; there just isn't any money in it. We were ready to skedaddle when services ended. Besides, we made fifty cents mowing lawns or carrying garbage. We were ready to get back to town to earn money, or maybe, get up a baseball game. Three hours of a holy water ritual and praying for the dead were enough for an entire month, let alone one day.

Holy Thursday was difficult, but it started all over again on Good Friday when we assisted Father in the morning, had the afternoon free, then served again in the evening. Those services were easier, though, because we didn't have all that water to tote, but they still lasted two hours. Again we prayed for all the evils of St. Columbkills and Holy Trinity, and we purged ourselves of sins until we couldn't purge anymore. Easter Sunday was coming and we had to be ready for God, because Father said God wouldn't rise again, and he certainly wouldn't visit Goodhue if we hadn't sufficiently purged ourselves. We devoted considerable time to telling Father and God how sorry we were for our sins.

It seemed then as if the altar boys committed more sins than anyone else. That meant confession again. Although confession was difficult, eventually it ended and for a few days we lived free. We wouldn't have to confess for another week. There was no feeling like finishing confession. You dreaded it for days ahead of time; afterward, you felt you had been awarded a new life—the clouds blew away, the sun came out, the humidity dried up, a nimble step returned to your walk. Eighty-year-old men who during the course of a normal day couldn't walk a block without the help of a cane, exited the confessional doing cart wheels and skipping down the street. Those men *crawled* into the confessional but danced out doing cart wheels. Miracles happened right there at Holy Trinity.

When Holy Saturday finally arrived, I usually had discussions with sister Rose and brother Tom about whether we could end our Lenten *give-ups* at noon, or whether we needed to wait until after Easter Sunday Mass. This was an area of theology in which the Church was unclear and, once again, we couldn't find an answer in the *Baltimore Catechism*. We were on our own. It was one of the few issues we could decide for ourselves. Those of us having less perseverance and patience—Tom and me—usually gave in about Saturday noon to eat a Hershey Bar or Nut Goodie, or drink a bottle of Squirt. It was just too hard to wait another twenty-four hours. Rose was a theological purist. She wouldn't give in on Saturday, electing to wait until Sunday all the while lecturing us that we were poor souls doomed to hell, or at least a lower place in heaven than what she was expecting.

Heaven held a special place in the hearts of Goodhue Catholics. It didn't simply exist as a generic, all-purpose heaven. No, there were levels which our elders certainly told us about. One didn't simply hope to get into heaven—you hoped to gain a higher level, up the stairs and closer to God. I often wondered how those level-one souls felt. Did they feel bad because they were only on level one, or were they happy because they were in heaven? How many times did I hear Mother say that if I did a good job of mowing the lawn, if I washed the dishes without complaining, if I was polite to the neighbors, if I helped old ladies across the street, if I said my prayers every night that I would, ". . . get a higher place in heaven." Remember, here was a boy with ten to fifteen impure thoughts a week. I figured I would be happy just getting into heaven. Level one would be all right.

By Sunday, I had navigated the biggest swells in the liturgical sea. I had finished those endless days of Thursday, Friday and Saturday, and now all I had to do to be free was serve one more Mass after which I would eat candy and drink all the pop I had given up, and free to watch the town team beat Mazeppa on Sunday afternoon at the ball diamond.

Easter Sunday was a particularly nice day, because after having survived a bitter, arctic Minnesota winter, it was nice to have winter and Lent ending at the same time. God sure made a wise decision when he scheduled Easter at the same time as the ending of winter. It was a time of renewal, a time of rebirth. We had prayed for six weeks, had given up everything in the world, and had been on our knees so much I had scabs from foot to knee.

Our family walked to Holy Trinity together on a day when the women wore their new spring hats, the hats they had purchased months ago but had waited anxiously to display at Mass. Mother wore her new pillbox hat; Dad wore his one-and-only pinstriped Sunday suit and painted tie. Tom and Rose and I had new clothes to wear. I wore a new red spring jacket. Red wasn't seen much in the village in the forties. Most colors were gray, dark green, dark blue and black. Dads wore gray and priests wore black. But my jacket was cardinal red. I wore it proudly that Sunday and for several years afterward. I did take it off, though, for one last service.

Mass was easy because Father had talked himself out by Sunday. Even *he* was ready to get it over with. Finally, Mass ended, the parishioners filed out, and as was so typical, stayed for a long time to talk on the lawn. Mass certainly was significant, but talking after Mass ran a close second. For the townsfolk and farmers who came to town once a week, the time after Mass was a time to converse, a time to find out what had happened since last Sunday, a time to find out how neighbors' corn and barley were doing, a time to talk about the lack of rain, the price of corn, wheat, and barley. The only thing Catholics did more that pray was talk.

Easter Sunday brought the end to six weeks of agony for a boy. He had stored up enough grace, indulgences, and goodwill to earn him at least level one, maybe even level two in heaven. It was a good Lent. It was a good Easter. It was over.

Chapter 13

The Greater Goodhue Hotdish Challenge

Ladies of the Club

GOODHUE WAS OUT-OF-SORTS. THERE HAD BEEN considerable scuttlebutt floating through the town for several weeks; church socials were unusually subdued, Bridge Club and Five Hundred Clubs conspicuously silent. What was happening? It was the impending July 4 Greater Goodhue Hotdish Challenge.

217

1

The Challenge

Our mothers had been making hotdishes their entire lives, but this event was new. A hotdish was, and is, a Minnesota tradition. Mothers couldn't be official mothers without fixing hotdish. They couldn't attend the Ladies Aid Society or the Bridge Club or the American Legion Auxiliary or a Sunday family picnic without fixing one. "We're getting together Sunday at Colvill Park, Lucy."

"What should I bring?"

"Oh, just a hotdish."

That was all the explanation needed. If you lived in Minnesota you automatically knew what a hotdish was, but an out-of-stater probably wouldn't know. Locals didn't ask, "What should I put in my hotdish?" But it was all right to exchange recipes. They shared them at social functions then filed cards in recipe boxes. And that recipe box was more valuable than stocks and bonds in a safety deposit box. Mothers and grandmothers guarded their recipes with a vengeance. It took an entire lifetime to collect them; they were not to be treated lightly.

Mother kept her recipes in a Red Dot Cigar box. Dad smoked an occasional cigar after supper, or more likely after Sunday dinner on the front porch, so she confiscated one of his empty boxes . . . RED DOT, MANUFACTURED BY THE FEDERAL CIGAR COMPANY, RED LION, PA. A CIGAR THAT'S TRULY DIFFERENT . . . was emblazoned on the side with a picture of a red-haired lady looking lovingly at the purchaser of those cigars.

Mother organized her cigar-recipe box into sections for a variety of foods, plus a section for non-food items: How to preserve fall leaves, how to keep evergreens green, how to take the stain out of the living room rug. There were Hints from Heloise, a few tattered S & H Green Stamps, an ammonia solution for washing walls during spring cleaning, a concoction for making wheat germ, and even a recipe for stomach cramps—1 tsp. vinegar, 1 tsp. sugar in a glass, 3/4 tsp. soda and 1/2 glass water. If you didn't have the cramps before swallowing this solution you surely would afterward. There was a cough syrup recipe calling for equal parts of honey, lemon juice and whiskey but, "Eliminate the whiskey if you're giving the syrup to the kids!" There was a concoction from Heloise for unplugging a sink drain if you didn't want to call a plumber. "Buy a pound of washing soda at your grocery store and dump the whole box down your drain. Let this set a minute or so. Then heat two or three gallons of water until it boils and pour it down the drain. This will usually help a sluggish drain pipe. And if that doesn't work, there are commercial products on the market. If they don't work, woe is me! I guess you'll have to call a plumber."

But the most important sections were the recipes. Village mothers had collected them from their mothers and their mother's mother. Recipes had been handed down from generation to generation, some even coming from the old countries. They were more important than the deed to the farm. Let the farm go, but save those recipes for meat loaf, candies, canning, desserts, cookies, pies, pickles, relishes, salads, soups, wine, vegetables and hotdishes.

I'm uncertain, even today, how the challenge began, but it would be easy to speculate about its beginnings. Some of the ladies at the Bridge Club party probably began talking about or exchanging recipes when someone, maybe Agnes O'Reilly, innocently commented that she had recently made her best hotdish, having received a recipe from a relative in Pine Island. "It was just the best hotdish there ever was." Now, those were strong words. Making a statement like that at the Bridge Club took courage because every woman there believed her hotdish to be the best. Imagine the retorts . . .

"Ag, your hotdish might be good, but I make a fine one myself. I include special ingredients till it's the most delicious dish you've ever tasted," from table one.

"I've a good recipe, too . . . came from a cousin in Hager,

Wisconsin. I'll bet it's as good as yours, probably better!" from table two. The temperature in the room was rising above that outside. Those were fighting words.

Your hotdish better than mine? Come now, that can't be.

"Your hotdish is probably good, but my grandmother's recipe can't be beat." Suddenly, every woman at the party became involved, all talking at the same time. Mary Haas was hosting that day, but was in the kitchen fixing another pot of boiled coffee when she heard the sudden commotion erupt in her living room. "Ladies, ladies, what on earth is going on?" Mary shouted.

"Ag just said she had the best hotdish recipe in town, and I don't believe it," from table one.

"I don't believe it either. My grandmother had a wonderful recipe in Wisconsin; in fact, it won first prize in the Hager Recipe Runoff when she was a young woman," from table two.

"Ladies! Let's settle down here. I've new coffee and fresh apple pastries. Let's see if we can settle this issue like adults while we have a little lunch," Mary intoned.

"I don't know. Ag shouldn't make a statement like that. She's a good cook and all, but I've a dandy recipe myself."

"I'm sure your recipes are good, but we don't have to decide which is best," Mary admonished.

"Why not?" Agnes demanded. "My hotdish *is* wonderful; in fact, I would bet it's better than anyone else's here." The challenge! There was to be no more negotiating after that statement. "All right then, Ag, I'll just take you up on that challenge," from testy table one.

"Me too."

"If I can't bake a better hotdish than you, I'll move out of town," from table two.

"Calm yourselves. Don't go that far," Mary proclaimed. Even Mother got in on the act. She had her favorite Red Dot recipes, but wasn't one to become involved in such challenges. However, Ag *had* challenged everyone and Mother was proud of her recipes and she had *her* mother and grandmother to think about. She had to uphold the Franklin and Haustein names. "Ag, we've been friends for many years, and we've exchanged recipes for cookies, meat loaf and pies, but I must accept your challenge. I am sure as I'm standing here, sure as Jesus on the cross that I can bake a better hotdish. I challenge you to a bake-off!"

"Me too!"

"And me!"

"Count me in!"

"I'm in this challenge!"

"Well, that's it then, Agnes O'Reilly. It looks like you've been challenged," Mary said. Agnes couldn't back down now. She had made an outrageous statement about her hotdish, and had been challenged by the entire Bridge Club.

On a sleepy, Friday afternoon at a normally serene Bridge Club party, the hotdish challenge began stewing.

2

The Announcement

Within the hour, word of the challenge spread through the village like wildfire. The Lutheran Ladies Club heard about it. The Methodist Ladies Social Club got word of it. The Catholic Aid Society heard the news. St. Luke's Ladies Club was informed. The Women's Study Club heard the news. The Norwegian Society and the Swedish Society got word of it. It soon became evident the challenge would be too big to confine it solely to the Bridge Club. Almost every woman in the village wanted in. Every mother knew she had the best hotdish recipe and was anxious to prove it.

Mary became increasingly concerned after the Bridge Club commotion. She had confirmed the challenge before the ladies left as a means of solving the dilemma, but she had only a friendly social challenge in mind, one they could conduct at the next bridge party. But this hotdish challenge was boiling over. The Lutheran Ladies Club, the Swedish Ladies Club and the Norwegian Ladies Club now wanted to be included. Mary was inundated by requests.

She needed help. She rang up Bill Mans, Goodhue's mayor, "Bill, I have a problem. This hotdish challenge started out as a little event we were going to hold at our bridge club, but now every woman in town wants in. Do you have any suggestions?" Bill leaned back on his heels and thought for a good while. He was normally a reticent man, because he was a fisherman; anglers don't talk much, or fast. "You there, Bill?" Mary inquired.

"Yes, just thinking about what you said."

"I need help; this thing has gotten too big."

Bill had an idea and was pondering, mulling it over but was moving too slowly for Mary. "Bill, you still there?"

"You betcha, just thinking a bit here, Mary. You know, July 4 is in a few weeks and the village will be having its annual celebration. We're getting together tractors, wagons and trucks for a parade—John Deeres, Internationals, Allis Chalmers, a couple of Ford garden tractors, some hay racks decked out in red, white and blue bunting, a New Deal combine and our fire truck. About dusk the volunteer firemen will have a fire hose tug of war contest with the Zumbrota firemen, and we'll finish off the day with fireworks over the railroad station. I'm thinking here, Mary, that we might just be able to work in that hotdish challenge after the parade and before the tug of war. Anyone who wants to enter their best hotdish could do it. We could advertise in the *Goodhue County Tribune*, and have the final judging on one of the hay racks in front of the railroad station. We could hire a judge from out of town to get an unbiased person, then crown the Greater Goodhue Hotdish Queen right then and there. Why, it would make all the papers. It might even be a bigger event than crowning the Dairy Princess Queen, or selecting the Goodhue County Artificial Breeder's Association Queen. What do you think of that idea?"

"Golly, I didn't plan on it getting that big, but it does sound like a good idea. Let's do it!"

The first, to be annual, Greater Goodhue Hotdish Challenge was on the front burner. Bill presented his idea to the Village Council at their next meeting; they adopted it immediately. The announcement made front page headlines in the *Tribune:* "Attention Hotdish Lovers! You are cordially invited to enter your best hotdish in the Greater Goodhue Hotdish Challenge to be held on July 4. Contestants should bring their hotdish to the hay rack in front of the railroad station by 10 A.M. the morning of July 4. Label the hotdish on the bottom of your casserole dish, register it with Mary Haas at a table inside the station, then place your hotdish on the table for judging. Enter only one dish. Complete the coupon on the bottom of this page and mail to Mary Haas by July 1."

When the *Tribune* hit the streets, the village began buzzing with excitement. I don't believe there had been that much excitement since the basketball team of '44 won the District Tournament. But a change suddenly took place—women went into hiding, socializing stopped, the Bridge Club didn't meet, the Catholic Aid Society didn't meet, the Lutheran Ladies Club didn't meet. The ladies were too busy, too secretive to be meeting. They were in their kitchens, curtains and shades pulled, perfecting their best hotdish.

The aromas infiltrating the village two weeks prior to July 4 were intoxicating. The village took on a new essence. The dry, dusty odor of the dirt streets, the acrid smell from the grain elevator, the brackish odor of the sewage plant, and the manure stench floating into town from outlying pig sheds were still unmistakable, but were now mixed with new fragrances. My nostrils were bombarded with a multitude of scents—allspice, basil, oregano, thyme, chives, garlic, onion, curry and paprika in tuna fish hotdishes, hamburger hotdishes, pork and veal hotdishes, veal-rice hotdishes, sausage hotdishes, pork and bean hotdishes. The aromas were different every day, because in those sequestered kitchens, mothers were experimenting with recipes. Telephones seldom rang and even if they did, they weren't answered. Central didn't have anything to do but knit sweaters for her grandchildren. Shades were drawn and doors were locked for the first time since anyone could remember.

3

Testing Recipes

Mary Ellen O'Reilly labored feverishly perfecting her entry, a pork hotdish recipe that had been passed down in the family for generations. She added her own touch to the recipe, but most of it had been her great-grandmother's. She was sure she could win the challenge. It called for: "One and a half pounds of pork and veal mixed. Boil one package of noodles in stock from broth. Then add one-quarter cup grated cheese, one can chicken noodle soup, salt and pepper and onion to taste. Sprinkle cereal over the top and bake."

Agnes had started the whole thing, but was now getting anxious. She baked her hotdish ten different times during the two weeks before the challenge. The O'Reilly family was completely saturated with hotdish from her experimenting. In fact, there wasn't a person in town who wasn't sick of hotdish by the Fourth. Villagers had consumed so much hotdish that the actual challenge was anticlimactic, at least for the men. Most men couldn't stand to smell or eat another hotdish by the time the parade finished and the judging began. But the women persisted. This was life and death to them; the men would have to tolerate hotdish for a few more days. After July 4, the recipes could be placed in the back of the recipe box for a few weeks, but only a few weeks. Hotdish was too much of a staple to be put away for very long.

Ag's dish was a ground round steak hotdish. In tight financial times it was a hamburger hotdish, but she would need to go all out for the challenge. Every day for two weeks she walked to Heaney's Market to order round steak. Of course, she purchased other ingredients to throw Dody off track. "Hi, Ag. How are you today?"

"Fine, Dody, just fine."

"How's your hotdish coming? Think you'll win?"

"Sure do. Nobody, but nobody makes a better hotdish than I do."

"What kind are you making?" Dody inquired.

"Oh, you know I can't tell you that."

"Well, what'll you be buying today?"

"Give me a pound of hamburger, three pork chops, a ring of that sausage, some head cheese, and throw in a couple pounds of prime round steak."

That will confuse Dody. She won't know what kind of hotdish I'm making.

"Sure sounds like a concoction, Ag. That'd be quite a hotdish."

"Thanks, Dody, see you tomorrow."

Agnes experimented endlessly with various ingredients to get her dish tasting just right. Her recipe called for: "One package of 8 oz. wide noodles, one can mushroom soup, one can milk, half cup of grated cheese, stuffed olives, a little pinch of diced onions, and about a third of a pound ground round steak. Top it off with chow mein noodles and salted nut cashews." That was the real secret of her hotdish—chow mein noodles and cashews. Folks didn't expect that. Round steak was common enough, but most ladies didn't garnish it with chow mein noodles and cashews. She knew she would win.

It was now only three days until the celebration. The tension was becoming unbearable for the ladies, and the tension in the stomachs of village families had reached the breaking point. Never in the history of the village had so much hotdish been consumed in such a short period. The per pound average weight of Goodhue men increased by four pounds by celebration day. But there were still three days remaining before judgment day arrived. That meant more cooking, more baking, more experimenting, more hotdish. Hotdish for breakfast, hotdish for dinner, hotdish for lunch, hotdish for supper. The village was being consumed by hotdish. And there were more recipes to be tested before the big day.

Dody Gorman was working on her veal-rice hotdish, but having trouble getting the flavor she wanted. Leone Ryan was working feverishly on her hamburger hotdish, but even though she knew it was excellent, she lacked confidence in it. She had difficulty adding the proper amount of seasoning, and it was the seasoning that was bothering her now.

Jesus, Mary, and Joseph, help me get this right.

Special ingredients in her recipe were cut-up onions and green peppers covered with tater tots. The tater tots set Leone's hotdish apart from her competitors. Mrs. Haga decided to go with the sausage hotdish recipe handed down from her Swedish great-grandmother. She was confident it would win the challenge for her. She used several secret ingredients, but it was the crushed Ritz crackers as a garnish that made her hotdish stand out. Mrs. Sawyer decided to place her stock in a ground round steak hotdish, like Ag, but it wasn't only the ground steak that made it special. She used grated cheddar cheese, beaten eggs, pimentos and parsley in her recipe. I could smell her hotdish baking slowly as I walked past her house. Every day that savory aroma reached my nostrils about the time I passed Holy Trinity. Every day it got better. Mrs. Sawyer was going to be hard to beat.

Mary decided to bet on her hamburger and onion broth hotdish. It had been a winner in her family for years, and if Luverne was happy with it, then maybe the judge would be also. Her special ingredients were the fresh raw potatoes she added. She also included sliced carrots and a pinch of garlic powder, but only enough to make the judge take notice. Ardis Banidt chose her hamburger hotdish also. Many chose hamburger for their main ingredient. That's not surprising; by nature, a hotdish was inexpensive. Ladies put anything into a hotdish; in fact, that was the purpose—get rid of refrigerator leftovers but make it tasty. Dishes included roast beef leftovers from Sunday dinner, hash from Thursday's supper, carrots and potatoes from Wednesday's lunch. Anything could and did find its way into a hotdish, and they weren't exotic ingredients like shrimp or crab, either. The artistry came in preparation. Ardis spiced her's with soy sauce. Folks didn't expect soy sauce in a hotdish, but that was one of Ardis' secrets. Laura Mans chose her pork and beef combination hotdish. She added chicken soup, mushrooms, wide noodles, part of an onion and seasoned peas. The fresh seasoned peas made her hotdish different.

After several days of deliberation, Margaret decided on veal. Her mother Mary had made the dish often, and with it being so popular with the McHughs, Margaret had confidence it could win. Most ladies didn't cook veal that much, so Margaret had a leg up on them. She also included celery and a teaspoon of soy sauce. She cooked it at 375 degrees for thirty minutes then turned the heat down to 250 for the last fifteen to give it a unique oriental flavor.

Gladys chose a tuna hotdish. She knew most ladies would be preparing a meat dish, so she developed a special flavor with tuna. She added mushrooms and chow mein noodles, but it was the special seasonings that helped her get the flavor she wanted. Finally, she added oregano to garnish the dish.

Mother had been in a stew ever since the challenge began. She was a wonderful cook, but was having considerable difficulty deciding on her best recipe. She conferred with her sister Lillian, she talked with her brother Bert, and she conferred with Jesus every night, praying she would make the right choice. But then mother prayed for everything: good health, a higher place in heaven, the poor souls in purgatory, above average children, and she wasn't about to leave out praying for the best hotdish. She began a novena the moment she left Mary's house. Three days before July 4, she decided on a ham hotdish. Ham had been a staple in the Haustein family for many years, ever since her grandfather arrived in Red Wing. She toiled over the stove into the wee hours of the night perfecting her recipe. She experimented with adding the right amount of carrots, raw potatoes and green peppers. She diced onions and beat three eggs to the proper consistency, added milk and finally topped it off with bread crumbs. She baked it carefully at 300 degrees for one and a half hours, then let it cool for the last thirty minutes at 250.

Ladies were baking chipped beef hotdish, Spanish hamburger hotdish, chicken hotdish, beans and hamburger hotdish, pork and chicken hotdish, hamburger and peppers hotdish, veal and pork hotdish. By the Fourth, every possible combination of hamburger hotdish had been baked.

4

The Fourth Of July

The day began as a typically hot, sultry Minnesota day, not the best weather to be fixing champion blue ribbon hotdish, but the ladies couldn't control the weather, and there was no sense fussing about it. After all the experimenting, hotdish breakfasts, lunches, and dinners, the time had come to prepare their final dish. Most were out of bed and in their kitchens by five o'clock. Lights blinked on all over town. Mary Ellen sprinkled crushed Rice Crispies over the top of her pork and veal dish. Leone sprinkled a few tater tots over her entire recipe. Agnes nervously diced onions and then stuffed olives with special seasoning before sprinkling over the top. Aromas filtered through the village like fog creeping in on a September morn'. Boys, girls and men were wakened from their sleeps as their nostrils twitched with the scent of oregano, stuffed olives, parsley, onions and garlic.

Mother was up by half past four. She couldn't sleep anyway—fidgety, agitated. She had her rosary out and was trying to prepare her hotdish and say five decades of the Sorrowful Mysteries at the same time.

All of the experimenting, preparation, secrecy and praying were about to end. The hotdishes were to be at the railroad station for registration by ten. At half past nine kitchen doors were opened for the first time in two weeks sending a gush of aromas through the streets. Dogs and cats twitched their nostrils and began trotting downtown, sidewalks suddenly jammed with women carrying covered dishes to the station.

There had been considerable consternation about procuring a judge. Some thought the judge should be a local, others thought she should be from Goodhue County, while others thought she should be from out-of-state. The town council squelched that last idea, though, because they didn't have enough money to fly a judge in from a long distance; besides, the village didn't have an airport, only the grain field behind Streater's Lumber Yard where that Piper Cub had landed. Bill Mans came up with a better idea. "Heloise writes a food column for the *Daily Republican Eagle*. She's an expert on food and hotdish, and she lives just up the road in Minneapolis. Why don't we ask her to be our judge?" Bill's idea had merit, so everyone on the council voted for his proposal as did the plethora of ladies clubs. Heloise graciously accepted.

The contestants converged on the railroad station carrying secret hotdishes under secure casserole covers. Dody, Bessie, Mrs. Haga, Ardis, Leone, Gladys, Laura, Mary, Margaret, Agnes, Lucy, Mary Ellen and seventy-five other women from the Lutheran Ladies Club, the Methodist Social Club and the Swedish Bridge Club descended upon the station like rush hour at Grand Central. Ninety-eight ladies had accepted the challenge. They registered their entries then placed their dishes on tables inside the station. The day was already hot and muggy, and the judging wouldn't be until the parade was finished. The ladies were concerned the heat and humidity would affect the texture and crispiness of their dishes.

The parade began at half past ten from the high school, the fire truck leading, siren wailing, volunteer firemen waving to the villagers. Mayor Bill Mans followed in his 1945 World War II Jeep. Then the Artificial Breeder's Association float appeared followed by the Sheep Breeder's float. Actually, it wasn't a float at all; rather, thirty-five sheep were being herded through the street. The shepherds had difficulty keeping the sheep together, though, and there was sheep manure littering the street making it difficult for the Girl Scouts to march. John Deere tractors, Allis Chalmers combines, quarter horses, cats and dogs appeared in the parade. Even ol' Buck had enough gumption to leave his shady spot by the jail to join in. The last tractor-float passed the reviewing stand (Bill O'Reilly's truck bed) in front of the jail signaling the end of the parade.

The entries had been placed on folding tables in front of the station, and folding chairs from Ole's Funeral shop had been set up for people to view the judging. Most contestants took seats, but Mother was too nervous to sit. Folks fanned themselves with handkerchiefs, paper plates or whatever they could find. Bill Mans walked to the front of the stage to begin the ceremonies. He introduced Heloise of "Hints from Heloise" fame as the honored judge. Heloise said a few words about how excited she was to be in Goodhue and to be the judge of the first challenge, "I've traveled all over this country judging recipes at county fairs and church socials, but I'm sure I'll find the very best hotdish in the country right here."

Agnes adjusted her corset.

"It's going to be a difficult job picking a winner, but that's what I'm here for."

Bessie coughed lightly into her handkerchief.

"While you folks were watching the parade, I went through the entries tasting each and making notes on each of them, so I've already done some of my work."

Leone crossed her legs, twitching nervously.

"Out of the ninety-eight entries, I've narrowed it down to ten for the final judging."

Lucy pressed harder on her rosary.

"I'll now call off the ten finalists."

Edna shifted nervously in her seat.

"The ten finalists are: Julia Swederholt . . ."

"Where is she from. I've never heard of her?"

"Inga Gustafson."

"Why she's a Methodist. How can *her* hotdish be a finalist?"

"Mrs. Willis Sawyer."

Edna leaned toward the stage.

"Bessie Benda."

Mrs. Haga wiped her sweaty brow.

"Mary Ellen O'Reilly."

Thank the Lord on my Bible, Mary Ellen whispered.

"Margaret Hart."

Agnes felt a palpitation in her heart.

"Agnes O'Reilly."

Mother squeezed her crucifix.

"Leone Ryan."

The crowd buzzed; there were only two names left.

"Mary Haas."

The crowd grew restless. The sun was high noon, beating unmercifully on the shadeless audience. "Before I announce the last finalist, I just want to say that all the hotdishes were absolutely scrumptious. I hate to eliminate any, but I'm here to pick a winner. I didn't come all the way from Minneapolis to be a wimp, did I?"

"You got that right!" someone hollered from the crowd.

"And now . . . for the last finalist . . . Lucille Franklin!"

Jesus, Mary and Joseph, my prayers have been answered, at least for awhile.

The crowd burst into a big cheer, hooting and hollering from the Belle Creek ruffians, polite applause from the German Lutherans. Some ladies wiped tears with crocheted hankies, while others received hugs from understanding husbands. "From the ten finalists, I'm going to award prizes to the top three. Now, you all understand that everyone of these finalists could be the winner, but as I told you earlier, I didn't come here to be a wimp, now did I?"

"You got that right. Get on with it, Heloise!"

"Would the finalists please come forward to join me on the platform?"

Ten ladies left the audience, and one by one, joined Heloise on the hay rack. They were dressed in their finest Sunday dresses and hats to shade themselves from the blistering sun.

Heloise walked up and down the line tasting each hotdish a final time. She stepped in front of Bessie's, tasted, smiled. She moved to Mary's touching the crumbs to her lips. She shuffled to Leone's, Lucille's, Inga's, Julia's and Edna's. She tasted each, wiped her fork and smiled at each finalist. The tension in the finalists and audience was unbearable, and it had become deathly quiet, so quiet you could hear wheat stocks quaking on the edge of town, leaves rustling in the elm trees, flies buzzing around the hotdishes, flags fluttering in the hot breeze, the shuffling of Heloise's feet and the smacking of her lips tasting . . . tasting . . . Finally, she was finished. She moved slowly to the microphone.

"In third place with a delicious, and I do say 'delicious' pork and veal hotdish is . . . Mary Ellen O'Reilly!" The silence was broken, for a moment, as the crowd erupted in joyous applause. Mary Ellen gingerly stepped forward to accept her white ribbon, congratulations and a hug from Heloise. Silence again, except for the buzzing flies. The crowd had grown in size, a couple hundred milling around the railroad station.

"In second place, with a scrumptious, the best ham hotdish I've ever eaten . . . Lucille Franklin!"

"Way to go, Lucille," Uncle Dave hollered from the back of the audience. Mother walked slowly to the front of the stage, accepted the red ribbon from Heloise, then looked to the heavens for a moment. I don't know if that was *thanks* for coming in second or pleading for first.

"And now, for the Grand Champion hotdish, the best hotdish in Goodhue, the first place winner of the first, to be annual, Greater Goodhue Hotdish Challenge is none other than . . . Agnes O'Reilly!" The crowd erupted. Fire sirens whined. Dogs howled. Agnes almost collapsed. She was about to faint when her son Lefty leaped to the stage to catch her. Heloise handed her the blue ribbon, but Agnes was so faint she couldn't speak. She smiled and waved to the crowd while receiving its thunderous applause. Bill Mans came forward to crown her Hotdish Queen.

Agnes had met the challenge. She had set it three weeks ago at Bridge Club, and had now met it. But then in another sense, all the ladies had met the challenge. They had baked their best hotdish. They were all winners. The first Greater Goodhue Hotdish Challenge was history.

The Bridge Club met at Bessie's home the following Friday afternoon. They were all there—Bessie, Mary, Leone, Lucy, Mrs. Sawyer, Margaret, Mary Ellen, Laura, Agnes. Bessie brought out an angel food cake with twisted, pink candles on it and set it in front of Agnes. The ladies burst into song . . .

For she's a jolly good fell . . . lady,
For she's a jolly good lady,
For she's a jolly good lady
That nobody can deny.

"Bessie, this is absolutely the best angel food cake I've ever eaten," Ag said humbly.

"Oh, I don't know about that. I make a pretty good angel food myself," Leone uttered.

Chapter 14

Sex Education

Everybody's Drive-in Theatre

GROWING INTO MANHOOD WAS ESPECIALLY DIFFICULT, awkward and troublesome in our sequestered burg. It meant finding out about sex, a task next to impossible. Where could I get information? Priests didn't talk to boys about sex. Dads didn't talk to boys about sex. Mothers didn't talk to boys about sex. Today, PG means a Parental Guidance movie rating, but in 1948 it was the term mothers used for *pregnant*. They couldn't even say *pregnant* in our presence, because the word was too potent for youngsters. But merely being difficult didn't stop a boy from wondering about the natural process of becoming a man. *PG* didn't stop it at all.

_____1

Puberty

In late '48, the primitive television shows were extremely tame compared to today's programming—no revealing gowns or swim suits. Nothing. We watched the Ed Sullivan Show, Dragnet, Sid Caesar and Imogene Coca, Red Skelton, and Milton Berle, enter–taining shows but no halter tops, no short shorts, no bikinis, absolutely nothing to satisfy a boy's curiosity.

Most of my sex education came from older guys and farm boys who grew up watching cows, pigs and horses getting together on the back forty. The farm boys had stories. They lived with farm sex daily, and even if they didn't fully understand what was happening, they at least saw mating in the pasture. If they were intelligent enough to put two and two together, they could also figure out what people did. But I lived in town. I didn't see cattle roaming the streets. Dennis had cattle pens behind the slaughter house, but the steers and heifers were separated by fencing. Segregation. I visited friends and relatives on a farm occasionally, but seldom was fortunate enough to see cows getting it on.

Upperclassmen were forever boasting about sexual con-quests, simultaneously taunting us younger guys. I didn't know what *gettin' any* meant when I was a wet-behind-the-ears fresh-man, but if they asked me, I sure said, "You betcha, I'm gettin' some!" You had to be of strong mind to stand up to those farm boys who knew what cows did, what horses did and most likely knew what men and women did. The town boys had to appear knowl-

edgeable, so we talked with confidence and assertion in the locker
room . . . "Hey, guys, I made out like a bandit Saturday night."
    "Big deal, I'll bet you did."
    When that pubescent urge began creeping through my loins,
I needed to find a way to resolve it. I couldn't talk to Father Smith.
He was the last person I would talk to about sex. Priests didn't talk
to children about sex, anyway. They were excommunicated on the
spot if they ever did. It was written in the Vatican Encyclical on
Sex, *E Pluribus Sexium*. *Priests shall never, ever speak to young
boys and girls about sex.* We were expected to learn by divine
revelation through the Sex Spirit. Generation upon generation
grew up waiting for that special moment when the Spirit would
descend, anoint them on the head to be endowed with all knowledge about sex—about girls and boys and what they did and
makin' out. I waited. I prayed for the Sex Spirit to hover over my
bedroom. Never did. But I had Eddie's Drugstore and the few girlie
magazines he stacked on the back shelf.

2

Eddie's Drugstore

Eddie Fischer's Drugstore stocked girlie magazines on a shelf in
a dim, back corner behind the Epsom salts and castor oil. That was
absolutely the only store where I could look at girlie magazines.
Oh, we called them girlie magazines, but they were tame by
today's standards. I don't remember their titles but who was
reading? If I wanted to read I purchased *Spiderman* comic books
or the *Republican Eagle* or the *Goodhue County Tribune*. When I
strolled to Eddie's I was looking for photos, trying to find out what
was underneath all that clothing girls wore. Remember, this was
Minnesota where winter lasted nine months of the year, where
women wore multiples layers of clothing. How was I to find out?
"Hey, Jim, you been gettin' any lately?"

"You bet, had a date Saturday night."

"Oh sure, I'll bet you're not gettin' any, though!"

Eddie's was only a dilapidated rural-style store, the same brick, two-story functional building that dotted every small town in the Upper Midwest. It was named after the Andersons or Quasts or Aherns, I don't know which. When Goodhue was incorporated in 1897, store builders must have thought they were important because they named the buildings after themselves. Even today you can saunter through downtown, look to the top of the buildings and see the names chiseled in stone.

The inside was long and narrow with a wood-slat floor that creaked. A couple of slats in front of the girlie magazines had a particularly loud squeak; I had to be light on my feet and adept at avoiding those boards lest I tip off Eddie on my sojourn to the magazines. The store had fifteen-foot ceilings made from dishwater-gray corrugated metal in geometric designs.

Eddie's place had acquired its own peculiar aroma. Drugs, concoctions and the paraphernalia he stored in the back room emitted unique odors. Heaney and Gorman smelled of fresh ground meat, smoked hams, pork chops and sawdust; Bill Huebner's Blacksmith Shop smelled of horse manure and hot, molten iron. Funeral parlors have their own odor, one considerably different from a blacksmith shop, meat market, grain elevator or drugstore. Ole's funeral parlor aromas were questionable because I never knew what I was smelling. Sidney's Shoe Shop smelled of stained leather. Husbyn's Hatchery smelled of chicken . . . well. Each store emitted its particular fragrance, but Eddie's was a bizarre mixture of hydrogen peroxide, smelling salts, lye, dimestore perfume and formaldehyde, odors that stung my nostrils.

Glass display cases along the walls contained glycerin balm, Mentholatum balm, Vicks Vaporub, Dexamyl, quinine, aspirin, boric acid, camphor, hydrogen peroxide, tincture of iodine, Mercurochrome, carbolic acid, Lysol, mycomycin, streptothricin, sulfadimethoxine, castor oil, Epsom salts and Milk of Magnesia. Eddie stocked enough drugs and concoctions to fix any known ailment. He sold drugs for curing infections, pestilence, seizures, fever, prostration, anemia, convulsions, arthritis, rheumatism, laryngitis, hepatitis, gout, chlorosis, dysentery, cholera, chicken pox, smallpox, German measles, bronchitis and pneumonia. The display cases were ancient and worn, but then they had been there for many years. A drugstore was one of the first stores to set up business in town, because folks needed drugs for their aches and consumption. Eddie proudly displayed his stock of Colgate toothpaste, Palmolive soap, Bayer aspirin and items women purchased in brown packages.

His regular magazines were displayed in front by the window. It was easy to read those where Bessie Benda or Bill Hennings might see me upon entering, but girlie magazines would have been difficult to look at in the front. A fellow can be casual when reading about a new bandsaw in *Popular Science,* because everybody in town expected him to be interested in that, but magazines about what was underneath girls' sweaters was different. It was hard to be casual then. It took time and training to become nonchalant about getting a look. If the girlies had been in the front rack when Lydia Moran or Esther Kyllo walked in to buy Epsom salts, it would have been even harder. I don't know if I could have handled that. But I learned there were solutions to such predicaments, even in back behind the creaky floor boards.

I realized a good way to remain calm was to first stop at the front magazine rack where I would pick up a *Popular Science,* begin reading about band saws or the new Ford V8 engine, then casually make my move to the rear. I would capture a girlie magazine when Eddie was in back preparing a prescription, insert it between the band saws and V8 engine, and I was home free. Now, if Lydia walked in or if Eddie shuffled out of the back room or if Bill Hennings, my neighbor no less, saw me, no problem. "So, what are you reading then, Jimmy?"

"Oh, just about the new V8 engine Ford is producing this year."

"That so? I didn't know they were producing a V8. That's a pretty big engine."

"They figure they can do it now that the war is over. They've got more iron to work with, and we don't have gas rationing anymore, so the V8 is a pretty good deal."

"Sounds like a heckuva deal to me. You have a picture of it there?"

"Oh, no . . . this is just a story. They won't have a picture of the new engine until next month. See you around, Bill."

Wow, that was a close shave!

It wasn't the best system, but better than standing in front of the window looking at a girlie magazine. I wasn't ready for that yet.

Eddie was five foot ten inches tall, thin and lanky with close-cropped salt and pepper hair parted down the middle, a few strands falling over his eye. Those strands never stayed in place even with a healthy dab of Wildroot Cream Oil. But the most distinctive thing about Eddie was his walk. He had a hitch in his get-along, but didn't use a cane and could move reasonably fast from the back room to wait on a customer, or shuffle to Florence Taylor's Eat Shop for lunch. His limp made its own peculiar sound—shaboom, shaboom, shaboom—a sound advantageous for me, because I knew when he was shuffling from the back room where he prepared his prescriptions and did whatever it is that druggists do when they're hiding from the public. When I heard shaboom, shaboom, I could move quickly from the girlie magazines to the comic books.

Eddie wasn't a big talker which was remarkable for a Goodhue merchant. Most would talk your arm off, but he was raised in Featherstone Township where folks were of a different persuasion. The word around town was that Featherstonians were more inter–ested in thinking than talking, an odd characteristic for our village. Sometimes he would simply stand behind the counter gazing out the window toward Sydney's, or down the deserted street toward Tomfohr's International. Maybe he wasn't even thinking about the drugstore during those moments. Maybe his mind was off in Australia. Maybe he didn't want to be operating a drugstore in Minnesota. Maybe he was wishing he was somewhere else where people didn't talk so much. "Hi, Eddie, how are you doing today?"

"Can't complain." His reticence made it difficult to distract him. "What can I do for you, Jimmy?"

"Oh, I don't know. I thought I'd just look around for awhile. That be okay?"

"Sure."

I had to be astute. It was hard acting natural while making a move to the magazines so Eddie wouldn't notice, or Agnes O'Reilly or heaven forbid, my mother, suddenly walked in.

Fortunately, Eddie stacked the comic books and the girlie magazines only ten feet apart permitting me to make my first move to the comics. Safety. I would feign interest in *Spiderman* or *Superman* while eyeing the hot stack down the counter—one glance at *Spiderman*, a glance to the door, a glance toward the back room . . . *Coast is clear. Go for it, Jim* . . . a darting move down the counter. Girlies! Flip open. Search! Find out . . .

First page, nothing.

Second page ad about hair removal cream.

Third page ad about Charles Atlas developing big muscles. Damn!

Three pages and no photos.

Eddie's coming back.

Dart back to *Superman*. Mission unaccomplished.

Week after week, month after month I would trot to the drugstore to get educated, to develop a limited sex education. I wasn't old enough to drive to Red Wing or Rochester for magazines. There was no alternative. "You back so soon, Jimmy?"

"Mother needs a bottle of aspirin. You have any aspirin, Eddie?"

"Sure. How many?"

"Oh, just a small bottle. Her headache isn't big."

I would buy a bottle, saunter around the display cases for awhile, shuffle toward the comic books hoping Eddie would shaboom to the back room to prepare a prescription. Look left, look right; no one in the store. A beeline to the magazines. Pick one at random.

I'm in luck . . . Wow!

Flip another page, eyes bulging out of their sockets. Turn faster. Boobs, knockers, fannies, more boobs. God! I felt weird, different than when playing rubber gun wars. This was very different. The farm boys were right. Something was happening. More boobs.

Eddie's coming! Back to the comics.

"Well, I guess I'll be going, Eddie. Mom's headache is pretty bad; she'll be wanting these aspirin."

"All right, Jimmy."

"So long, take 'er easy."

I purchased considerable aspirin and toothpaste during my adolescence, creating a stash under my bed to last many years. Mother would never have had enough headaches in her lifetime to use all the aspirin I purchased. But I had to buy something. Eddie's wasn't like Heaney and Gorman where I could walk in and just talk. Eddie's place was antiseptic, just like the drugs he sold. He didn't have a rocking chair to sit in by a potbellied stove. If you went to Eddie's, you went to buy aspirin or toothpaste. But I was learning a little about sex, something I knew nothing about—girls, how they felt, what they thought about sex. If it hadn't been for the Drugstore I wouldn't have learned anything. I would have believed whatever Fr. Smith said bout sex—nothing. The Church simply said everything would be fine once you were married. God bless the Sex Spirit.

I was growing up. My head was changing, my body was changing. I felt different looking at girlie magazines than I did when reading about atomic rings and crystal radios in my *Johnson-Smith Catalog*. Those feelings kept bringing me back to the drugstore. "Mom's got a headache. Any aspirin, Eddie?"

3

Tall Tales In The Locker Room

My body changed over the next several years precipitating an increasing interest in girls. With the advent of *Playboy* I became less interested in *Popular Mechanics*. I started dating and holding hands, even putting my arm around my dates at the Rochester Drive-In Theater, fondly known as The Passion Pit. I was slowly learning about girls.

By my sophomore year the farm fellows—Dale Buck, Leo "Beefsteak" Ryan, Ralph "Spade" Malloy, Roger "Bood" Buden—siek, Bill Gadient, Harvey "Farmer" Opsahl, Johnny Reese, Clemey Joe Ryan—were talking more about sex in the locker room. After football, basketball or baseball practice, the locker room became another avenue for my sex education. I was exposed, literally, to the flesh. There would be fifteen or twenty guys showering and talking about *makin' out* and *doin' it*. Those farm boys were the biggest braggarts, because they saw farm sex daily. And they weren't as dumb as we town kids used to believe. They came off the farm with hard facts and tall stories, and they strutted naked around the locker room like stallions in the back forty. They were a proud bunch, some as well-endowed as stallions and they liked to let us younger village boys know it. They showered then paraded around the locker room for an hour showing off, prancing like black stallions, boasting about Saturday night's escapades. But not the younger village boys who weren't endowed like stallions. We took our showers and dressed quickly.

Gradually, the locker room conversations began changing— less girlie magazine talk, more *gettin' some* and *doin' it*. On Mondays the conversations would begin . . ."Boy, did I make out Saturday night!" Reese shouted.

"Ya, I'll bet you did," hissed Buck.

"Really, I mean I did it. I went all the way!"

"Reese, you're bullshitting me."

"No, really. We parked in lover's lane behind Finney's Woods and did it in the back seat of my Merc."

The next fellow told a bigger and wilder story than the previous one—talk and challenge—only to be challenged by friends who never believed their tales of conquest. How many stories were true? "Hey, Jimmy. Did you get any Saturday night?" Buck bellered from the toilet.

"Oh sure, I really made out," I countered.

"Bullshit! I'll bet you didn't even kiss her goodnight."

"Really, Buck, I made out like a rabbit."

Of course I was *gettin' some*, but I didn't even know what the phrase meant. How was a teenager to know about *gettin' any* if he hadn't ever gotten any? Looking at Eddie's magazines was one thing, *gettin' some* was a big step beyond that. It was difficult parrying with the farm boys, the show-offs, the well-endowed, but I did begin wondering what they were doing in Finney's Woods. I was playing the game. We were all playing the game.

Although my sex education was slower than the farm boys, I eventually caught up. I never bragged, too timid for that, but I attempted to hold my own in the locker room. "Wow! was Saturday night ever hot for me. I really made out."

"Bullshit, Franklin."

"No really, I had this hot date from Zumbrota, and we had a time, I tell you . . ."

One story more farfetched than the next, but it was part of the process, part of learning about sex and why I discarded *Popular Science* in favor of *Playboy*.

4

Beyond Rubber Guns

My trips to Eddie's Drugstore gradually changed in focus. I still purchased aspirin, but I eventually moved from the girlie magazine section to another area. But it was very difficult asking Eddie for a package of rubbers. With all the locker room bragging that occurred, a fellow needed a package of rubbers in his billfold. I now knew what PG meant, and I knew how girls got that way. I wasn't about to get a girl, or me, into that predicament. It was time to buy some rubbers, to be ready; besides, a package in your billfold lent status in the locker room.

I had heard ample Dale Buck stories, enough Leo Ryan examples. I had now seen cattle go at it on O'Neill's farm; I finally had it figured out. And I also had a few years experience holding hands, spinning the bottle and tussling with girls to find out a little of what they felt like. That's why junior high kids fight so much on the playground. They are trying to get a feel. Fighting and tussling are fair game. I had tussled with the girls and liked the experience. It was time for the next step. "How you doin' today, Eddie?"

"Could be worse. What can I do for you?"

"I need toothpaste, cough drops, and I guess I could probably use a small bottle of aspirin."

"You sure have been buying lots of aspirin, Jim. Are you having headaches?"

"Nope. They're for Mother. She has arthritis in her knees."

"Oh. I'll get you some."

How am I going to do this? I've never bought rubbers before. What's Eddie going to think of me? What does he think I'm going to do with them? What if he asks me what size I want? The guys at school said they come in small, medium and large. I don't think I've got the nerve to ask. I'm embarrassed.

"Have your aspirin, cough drops and toothpaste here. Will there be anything else?"

Now's the time. Can I do it? How many do I need? How many come in a package? I wish Dallas was with me; he'd know. He's so much more experienced than me. Hurry up, Jim, make up your mind.

"Did you hear me, Jim? Do you need anything else tonight?"

Where does Eddie keep them? If I could just see a box maybe I could decide. They must be behind the counter. If they were on a shelf, I could pick up a package and casually place them on the counter along with the cough drops and say, 'Oh, I guess I'll take a package of these along also.'

"Jim, you must be day dreaming. I've asked you twice if you needed anything else, but you're just looking off into space."

"Sorry, Eddie. I was thinking about our basketball game tonight against Wanamingo. Big game you know. No . . . well . . . that'll be all for today."

Damn! I couldn't do it. I lost my courage.

"Thanks, Eddie."

"All right, Jim. Have a good game."

"You betcha." I walked out the door, downcast, discouraged.

How am I ever going to buy rubbers. It's so embarrassing. He'll know for sure what I'm going to do with them. He'll probably tell everyone who comes into the store, then everybody in town will know that I bought my first package. Would Eddie tell? Did pharmacists take a vow like priests? I don't want him to know what I'm going to use rubbers for, but it would be better if only he knew, if he didn't tell other folks.

We beat Wanamingo by two points. I had a good game even though my mind wasn't focused. I was shooting free throws while thinking about purchasing my first package of rubbers, and I didn't even know if I would have an opportunity to use them. Nevertheless, I needed a package. I wanted to be prepared. In the locker room after the game I mustered the courage to ask Dallas how he purchased his rubbers. "Dallas, I need to talk to you. You've bought rubbers from Eddie before. How do you go about it?"

"First you walk in, pick up a bottle of aspirin . . ."

"You buy a lot of aspirin too?"

"I've got enough aspirin under my bed to last a couple of years. Anyway, get yourself a bottle of aspirin, place it on the counter and then when you're ready to pay Eddie say, as if it was a second thought, 'By the way, Eddie, throw in a package of rubbers, too.' That's all there is to it. You have to ask like you were doing it everyday, like you were asking for toothpaste or aspirin."

"It sounds so easy for you. You're so experienced and . . . Big D, do you think you could . . . I mean . . . maybe . . . for me . . . . oh, forget it. I guess this is something I'll have to do for myself."

Dallas and I were double dating tomorrow night. My date was a cute Zumbrota girl and Dallas' was a Wanamingo cheerleader. We won our game against Pine Island on Friday night so I was feeling good, looking forward to my date. It was time for a young man to have a couple of rubbers in his billfold.

At Heaney and Gorman Saturday morning, I trimmed meat, waited on customers and delivered groceries throughout the village. But my mind wasn't on work. I needed that security for tonight, and I needed to devise a plan for getting away from the store momentarily to run up to Eddie's. We normally took a morning break about ten, another about half past three. The morning went by so rapidly that I didn't get a chance to leave. I was getting increasingly nervous. The siren sounded for high noon. I looked through the front windows to see Eddie shuffling to Taylor's Eat Shop for lunch—shaboom, shaboom, shaboom. I walked out of the store, waved to him across the street, "How you doin', Eddie? I'll see you later. Need more aspirin."

I hope that's an ice breaker. Now he will know I'm coming up to his store this afternoon. I feel better. This time I'll do it.

Quarter past three. Only fifteen minutes until afternoon break time. "Jim, are you ready to go to lunch with me at Swenson's?" Dennis inquired from behind the cutting saw.

"I've got to go to the drugstore to get something for school on Monday. I'll have to skip lunch today."

"What do you need?"

"No big deal . . . I'll be back in a few minutes."

It was only a block from Heaney and Gorman to Eddie's Drugstore, but I wished it would have been ten miles so I would have had time to think.

Slow down feet, don't move so fast. Breathe slowly, Jim.

I passed the Shell station; Luverne hollered, "Where ya headed, Jim?

"Hi, Luverne. Just need to get some aspirin at Eddie's."

If he finds out I'll never live it down. He'll tell everyone in town, even my mother.

I skirted Marshall-Wells, passed the bank until only a few feet remained.

Here goes.

"Hi, Eddie, did you have a good lunch?"

"Light lunch—roast beef, mashed potatoes and gravy, green beans, salad."

"All of that for lunch?"

"What can I do for you?"

"I need more aspirin and you know, we're having a special experiment in chemistry class at the high school on Monday morning; I was wondering if you had a few supplies I need."

"Yes, what do you need?"

This is it. Mother of God, pray for me that I can get through this.

"We're having an experiment in which we're using chemicals to see if they will react to each other when mixed, but before we mix them we need to keep them in separate containers, something flexible like soft rubber. Our chemistry teacher said it would work."

"What supplies do you need?"

"Our teacher said that if we put the two liquids in separate flexible containers and lay them together, the heat transmitted between them will start a fire."

"Sounds like a good experiment, Jim, but *what* do you need?"

"I need a bottle of hydrogen peroxide, a small bottle of rubbing alcohol, a package of cotton swabs, a bottle of aspirin and throw in a package of rubbers."

There, it's out. I've said it. What's going to happen now? What's Eddie going to do? Did he hear me say rubbers? *Oh, Lord.*

"Here's the hydrogen peroxide, rubbing alcohol and cotton swabs and aspirin. What size rubbers do you want?"

"Oh, a pretty big bottle, I guess."

"Not the hydrogen peroxide, the rubbers?"

"Gosh, I don't know, Eddie, what sizes do you have?"

"I've small, medium and large?"

"Oh, I guess I could use the large. Give me a box of large."

"All right. Do you want a small package or a gross?"

Gross? How many rubbers in a gross? Why didn't Dallas tell me about package sizes?

"Well, we may do the chemistry experiment several times, so I guess I'll take a gross." Eddie went behind the counter, reached over to the lowest drawer near the floor, opened it slowly and took out a package wrapped in brown paper. He placed it on the counter, tallied up my bill, wrapped all the packages together, gave me change and as I walked out the door said with what I though was a breaking smile, "Hope you have a good experiment, Jim."

___5

Kissin'

As I sauntered back to Heaney & Gorman with my *burning* pack–
age, I began thinking . . . about my progress and achievements
since grade school in finding the Sex Spirit, about those first
photos in the tree house, about that first kiss while playing spin the
bottle, about Eddie's girlie magazines, about stories in the locker
room, about my first urges starting back a few years ago, about
necking, about being sixteen and never having done it, and now my
first package of rubbers . . . .

About seventh grade I began developing a serious interest in
girls, realizing there were things of greater interest than sliding into
second base with a double. I acted like my classmates—teasing,
tussling, pinching girls in my class. I didn't know then what I was
doing, but something was propelling me forward. I began waltzing
and fox trotting with girls at sock hops after basketball games in the
old gym, getting closer.

I never had what one would call an actual date throughout my
junior high years, a time when I asked a girl to have a hamburger
and malt at Swenson's, or take in a movie at the Chief Theatre in
Red Wing, or invite her to sit on a blanket at the free movies. But
we did have house parties under scrutinizing parental eyes at
Janice Cook's, Bettie Lunde's, Mary Benda's, Larry O'Reilly's,
Bob O'Reilly's, Bev Moran's, Lee Johnson's and Joanne Mans'
houses. We played Monopoly, Canasta, Charades and Spin the
Bottle, innocent activities, but beneficial for trying to get closer. If
the Irish, Norwegians, Swedes and Germans were going to prolif-
erate in the township, it would be necessary to get closer.

Sometimes we turned the lights lower, sat in a circle and played Spin the Bottle. How do you kiss? Do you keep your mouth shut or open it? Mother didn't talk to me about kissing, Dad certainly didn't and Fr. Smith was under strict orders to abide by *E Pluribus Sexium.* Was I supposed to know all by myself?

Oh, bottle, don't point at me.

My first Spin game was at Lee Johnson's on a blustery Friday night in February of 1948. Janice, Lee, Gladys, Jack, Beverly, Mary, Bettie, Bob, Larry, and I were there up on water tank hill. Lee mustered the courage to turn off a few lights in his living room then light a candle. We had pop and popcorn, but soon it was time to begin. I wasn't especially nervous when the game began, because I thought the odds were in my favor. I wanted to kiss a girl, eventually, but not tonight. It could wait a week or two.

Lee found an empty Grain Belt bottle in the basement and placed it in the middle of the floor. I could tell the boys were nervous. The girls didn't appear to be so. Maybe they had kissed before. Lee gave that bottle such a spin that it twisted out of the circle. Again. Spin.

Don't let it point at me. I want to kiss a girl, but I need a little more time. Please, not tonight.

The bottle was slowing considerably. It spun toward me but passed by stopping between Bob and Mary, pointing to neither. Lee again spun the bottle.

This is like Russian Roulette. What will I do if it stops in front of me?

It rotated slower and slower.

Looks like only one more revolution before it stops.

It crept around the circle in my direction.

Will it stop this time? No, I'm saved, it's going past.

It stopped in front of Janice. A deathly quietness enveloped the room. We could hear the wind howling as sleet battered against the window panes. What was Janice going to do? She rose to her feet with deliberate speed, glanced in my direction, looked beyond, then ever so slowly moved toward Lee. Lee was ashen. I had never seen him this sallow before. I caught a glance from his eyes just before Janice stood in front of him. They connected with mine in a look of desperation as if to say, *"Sorry, Jim, it was good knowing you."* Methodically, Janice kneeled on the floor and maneuvered her face toward Lee's. I don't know if he had kissed before, and I didn't know what you were supposed to look like when kissing, but he looked pained, sad. I couldn't see Janice's face because she had her back to me, but through the candles' flickering light I saw Lee brace.

Oh, I hope you make it, Lee, so we can play basketball tomorrow.

Then he relaxed, tension leaving his legs and back. Janice skittered quickly back to her place in the circle. I now had a full view. He looked bright, no longer ashen, red face glowing and hair glistening in the flickering candlelight. I had never seen him look so peaceful before. I was confused. Did a kiss have that much power?

Lee was in a daze so Jack got up to spin. He spun it even more vigorously than Lee. Around and around it whirled but stopped without pointing at anyone. Jack spun it again. This time it seemed to rotate forever, but I had a dire feeling it would stop and point directly at me.

Could I kiss? Should I run now? Should I go to the toilet before it stops?

It spun slower until it was apparent there was only one more revolution. It passed by, creeping to a halt in front of Bettie. I wiped the sweat from my brow and let out a sigh of relief. I heard, for the first time, Hank Williams' *Your Cheating Heart* playing on Lee's phonograph. Had that music been playing all this time? A spreading smile covered Bettie's face. She seemed so confident, so sure of herself. Where did she get that confidence? Did she know I had never kissed a girl? She glanced around the circle with darting blue eyes glancing at Bob, flirting with Larry, Jack, Lee, then . . . her sparkling eyes settled on me. I stared at the floor trying desperately to listen to Hank Williams, but when I brought my eyes back up into the candlelight, she was on her feet, gliding toward me, a twinkle in her eyes. Maybe she wouldn't stop in front of me. Maybe she was heading toward Bob on my left or Larry on my right. No such luck. I began shaking. Much too quickly, she was sitting cross-legged directly in front of me, eyes twinkling, lips wet and only inches from mine. I had never seen a girl's face that close before. It was as if I had never seen her before, yet we had been attending school together since first grade, one of The Five. A smile curled from the corner of her mouth as she moved yet closer—Ten inches, nine, eight, seven.

What am I suppose to do? I don't know how to kiss.

I stiffened. When her lips were only two inches from mine, I sensed something. Even though our lips hadn't touched, I felt . . . electricity, a connection I had never felt before. Then, it happened. My eyes were closed when I felt something touch my lips.

It must be Bettie. No one else is this close to me.

She had her lips slightly parted and a little bit wet as if she had just taken a sip of Pepsi. When they touched mine, she pressed and twisted and at that moment, I felt the strangest sensation move down my body starting in my lips, moving to my neck, then down across my chest through my tummy and down into my growing parts. Wow! Then it was over and Bettie was sliding back to her place in the circle. As she turned she looked at me from across the shadowy room, a smile spreading across her pretty face. She winked. I winked back.

I felt experienced then, having had my first kiss. I floated down the hill, feet lightly touching the ground. Was I in love with Bettie? Does one kiss make a boy and a girl lovers?

Well, it was a breakthrough, but I didn't become an instant master kisser. I had wanted to but had difficulty generating the necessary courage. There were a lot of hit-and-run kisses over the next several years, the type where you walk your date to the door after a movie, stand nervously on one foot then the other wondering if you have the courage to kiss her goodnight. But it was an unwritten rule around GHS that a fellow at least kiss his date goodnight. If he couldn't do that much, he wasn't making progress toward his sexual learning, and it would be hard talking to the guys in the locker room.

Kissing continued to be awkward for me during those early high school years. If I were double-dating in the back seat of a Chevy I tried to kiss my date before arriving at her home, because that way I could take pressure off having to do it at her doorstep. Nevertheless, kissing my date in the back seat felt direct and forward for a shy altar boy. If I simply turned and kissed her, what would she think? Would she slap me across the face? But everyone at GHS knew you were supposed to kiss your date goodnight. "I had a nice time tonight. It was a good movie."

"Me too, Jim, and thanks for the hamburger and malt."

"Oh, no big deal."

"Well, I guess I better be going in the house."

"I guess so. Well . . ."

Can I do it? Do I have the courage to give her a goodnight kiss? Just close your eyes and do it, Jim.

"Goodnight. I'll see you in school on Monday. Got to do my algebra homework yet tonight."

"Okay, Thanks for the movie."

Now, make your move, Jim. Move toward her and kiss her on the lips. Hit and run. No embrace yet, no hand holding or hugs. Good . . . You did it. Wow!

"Goodnight."

"Goodnight."

Hit-and-runs were gradually replaced by longer kisses accom–panied by considerable hugging. As I gained more experience, I began having different feelings. I was still listening to the fellows in the locker room talk about their conquests, so by the time I was a junior the conversations had moved beyond hand holding and makin' out. The guys weren't satisfied with a simple goodnight kiss or two anymore. They were looking for more action, another step in our stairway to sex education, a stairway long and steep but worth the climb.

On my dates I had now progressed to sneaking my arm around her in the back seat of Hutch's Volkswagen or Dallas' Chevy, two guys with hot cars . . . well, cars. I didn't have access to wheels, so when I managed to get a date it was a double date. That wasn't bad, though, because it gave me an opportunity to develop my necking technique. I could gradually slip my arm around the top of the seat and casually let it fall down around her shoulders. Once in place it froze in that position lest it became obvious to her there was an arm around her shoulders. Initially, the technique wasn't so much makin' out as simply moving closer. The more I initiated it the easier it became—back seat of a jalopy, arm around your date, kissing, holding hands, hugging, and . . .

I began to think there was more to dating than kissing. I certainly liked it but something was happening to me during those embraces that needed attention. I was becoming accustomed to squeezing, fondling and hugging, but I felt something else was supposed to happen. I remembered those pictures at Eddie's, and the locker room braggarts were continually spouting off about *gettin' some*, but there's a big difference between talk and action, between boasting in the locker room and coming face to face with it in the back seat of a Volkswagen.

I developed a creeping urge to find out what that other *something* was. Makin' out became more intensive. The kisses became longer, harder, wetter and my arm didn't stay around my date's shoulders in one frozen position anymore. It began moving, arms and hands began wandering. I knew what was under that heavy winter clothing, but I hadn't experienced it. I was hoping to find out.

. . . By the time I returned to Heaney and Gorman from Eddie's, that brown package in my pocket was scorching my hand. I finished the afternoon trimming meat and cleaning the block, then hurried home to clean up. Dallas would drive by to pick me up soon, then we would head to Zumbrota and Wanamingo for our dates. We took in a movie at Rochester, then stopped at the Wagon Wheel Drive Inn in Zumbrota for burgers, malts and deep fried onion rings. Hank Williams was on the jukebox, onion rings were deep frying, and I was loaded for action.

Dallas' date lived on a one hundred sixty-acre dairy farm near Wanamingo. We drove through a country lane, over a hill and down into a small valley—Lover's Lane. Dallas was more experienced than me, at least that's what he told me, so when we neared her place he put his Bel Aire into park on a tree-lined secluded lane. Big D was not a timid soul, so as soon as he slipped that Power

Glide into Park he moved over. I was slower, fussing around, talking before I generated enough courage. However, I had grown tired of only putting my arm around my date and kissing a few times. I was ready to move up a few stairs on that stairway to sex education.

I was excited, nervous and inexperienced. I had heard the stories, seen the photos, but I had never done *it*, and I didn't know how to go about *it*. Should I ask her questions, or should I just make my move? We were makin' out and Dallas had disappeared from sight in the front seat. I was on my own. I began tussling like I did back in eighth grade. I thought if I did that I might accidentally brush a part of her body I had never touched before. I moved in closer, always aware of whether I would get a slap across the face. I moved my arm and hand down from her shoulder and held her around her tiny waist. She didn't stop me . . . yet. I moved cautiously. Slowly, very slowly and tenderly, I moved my hands upward from her waist. She felt good. I was excited and the cute Zumbrota cheerleader seemed to be enjoying it. Over a ten-minute period I managed to move my hands upward from her waist to *that* area. I wasn't in any hurry, and I couldn't see Dallas, anyway.

Then . . . it happened. I felt something I hadn't felt before. I was momentarily confused. I was sixteen and had spent countless hours in Eddie's Drugstore, had succeeded in purchasing my first box of rubbers, but at this moment I was in foreign territory . . . alone. Dallas was busy. My date wasn't fighting me off. I had a green light. I moved my hand up to her chest and lightly touched her left breast. Tension, suspense. Was she going to stop me? Did she like it? My hand froze for several minutes. I couldn't move. I was afraid to move. I didn't know what was going to happen next. We were kissing madly when I finally moved my hand. It was all right. She was climbing a few stairs herself. We were climbing that stairway together.

Chapter 15
Class of 1954
High School Years

Doris Bremer & Jim Franklin, Prom 1951

THE CLASS OF '54 GRADUATED IN THE SPRING IN OUR new gymnasium, the first class to graduate from the only school addition built since 1936, our birth year. We began first grade with five snotty-nosed kids, gradually added classmates from the country, boys and girls who boarded the bus each morning kicking cow manure from their shoes, until we accumulated twenty-one in the graduating class. We processed through the gym that May evening having successfully passed through *Dick and Jane*, the Palmer method, geography, history, algebra, geometry and physics. We had completed our formal education; much too soon we would be bidding farewell to each other, each going his own way after the ceremonies. But before we did we had to listen to the commence–ment address by The Honorable Edward J. Thye, Senior Minneso–ta Senator to the U.S. Congress speaking about, "What Makes America Great."

As I sat on the stage with my classmates, I glanced left then right and thought back to day one when Bob and I walked to school together in the fall of 1942. I thought about The Five and The Twenty-One, and wondered where all the years had gone. How could they have passed so quickly? I hadn't liked studying very much, but I liked school and I liked my classmates; seventeen was too young to go out into the world. I *heard* the senator but I wasn't listening. I was reflecting about the past twelve years, thinking about all we had done, all we had experienced together. I was sitting on the stage, but my thoughts were elsewhere. I was thinking . . .

____1

Assembly Hall: Miss North, Miss Cree, Charles Wood

. . . About our first day of high school in the fall of 1950 when we were pimple-faced, knock-kneed, gangly freshmen hoping to survive the GHS Assembly Hall with junior and senior country bullies from Bellechester, Belvidere and Belle Creek Townships. The entire high school congregated in the second floor Assembly Hall at the beginning of every school day. I had never seen so many students together in one room before. For the previous eight years, we had attended individual classrooms, fifteen or twenty students in a room, but all high school grades gathered together in the Assembly Hall. There must have been one hundred students in that room. Freshmen sat on the left side, seniors on the right. Between us were sophomores and juniors. Sister Rose was on the right, brother Tom in between. The odors emanating from that room on a muggy September morning were poignant. The odors in the sophomore section—Class of '53—were particularly pungent. There were teenagers who hadn't bathed for two weeks, students who had milked thirty Holsteins before coming to school in the same clothes and shoes, guys who arrived without changing jeans after cleaning the hog house. Oh, the *aromas*, and the sounds . . . students hollering across the Assembly to friends . . .

"HEY, BEEF–STEAK, MY ALLIS CHALMERS BROKE DOWN LAST NIGHT, BLEW A PISTON!"

"WELL, BUCK, THAT OLD TRACTOR IS JUST A BUNCH OF BALING WIRE ANYWAY. IT DOESN'T DESERVE TO RUN!"

"UP YOURS!"

"All right now, settle down. Get in your seats and be quiet."

The unfortunate teacher assigned the task of monitoring the Assembly at the beginning of each day had an unmerciful task. Imagine getting one hundred students into their seats, especially GHS students. Sometimes Ray Battie had the assignment, other times Miss Cree or Miss North. Superintendent W.E. Hubert rarely handled the job; mostly, the task fell to Charles Wood our principal and band director. But we eventually settled down, roll was taken then classes were released to individual classrooms for first period.

Freshmen first hour was typing class with Miss North . . . A S D F G, then J K L over and over again. Move up to Q W E R T Y, over to U I O P then down to the bottom row, Z X C V B and N M. "Ouch! Who threw that spitball?"

"Miss North. I got hit on the back of my head with a spitball. Digger Dave threw it!"

"Did you throw that spitball, David?"

"It wasn't me, 'cause I was doing my QWERTYs. I saw Bremer throw it!"

"Did not. Dewey threw it."

"I don't care who threw it. Behave or you'll all stay after school; get ready for a speed test."

Miss North could get her mouth twisted and set in a smirk that would send shivers down my back. She paced back and forth in front of the typewriters probably wondering how she ever got into this mess of trying to teach typing to Goodhue hayseeds. The bell finally rang releasing a mass of humanity into the halls—freshmen, sophomores, juniors, seniors—for a few minutes before the next class. We survived freshman year, all that is except Miss Cree.

"My name is Miss Cree. That's spelled C R E E!"

I believe that was the only moment all year she held our undivided attention, because she didn't know how to handle village children, and she certainly didn't know how to handle farm ruffians. She was a pretty woman with long, black hair, and pretty dresses, but she couldn't discipline "Digger" Dave Majerus, Neil Bremer, Mike Ryan or Jimmy Franklin. She didn't know what to do when we started acting up, so mostly, she cried. She wrung her hands and paced and cried and went home every day vowing never to return to teach such hooligans.

She graduated from River Falls Teachers College in Wisconsin, but those Wisconsin professors didn't know about us. They didn't prepare her for the behaviors of country bumpkins—earthy fellows who slushed through cow and sheep manure and talked about horses and cows screwing. Miss Cree wasn't ready for GHS. She didn't make it. She finished her first year and was never seen in town again.

RRRrrrrrrrrrrrrrriiiiiiiiiiiinnng!

The bell rang loudly as Miss Cree was trying to teach us how to conjugate verbs, but she didn't have a chance to finish. Once we heard that bell, we were gone. Tom Manahan, normally a quiet and gentle fellow, hopped over Gladys Holst on his way to the door. Dewey Jonas bumped Rita Diercks knocking her English book to the floor as he dashed through the door. Roy Roble slid under Virginia George's skirt as he made a beeline to the hallway. Mike

Ryan grabbed Janet Kann's English and math books and threw them out the window as he passed her on the window side. Miss Cree started crying. She put her face in her hands and sobbed.

. . . I thought about third hour study hall for freshmen. It was called study hall, but many didn't study. Some of the more studious fellows and most girls did, but many guys didn't crack a book. Virginia George studied. Rita Diercks studied. Janice Cook studied. Pearl Decker always studied. Bob O'Reilly studied even though he walked to school with me. We toted books home daily, but Bob used his. I set mine on the dining room table then picked them up on my way out the door the next morning. "Hi, Bob. Did you get your English verbs conjugated?"

"Yes, did you?"

"Naw, guess I'll try to get them done this morning in study hall." What a joke, but every day I did the same thing—talk, joke, tease, everything but conjugate verbs. I had more important things to do like bouncing a basketball. I loved dribbling a basketball, and when I could do that, verbs didn't stand a chance. Isosceles triangles didn't have a chance. Book reports didn't have a chance. If my teachers had placed verbs and geography and Africa and Europe and algebraic equations on the outside of a basketball, I might have had a chance. They didn't. I didn't. But I could bounce and pass and shoot a basketball. I constantly cradled a basketball, but if I didn't have an official ball I used make-believe basketballs in the form of a spitball sailing across Miss Cree's classroom, basketballs in the form of a tennis ball slowly arcing across the Assembly Hall to Bill Center or Nick Delva or Ralph Malloy. If I were even more courageous, I would try a pass all the way over to Harold Pepper or George O'Reilly in the senior section.

I could bounce a basketball while chomping on a peanut butter sandwich or changing shoes or brushing my butch haircut or eating supper or listening to Ma Perkins. I could bounce a basketball while serving Mass or going to confession. I could bounce a basketball anyplace, anytime—down the street, across the church lawn, down the alley behind Art's Bar, through my legs, around my back, down the curb, up on the sidewalk, through Campbell's Hardware, into Eddie's, in the front door and out the back at Swenson's, over to Heaney's, ". . . two pounds of hamburger for Mother please" . . . make change, pay for the hamburger, whip around Lydia Moran at the checkout counter, drive to the door, dart past Blanche Cook, under my legs with hamburger in one hand, the basketball in the other, never stopping, never studying.

. . . I thought about Mr. Charles Wood's social studies class. Discipline was better in that class because he knew how to handle the ruffians, and he knew how to handle me. There was something unique in the way he stood and stared and spoke. He could discipline the bullies better than any teacher. Superintendent Hubert was severe—we stepped aside when he shuffled through the halls—but Charles Wood was the real disciplinarian. He was also the band director and with me a clarinetist, I thought I should behave in social studies—no spitballs, no hair pulling, no teasing, no basketballs. And Joleen Cordes, Pearl Decker, Gloria Holst, Beverly Muhlman, Mary Benda and Bob O'Reilly studied. Even "Digger" Dave studied. Not much I could do, so I studied, too.

Only one more class, Mr. Hilling's algebra class, before sports practice. He ran a good class, and most fellows behaved, because he was also the basketball coach. I didn't want to get into trouble; I loved basketball. No spitballs, paper airplanes, gum chewing or boisterous behavior.

2

Swenson's & Shelstad's Cafe

. . . I thought about our after-school, after-game hangouts and how high school students would congregate at Swenson's or Shelstad's Cafe for malts and burgers on snow-driven February nights. Those cafes were our hangouts, because they were the only places in town where we could congregate. We couldn't go into the Corner Bar or Art's Bar.

Heinie and Regina owned Swenson' Cafe, but son Dave fixed the malts. Dave graduated in 1948 from GHS, several years before our Class of '54. Thirty or forty high schoolers would descend on Swenson's after a game, all wanting quick service. "Dave, gimme a malt, big fries and hamburger. Hold the onions."

"Just hold on there a minute, Jimmy. I have eight malts and ten burgers ahead of you."

Swenson's decor was middle-America-rural, a row of stark booths on one side, bar on the other, a candy case up front and the griddle in back. We affectionately called it the Greasy Spoon. After a night at Swenson's, you could smell hamburger and onions on your clothes for days. The Assembly Hall smelled like fried onions. I could sit in English class and catch the aroma of onions wafting over the classroom. That aroma mixed with Digger Dave's boots was enough to send Miss Cree or Miss North reeling and retching from the room.

Swenson's—malts, burgers, fries, classmates, phone calls for a date; Whist and Euchre on drowsy Sunday afternoons.

3

Classmates

I stopped daydreaming for a moment to look at my classmates on the commencement stage listening to Senator Thye. I saw "Just One More Chance" Mary Rose Benda, "Making Whoopee" Neil Harold Bremer, "Toot Toot Tootsie" Janice Marvel Cook, "Simple Melody" Joleen V. Cordes, "Ricochet" Pearl Audrene Decker, "A-You're Adorable" Rita M. Diercks, "Five Minutes More" Virginia George, "Johnson Rag" Gladys Marie Holst, "Dance Me Loose" Gloria Mae Holst, "I'm Never Satisfied" Duane Curtis Jonas,

"Once In Awhile" Janet Kann, "Anytime" Marilyn Joann Klair, "The Moon Shines Bright On Pretty Red Wing" Bettie Jeanne Lunde, "Gold Digger of Broadway" David William Majerus, "Slow Poke" Thomas Patrick Manahan, "From Rags to Riches" Beverly Joanne Muhlman, "That Little Boy of Mine" David O'Neill, "It's In The Book" Robert R. O'Reilly. I looked at "Just A Little Loving" Roy A. Roble. And I looked at, "When Irish Eyes Are Smiling," Michael J. Ryan. I thought about the good times we had experienced together. I looked up and down the row again, but this time I didn't see young men and women in commencement cap and gowns; I saw friends, pals. I saw Mary Rose, Bremer, Jan, Jo, Pearl, Scoot, Ginny, Liz, Tully, Dewey, Janet, Klair, Bets, Digger, Walter, Bev, Dave, Bob, Roy and Mike. I thought back to that first day in fourth grade when all the new faces appeared and how I didn't want any new classmates. As I thought about them, moisture appeared in my eyes. Mother said later that she noticed the tears during the ceremony and was touched that I had responded to Senator Thye's speech, but that wasn't it. I didn't hear a word. I was thinking . . .

. . . About the '54 Yearbook we had recently received and how hard we had worked preparing the book that would follow us through life like a puppy, the book with notes and comments from friends, the book each carried to classmates and teachers for signing. I thought about the notes my teachers wrote . . ."Jim. Usually in third hour class, I looked as crabby as this picture, and one of the reasons, I am sure you know why! Best wishes for a happy and successful future." Mary Lou Woelfinger.

"Jim. You have done a find job in band and chorus and your good work has been appreciated. I wish you the very best." Sincerely, Charles Wood.

"Jimmy. When the basketball team takes the floor this fall, I know we'll miss Franklin. You're a great credit to the school in every way. Best Wishes." Gordon Foss.

"James. All we need are more like you. The best to you." Enoch Bennett.

Then I thought about the comments my classmates and friends wrote . . .

"Jim. The best for you always." Mary Rose.

"Jim. Best of luck." Neil.

"Jim. Good luck in college. It's been a real pleasure to have you as a classmate and buddy. Good luck, James." Dewey.

"Jim. Remember the good times in English class and all the other good times in school. Good luck in the future." Thomas Manahan.

"Jimmy. It's been swell knowing you these four years of high school that you have just finished, and I hope you keep on going! Be good this summer and don't ever forget the little deal we had about those cute Zumbrota people!!! Pretty sly! Good luck in the future!" Kittie Ryan.

I thought about those comments and how so many of my friends wrote about the future, because in our minds, that's what we had, a future and the "best wishes" and the "good lucks" to make it in the future, wherever that was. I guess it was from this moment on, after the droning, monotonous speech by the senator and after the graduation parties later tonight. That's when the future began, or did it begin right now?

I thought about our class motto . . . "Everything is possible with tomorrow; no dream too foolish, no goal too high." I guess mottoes are for helping us move into the future, to dream the impossible dream, to shoot for the stars, to conquer over all . . .

Hail, hail the purple and white,
Wildcat in spirit, Wildcat in fight.
Our true mo . . . tt . . . o . . .
We'll win over all.

Yes, we would certainly ". . . win over all" in the future. We had our entire lives ahead of us to be successful. I thought about that. I tried to gaze into the future. I wondered how accurate our Class Prophecy was. The entire class had toiled on it for weeks as each of us tried to determine where we would end up thirty or forty years down the road. We all had vision. We knew we would be successful. We knew we would be able to rise above the little village that had confined us for the past eighteen years. Oh, we liked our village. We would never be able to shake the dust from our shoes, but for now, at our commencement, we wanted to shake it off. We wanted to leave, to fly. We wanted to return someday on the wings of an eagle. We wanted to show the world how well we could do. So we wrote, we prophesied . . .

The scene is an enormous airport for space ships and rockets. Our pilot, Michael Ryan, is getting ready to make his first flight after ten years of strenuous training at the Belle Creek Space Academy.

I thought about a Class of '54 reunion twenty years from now and wondered if Mike would still be flying high at the Space Academy? I wondered which of my classmates came up with the phrase, "Belle Creek Space Academy." That took some far-fetched vision because Belle Creek was only a general store and a creek surrounded by thousands of acres of beans, wheat, corn and oats. The only *space* in Belle Creek was *spacious* farm land, certainly considerable land for a space academy, but hardly the technological center of the nation. But we had vision. We needed it to leave Commencement and go out into the world.

As the senator's speech dragged on unmercifully, I thought about the treasures the class had willed to friends we were leaving behind. We didn't have use for our gifts anymore, so we wrote the class' Last Will and Testament. We willed our most prized possessions, giving treasures away because we wanted to be remem–bered. We didn't want to have walked the halls of GHS for four years to be simply forgotten. We wanted our names to remain—to be displayed on the walls long after we had departed. We wanted our spirits to be floating through the old school long after we had fulfilled our class prophecy. We each left part of us behind, willing possessions to the Class of '55, Class of '56, Class of '57.

To our most beloved teachers, we leave our heartiest thanks for their patience and understanding.

To the Juniors, we leave our good times with hopes that they get through the next year successfully.

To the Sophomores, we leave our great integrity and enthusi-asm.

To the Freshmen, we leave our intelligence and courage.

We had individual things to will:

Bettie Lunde wills her voice at basketball games to Phyllis Buchholtz, and she leaves her "utter silence" to Rita Ryan.

Gloria Holst wills her Grand 4-H heifer to Arlene Henrichs.

"Digger" Dave Majerus wills his good times in English class to anyone who wants to take those chances.

Gladys Holst wills her extra pounds to Arnie Vomhof.

Jimmy Franklin wills his basketball ability to Martin Manahan.

Michael Ryan wills his ability to take out Zumbrota girls to Elroy Strusz.

Roy Roble wills his '49 Ford to anyone who can keep it running.

Robert O'Reilly wills his system of wire tapping to any communist.

. . . I thought especially about The Five who began school together in 1942, my close and special classmates. I thought about Mary Benda . . ."James Leo. For twelve years we have gone together to school. It's been lots of fun. Don't forget the night down at my house when Gladys O'Reilly stopped in. Way back when, huh? Be good, Jim, and make the best of your life." Mary Rose.

Janice Cook . . ."Well, we finally made the grade. It really doesn't seem possible. I'm sure glad that you plan to go on to college. I hope to see you again from time to time. May every success and happiness be yours." Janice.

Bettie Lunde . . ."Good luck, Jim. We've sure had a lot of fun through our school years. I hope you have a lot of pleasant memories. Best to you always." 'Bets,' '54.

Bob O'Reilly . . ."Best of luck at St. John's, Jim. Even though I'm going to St. Thomas, a much better and intellectual college! I've enjoyed being your neighbor and friend for the past eighteen years. The best of luck and success." Sandbox Bob.

I thought about the comments we wrote about each other in the yearbook, the peculiar quirks and peccadilloes each of us had. We tried to imagine. Just imagine . . .

Gladys Holst not having rip-roaring parties at her house
Mary Benda not attending one of those parties
David Majerus not eating candy in school
Dewey Jonas without a Scharpened-up remark
Jim Franklin going steady
Rita Diercks flunking an exam
Gloria Holst attending school as regularly as she attends 4H
Marilyn Klair not being married before Gladys' Silver
      Wedding Anniversary
Joleen Cordes telling a joke
Janice Cook not trying to get an "A" out of all the teachers
Bettie Lunde not trying to go out with older Red Wing men
Virginia George not flirting with men
Janet Kann with a poodle cut
Beverly Muhlman staying single for two years to teach school
David O'Neill without the nickname of "Baldy"
Roy Roble a midget
Mike Ryan conducting an orderly class meeting
Neil Bremer not having a car and a woman
Robert O'Reilly being a Republican
Pearl Decker sticking to one man
Thomas Manahan with straight blonde hair
The whole class with perfect attendance
The whole class agreeing

But we forgot one—*Just imagine school being over.* Was com–mencement an ending or a beginning? I thought a lot about that. Was I ending a lifestyle or starting a new one? What did commence–ment mean? It was hard to imagine ceremonies ending soon and not returning to school tomorrow morning. It was hard to imagine I wouldn't be playing basketball against Wanamingo or Zumbrota on this basketball floor next year. It was hard to imagine going off to a different town to attend college. It was hard to imagine not being with my classmates in English class or the class play or band or chorus. It was hard to imagine not meeting at Swenson's for a malt and hamburger after a game. Sure, we all vowed to attend every class reunion, but somehow I just knew that wouldn't happen. Oh, we would come back regularly for awhile, telling each other about our new schools, husbands, wives, children, jobs, cars, success and money, but as the years accumulated, some wouldn't return for a very long time. It was hard to imagine.

. . . I thought about my friends in the Class of '53 who had graduated a year before us and how much fun we had had double-dating, playing ball, partying, dancing—Roger Budensiek, Dallas Diercks, David Hutcheson, Doris Johnson, George Lee Johnson, Dennis Mahoney, Shirley Thomforde, JoAnn Mans, Beverly Moran, Jack O'Reilly, Larry O'Reilly, Lyle Puppe, Joan Dahling, Bill Gadient, Janice Hilan, Dale Jonas, Leo Ryan. I wondered what they were doing a year later. Had their prophecies come true in one year? How would I feel a year from now when the Class of '55 took their place on this stage? What would I be able to tell them from my vantage point of one year out?

4

Louis Schinnert

. . . I thought about Louis Schinnert, the long-time janitor at the school. The superintendent receives the exposure, the principal makes the decisions about student curriculum, but the janitor makes the school run smoothly. Louis was janitor when I entered first grade until he died in 1948 when my dad replaced him. His daily presence was comforting from that first day Bob and I walked to school and met the girls at the flagpole. He wore the same garb everyday; you could count on that. He dressed in an Oshkosh Begosh gray work shirt, top buttoned at the neck. His green work pants were held up with a pair of suspenders, and he kept his railroad watch tethered to a chain in his right-hand watch pocket. He looked at that watch often to keep on schedule, and Louis was surely a man to stay on schedule. He wore silver, wire rim glasses, a pair of Red Wing work boots, and always had a pipe sticking out of his left hand shirt pocket. When I looked at him I thought, *There is a nice man.* As Bob and I walked to the front door with Bettie, Janice and Mary, Louis was at the flag pole hoisting the flag for a new day, but he took time to wave to The Five. Every school day for the next seven years Louis raised and lowered that flag like clockwork. You could set your watch by it. At eight o'clock the flag went up, at four it came down, rain or shine, hail, sleet or snow. Unfortunately, Louis' systematic work habits caused him some anguish one eventful day in the fall of 1947. I remember it well, although I didn't have anything to do with it.

The eventful day started as a normal workday for Louis. He raised the flag at eight, then swept the hallways after the children had gone to their classrooms. Louis was persnickety about keeping the school clean. He liked kids but didn't like kids messing it up. After sweeping the hallways, he carried milk and graham crackers to the first graders for their morning snack, shuffled to the boiler room to shovel coal into the boiler, then went to the first floor restrooms to check out waste baskets and toilets. Louis did the same tasks in the same sequence every day, and as I said earlier, his systematic timeliness was his undoing this day. Some of the wilder high schoolers noticed his habits. These toughies were farm boys, but they knew enough to come in out of the rain. If Louis had been a banker, he would have been robbed clean, because people would have noticed him carrying money to the vault at the same time every day. Louis wouldn't have made a good banker—you have to alter your schedule periodically to be a banker. Louis should have altered his janitorial schedule.

John Yungers, Hilbert Reese, Harold Malloy, Junior Lunde, Erwin Jonas and Donny Hadler were the culprits. They developed an idea for a prank. Harold and his cohorts probably devised the initial idea. They knew Louis cleaned the first floor bathroom every day at half past ten after stoking the boiler. He picked up wadded paper towels from the floor, flushed toilets that dumb kids hadn't flushed, wiped around the urinals and sinks, then the last thing he *always* did before going back to the boiler room for a smoke was stomp the paper towels in the big galvanized waste basket with his right foot to make room for more crumpled towels. Anticipate! At 10:25 Donny and Erwin asked permission to leave the Assembly Hall to go to the toilet. Two minutes later John and Hilbert received permission. Two minutes after that Harold and Junior were excused. By 10:29 six ruffians were in the bathroom, each sitting in a toilet stall. Louis entered at 10:30. He picked up a paper towel in the corner, another underneath the sink. He wiped finger prints and Belle Creek manure from the toilet-stall handles, and Bellechester grime from the sink handles. He had only one more task. The guys knew it. They sat in the toilet stalls waiting anxiously. One more towel to pick up, throw into the waste basket, then head to the boiler room for a long smoke on his pipe. Louis threw the crumpled paper towel into the basket. He planted his left foot on the floor, grabbed the waste basket with left hand and brought his right foot up over the rim to stomp the paper to the bottom, a procedure that would get him and the basket through the day until he emptied it after school. John was anxious, Hilbert was beside himself with anticipation, Harold covered his mouth to keep from laughing. Louis thrust his leg and Red Wing boot to the bottom; something was drastically different this time. Louis knew it immediately. Water exploded upwards from the basket splashing into his face, across his chest, up his suspenders, into his pipe. That water gushed out of the basket like a walleye jumping out of the Mississippi River. Water splashed over his head and showered down on the guys in the toilet stalls. Malloy started laughing. Junior broke. Erwin lost his composure. Louis didn't.

GHS was short six students for one week. Superintendent Eyestone didn't think much of the prank; consequently, it was more quiet around school the following week. After a few days, though, Louis saw the humor in the prank. He forgave. He laughed, but never altered his routine.

____5

Glen Dankers' Oranges

. . . I thought about how rapidly our grade school years had passed. At the time they seemed to pass slowly, because we hadn't had any other temporal reference point. But now that I was seventeen and sitting on the commencement stage, in retrospect, those years had passed much too rapidly. I was startled out of my reverie momen–tarily to hear the senator tell us what a wonderful future awaited us . . . but I *smelled* oranges. I looked around to see who was eating an orange, but saw nothing. Then I realized I was daydreaming about fourth grade lunch hour, about Glenn Dankers and oranges. To this day, I can't eat an orange without thinking of Glenn. I can't walk into a grocery store through the produce section without thinking of Glenn. I can't pick up a Sunkist without thinking about Glenn, because he ate an orange during every lunch period. Although he brought peanut butter and grape jam sandwiches on Monday, Wednesday, Friday, and bologna sandwiches on Tuesday and Thursday, every day was an orange day. When I looked at him, I saw orange and smelled orange. It's just one of those things that stay with you.

____6

Goodhue Art

. . . I thought about our Art classes. In the forties our teachers knew little about art or the aesthetics of art. We finger-painted, colored line drawings with crayons, created sculpted animals from bath-size Ivory soap bars, and weaved flower baskets from discarded Popsicle sticks, but we didn't paint with water colors or oil paints. We knew about Norman Rockwell from the *Saturday Evening Post*, but didn't know about Picasso, Monet, Rembrandt or Gauguin. They were nonexistent names in our vocabulary.

In arts and crafts class, we used more Ivory soap for animal sculptures carving rabbits, sheep and cows than we did for Saturday night baths. I even carved a statue of the Blessed Virgin Mary. When I brought it home to Mother she dropped to her knees and said . . . "Jesus, Mary, and Joseph, I think its a miracle." She placed the statue on the dining room buffet; it stayed there for years until it yellowed so much she didn't think it fitting and proper. The Blessed Virgin began loosing her shape from heat and humidity. When I came home from school one day, it was gone. She had wrapped the Blessed Virgin in tissue cloth and put her away in a Red Wing Shoe box.

In 1922 a true artist came through Goodhue on the train. He disembarked one sizzling summer day as the coal-burning engine took on coal and water for the remainder of the trip to Rochester. He sauntered across the street to Cavanaugh's Pool Hall, the local watering hole, for a cool brew because his mouth was parched from the sweltering train ride. A couple of old-timers sitting on barrels in front of the saloon noticed that he looked and acted strange. They could tell he was an out-of-towner, because locals didn't look the way this dude looked. He wore black pants, a long black coat with tails, a floppy hat without a brim, and his hair was so long it covered his collar. His beard was cut in a most distinctive way, but the most discerning feature was the monocle he wore over his right eye. The old-timers had never seen anything like him around these parts; they were certainly taken aback as that gentleman sidled up to the bar and ordered a whiskey. Another thing. He was carrying an odd contraption under his arm looking something like a tripod. And he carried a small case about the size one would carry wrenches in, but it didn't look like a tool box; it had vivid colors splattered on it. Red paint covered the handle, yellow dripped down one corner, and purple paint splattered the underside. It sure was confusing to the old-timers. "Hey there, stranger, what are you doing in these here parts?"

"I am just passing through, my dear gentlemen. It is hot. I am in absolute need of a whiskey."

"Don't you go calling us 'dear,' and by the way, I don't believe I've seen you through here before."

"No, my dear man, you have not."

"Don't believe I've ever seen such a contraption as you're carrying there, either."

"No, sir, you probably have not."

"Barney and I here were sort of wondering what you've got there then."

"Paints."

"Paint?"

"Yes, my dear man, paints."

"Shoot, you can't paint nothin' with that kind of paint. It would take you 'bout ten years to paint one of our barns if you was to start painting with those little brushes."

"My dear gentleman, I do not paint barns."

"Well, just what kind of painting do you do then?"

"I paint pictures of barns and animals and corn-fields and pitchforks and farm folks. I don't actually paint the barns themselves."

"Well, I'll be hog-tied. I've read about people like you in the Post, but I sure haven't ever seen one of your kind up close."

"Sir, I do not doubt that."

"Figure you'll stay around here and paint one of our barns?"

"I do not have that in my current plans."

"Hey, you hear that, Barney? This guy here says

*he paints barns, but that he doesn't really paint them.
Ever heard of such of thing? Now listen here, stranger.
We've got some pretty nice lookin' barns, and lots of
corn and wheat and barley around Goodhue. Maybe
you'd like to stay for a few days and do some paintin'
around here."*

"It is possible."

*"I believe the hotel has a couple of vacant rooms.
Why don't you check in for a few days? Besides, we
could use some liveliness around here. I'd kind of like
to see you do some of that paintin'. By the way, what's
your name?"*

"My name is Grantland."

"Ulysses S. Grantland from Galena, Illinois?"

*"No, my good man. My name is Grantland Wood,
and I'm from Stone City, Iowa."*

*"Iowa? Stone City, and your name is Grantland
Wood? You'd better change your name, fellow, if you're
ever going to be successful paintin' barns and corn-
fields. Stick around for a couple of days, you hear?"*

"I just might do that, my dear gentlemen."

*"One more time there, Grantland Pershing, or
Wood, or whatever your name is, cut out that 'my dear
gentleman' shit around here. We don't take to that kind
of talkin'."*

*Grantland Wood from Iowa stayed for a few days.
The old-timers kept him in whiskey, and that's all
Grantland needed—that and a few picturesque barns
to paint. The old-codgers transported him around the
countryside in their buggy for several days while Grantland painted barns, cornfields and farms, but his finished paintings didn't look like Norman Rockwell's. It
was hard to tell what he was actually painting. Oh, if
you looked real hard you might recognize a barn, but
without a hint, you might not be able to tell. Grantland
called himself an abstractionist painter. The first time
the old-timers heard that term they thought he said*

"abolitionist" and they were ready to run him out of town on the next train. But Grantland explained to them that when he painted a barn he wasn't interested in painting it like Norman Rockwell; he was interested in painting it abstractly. He said he broke up the lines of the barn so that it didn't look like a barn. He said you had to use your imagination to realize it was a barn, because that was what was important about his art. He said the old-timers needed to use their minds and imagination to realize his painting was a barn. He said that if they knew it was a barn the first time they saw it, then he failed as a painter. He said all of that, but the old-timers were confused. They couldn't grasp this absolutionist or abolitionist or abstractionist painting style, so it wasn't long before they tired of traipsing around the township with this abstractionist. They'd had enough . . . "Well, stranger, Barney and me are getting kind of tired; besides, this wagon seat is getting sore on my bottom end. Think it's about time we put you back on the Great Western heading for Rochester."

"Whatever, my dear man."

"And another thing there, Grantland. I don't think you're ever going to make any money painting barns in an abstract style. Why, people want to know it's a barn you're painting. Take my advice. You start gettin' your paintings to look like real barns and real corn and real people and real pitchforks. You just take our advice here, and maybe you'll make something of yourself, young man. Another thing. Your name is too long. It's too stuffy. Shorten it up a bit. Call yourself Grant Wood."

Grantland caught the next southbound train out of town. He appreciated the whiskey and the roast beef sandwiches they had supplied him with during the last several days. The old-timers hung the "absolutionist" paintings in Cavanaugh's Pool Hall. They hung there for a few months until the townsfolk got tired of them.

They tried to understand the paintings, but it didn't work—they just couldn't do it. They wanted a barn to look like a barn.

Our fourth grade teacher told us that story about the only abstractionist to ever pass through Goodhue. She said that, supposedly, there was a painting or two still stored in Cavanaugh's attic downtown. She said that Grantland did shorten his name to Grant, and did change his painting style when he returned to Iowa. She guessed he took the old-timers' advice. It was a good story, and it did get us to wondering what a barn would look like if it didn't actually look like a barn.

7

No Real Indians In Goodhue

. . . I thought about the Indian unit we studied in sixth grade when our teacher taught us about their culture, one we knew little about. The village's ethnic diversity was limited to white; we didn't know black, brown, tan or yellow. The village was culturally insulated, so the Indian unit introduced us to a limited multi-cultural diversity. We read articles from *National Geographic*, wrote stories from the *World Book Encyclopedia*, modeled miniature campsites and pueblos from construction paper, constructed teepees from toothpicks, match sticks and Popsicle sticks, and built a room-sized teepee in front of the classroom with poles and bed sheets. We made drums out of Folgers coffee cans and painted them in zigzag patterns. But the best part of the entire unit was the Indian ceremony. Our teacher said we would complete the unit by inviting our parents to a special ceremony for which we made Indian costumes, headsets, drums and moccasins, learned chants, circle and deer dances for our special night.

Beverly Moran made a white drum with red diamonds painted around the outside of her Folgers' can. She made a pretty red headband with Indian feathers (actually feathers from Vieths' Grocery). She wore Indian beads around her neck (actually rhinestones from Diercks' General Store), and she wore a pair of patent leather shoes covered with brown feed sack cloth to resemble moccasins.

Sunkist Glenn made a yellow drum from an empty grease can; Joanne Mans made a blue drum from one of her dad's empty Quaker State Oil cans; Mary Benda made a distinctive headband with one large chicken feather sticking out the back; Lee Johnson wore a red bandanna around his neck; Marla Schulz wore beads from her grandmother; Larry O'Reilly used his mother's old quilt as an Indian blanket, but Sandbox Bob made the best Indian outfit. It was just like him to outdo the rest of us . . . ol' one-upmanship Bob. He liked fashion and it didn't make any difference whether it was Hollywood or Indian fashion. He made the biggest headset of anyone completely covered with red, blue and yellow beads and twenty of the biggest feathers he could find from his dad's farm. He dyed them bright colors then dipped them in varnish. It was beautiful. He also made an Indian shirt, special leggings and the best drum of all.

We carried invitations to our parents for a seven o'clock performance on Tuesday night. We began the ceremony sitting in a circle on the stage, an imitation fire glowing in the center under red cellophane. We began chanting . . . Un, un, un, un . . . Un, un, un, un. Beat the drum slowly. Sing the chant slowly. We danced the deer dance with girls as deer and boys as hunters. Janice recited an Indian poem. Bob gave a reading from inside the teepee. I did a tumbling act then we finished the ceremony bowing in a circle with the imitation cellophane fire glowing on the darkened stage.

8

First Prom: 1951

. . . I thought about girls, dances, proms and the difficulty of getting started in dating. Four years ago, I was an un-dated little freshman barely five-foot tall, one hundred five pounds trying to extend my stature, because there were dances to attend, dates to get, proms to attend. "You going to the prom, Jimmy?" Larry asked one spring day after school as we walked home.

"Uh, gosh, I don't know, haven't thought about it."

"Well, you have to get a date and go to the prom, because everybody does."

"I don't know. Guess I'll have to think about it. See you tomorrow."

Prom? What is this all about? I don't think I'm ready to ask a girl for a real date? How do you do that?

I was anxious because I hadn't actually asked a girl, face to face, for a date before. I didn't sleep much that night.

The next day I bumped into Larry in the hallway, "Say, Larry, you know what you were talking about yesterday, about the prom and getting a date?"

"Sure."

"Aah . . . are you going to the prom?"

"Sure. I'm going to ask Angie Mickelson."

"Oh."

"Are you going to get a date for the prom, Jim?"

"Oh sure, I'll have a date in a couple of days?"

"Who are you going to ask?"

"There are any number of girls I can ask. No big deal. So, I'll see you after school, then."

I was in a dither . . . couldn't concentrate on anything.

How do you ask a girl to go to the prom with you? What if she laughs in my face and says, "You've got to be kidding!" Mary, Janice, Bob, Bettie and me—The Five—had been playing together for the past eight years, but those weren't dates. Well, Larry said you bought her an orchid corsage from Ole's Funeral shop, borrowed a suit and tie, picked her up, double- or triple-dated in a friend's jalopy, danced to the Bennett-Greten band, rode around the township after the dance, parked in Lover's Lane behind Finney's Woods, then took her home about two o'clock. How was I going to get through that? Corsage? How do you pin it on? Do I do that or does my date do it? I guess Tom had done those things, Rose had done them, but they didn't tell me about proms. Who would advise me? Guess I'll have to bare my soul to Larry, tomorrow.

"Larry, you know, I've been thinking about the prom."

"Well what?"

"Uh, well, you see . . ."

"What is it, Jimmy?"

"Aah, there are lots of girls I would like to ask for a date, but well . . . you see . . ."

"For goodness sake, what is it?"

"I've never really . . . well, I've not . . . I've never asked a girl for a date before!"

"You're kidding!"

"Nope, I'm not kidding. Never have."

"Oh, it's easy. Just decide who you would like to ask, then walk up to her and ask her. It's no big deal."

"Really?"

"You got that right. No big deal."

I felt better. Larry said "no big deal," and he was more experienced than me.

Since my first days in the Assembly Hall I had noticed a cute little blonde-haired girl sitting up the aisle a few seats. She was a country girl who rode the bus. I had never talked to her, but I knew her name was Doris. She had a cute smile, curly blonde hair, a perky nose and I sort of liked her. She had smiled at me once at the water fountain; I thought she would be my best chance for a date.

I'll ask her tomorrow after algebra class.

I didn't sleep, tossing and turning throughout the night. I kept going over my approach . . .

"Oh, hi there, Doris, are you getting a drink of water also? By the way, when you're done drinking would you like to go to the prom with me?"

Or, *"Oh, hi. I'm Jimmy Franklin. What's your name? Doris? That's a nice name, and I was wondering if you would like to go to the prom with me?"*

Or, *"I guess you wouldn't have to, that is, if you didn't want too, because you probably have other things to do, but if you wouldn't mind, I mean if it wouldn't be too much of a problem, you could probably go to the prom with me, although you wouldn't have to then?"*

Or, *"Hi there. Larry and Hutch and Bob and Puppe are going to go to the prom, and they asked me to go with them, but I said I didn't have a date, and they said 'get one,' so I was figuring that maybe you wouldn't have anyone more important to go with, so I was figuring that maybe you would like to be my date at the prom, huh?"*

Seven o'clock, time to rise and shine, walk to school, go to algebra class, and time to . . . . I didn't hear a thing Miss Cree said in English class. I didn't hear a word Mr. Hilling said in algebra class, but I did hear the bell. My heart pumped faster. My head flushed and my temples pounded like a marching drum.

This is it. Can I do it?

I shuffled hesitantly toward the water fountain; as I anticipated, Doris was standing there chatting with Janice Jorgensen.

Gosh, it's hard enough to ask her, but I don't think I can do it with Janice standing there. It would be too embarrassing. I wish she would leave.

Janice finally left to talk with Forrest Wipperling. Doris was momentarily alone at the water fountain.

This is my chance.

I ambled over, *accidentally* dropped my books on the floor, picked them up and said . . . "Oh, hi there. Didn't know you like water too!"

"Yes, I drink it all the time."

"Gosh, that's nice. It's nice water isn't it?"

Come on, Jim, this is your chance. Out with it. There isn't anyone around to hear you right now, so give her one of the lines you rehearsed last night. Which one to use?

"Aah, Doris, that's your name isn't it?"

"Yes, that's right."

"Well, I was wondering if . . . I was wondering if . . ."

"Yes, Jimmy, what were you wondering?"

"Well, I was wondering if . . . if you really drink six glasses of water everyday?"

"What? Water? Sure I drink six glass every day!"

RRRrrrrrrrriiiiinnng!

"Well, it was nice talking to you. Bye. I've got to go to class."

Damn! I missed my chance. I couldn't do it. I didn't have the nerve to ask her to the prom. Now what am I doing to do?

"Hey, Jimmy, did you get a date for the prom yet?" Larry said as he sauntered up to the fountain.

"Well, not exactly. You see, I was talking to Doris and . . ."

"Did you ask her?"

"Well, I was just about to when the bell rang and . . ."

"Shoot, I bet you chicken'd out."

"No, really, I was all set to ask her, but the bell, well . . . you know, Larry, I was wondering if, I was wondering . . ."

"Come on, Jimmy, what are you wondering?"

"Uh, I was sort of wondering, not that you'd have to do it if you didn't want to, only if you wanted to you understand, but I was wondering whether you might, whether you might consider asking Doris for me. You wouldn't have to do it if you were too busy or anything like that, or if it were too much work, but anyway, I was wondering if you could do it?"

"What? You want me to ask Doris to go to the prom with you?"

"Ya, well, it wouldn't be any big deal would it?"

"Are you afraid to ask her yourself? Are you chickening out?"

"Well, no, but you see, I'm pretty busy and I've got to go to Heaney's right after school to sack potatoes and to clean the butcher block, and I haven't had a lot of time and the prom is coming up and . . . ."

"Okay. I'll do it."

"You will? You're a great friend, Larry. Thanks."

I had my first prom date, with Doris, and even though I didn't actually ask her myself, it was my idea so I do get some credit for that and . . . it was a beginning.

Prom preparations went on for several weeks. It was a custom at GHS for the junior class to present the prom to the seniors, although freshman and sophomores could also attend the dance. The juniors transformed the gym into a crystal ballroom over the next several weeks. They purchased all the available crepe paper in town to construct a false ceiling, and by the time they finished, the gymnasium looked as good as the ballroom at Oak Center, or maybe even the Prom Ballroom in Minneapolis. Larry instructed me to order a corsage from Ole's, and he told me to get a suit, white shirt and tie. I had a hand-me-down blue gabardine suit and several ties from Dad, so all I needed was a white shirt. Larry, Bob, and I made arrangements with Hutch to ride with him on prom night— four dates, eight people in one car—a quadruple date. His parents owned a four-door Plymouth; we thought we could all fit in by stacking girls upon boys.

Saturday night finally arrived. Hutch picked me up, then we drove throughout the countryside to get our dates. That was a two-hour job because of the four dates. Doris lived closest to town, so she was picked up last. By the time we pulled into her farm yard the car was already full of taffeta, orchids, flowing dresses, Woolworth perfume and Old Spice. I carried her corsage to the door and gingerly knocked. After what seemed like an eternity, she arrived at the screen door. I was stunned. I had seen her at school wearing jeans and sweatshirts, but I had never seen her look like this. I didn't know what to say. I stared at her because I had never seen such a gorgeous girl in all my life. She had chosen a long, pink formal that flowed in ripples to the ground, so far that I couldn't even see her shoes. Her evening dress had a semi-plunging neckline showing her delicate collar bones, and off-the-shoulder sleeves that hugged her shoulders as it curled around her back. Her blonde curly hair was fixed as pretty as I had ever seen it, and she wore elegant silver earrings. She wore bright red lipstick which exaggerated the delicate contour of her full lips. I think I fell in love with her at that moment. I didn't know what love was, but I think I was in it. As I gazed at her in awe, a tingling sensation spread from my head to my toes. My hands began shaking and my face felt flushed, and . . . "Hi, Jimmy."

"Uh, hi Doris. My, but you look pretty."

"Thank you."

"Here, this is for you." I thrust the corsage box into her hand then stepped back. Just then her mother came to the door and helped her with the corsage. "Hi, Jimmy, you sure do look handsome tonight in your suit and painted tie. Do you want me to pin your boutonniere on for you?"

"Sure. Thanks, Mrs. Bremer."

"You kids have a good time and Doris, don't stay out too late."

"We won't, Mom. Goodnight."

"Goodnight, Mrs. Bremer."

The evening was wonderful. I liked this prom stuff. I liked Doris and I just knew that the next time I wanted a date with her I would be able to ask her myself. I wouldn't need Larry's assistance.

We danced fox trots, waltzes, the Lindy Hop, slow ballads, and drank red punch. We had our picture taken under the crepe-paper trellis and we promenaded in the grand procession—two by two, four by four, eight by eight—under the crepe paper ceiling with spangled stars dangling in blue lights. With the lights as low as the high school teachers would permit, we were transported out of Goodhue to a far off exotic place. The evening passed much too quickly until finally, the band played Glenn Miller's *Moonlight Serenade,* and as I looked around the dance floor, I saw couples dancing a lot closer than they had earlier in the evening. I looked at Doris, slid my arm around her tiny waist, pulled her a tad closer, closed my eyes and shuffled slowly to the strains of *Moonlight Serenade.* As the song ended and with my eyes closed, I felt a tender kiss on my left cheek. It was soft and it smelled nice and I liked it and I was glad Larry asked Doris to the prom . . . for me.

9

Third Prom: 1953

As Senator Thye droned on about pork bellies, corn subsidies and per bushel price of wheat, I thought about later proms. It became easier to ask for my own date during my sophomore year, and even easier during my junior and senior years. The trellis was brought out for each prom, giving us an opportunity to take the obligatory photograph with our date. The trellis' crepe paper was eventually replaced with imitation paper stone. During my junior year, when the Class of '54 was responsible for decorating the gym and presenting the prom to the Class of '53, I took on additional responsibilities as toastmaster at the junior-senior banquet.

Being toastmaster was an honor because I got to stand in front of my classmates and teachers to speak as if I had been doing it my entire life. I never had trouble talking, in or out of class, so I suppose that's why Mrs. Woelfinger asked me to do it. She and I prepared that speech several weeks prior to the banquet. If you want to know the truth, she wrote it and I memorized it . . .

"May I say to all our guests tonight and especially to you, seniors, the simple words of 'Welcome'. We receive you into our midst with gladness. As you entered our Oriental Garden, I hope that you laid aside the cares of America and that you are thinking only of the brightness and beauty of the Orient. The thought came to me as I looked at all the colorful flowers, that I was really looking through rose-colored glasses, and I hope for each one of you here tonight, life will indeed look rosy. However, I am sure you will agree with me that you, too, must be in a receptive mood. Someone has said: 'The way that you look at something is the way it looks at you. If you look upon it brightly, it takes a rosy hue. So all you lovely seniors, who come to eat with me, will find a rosy shadow on everything you see."

We had spent several weeks decorating the gym, so by the time banquet night arrived our Oriental Garden was ready. We had transformed the gymnasium ceiling into an oriental garden using blue crepe paper, and we had hung colored oriental lanterns from that ceiling. While I droned on with my speech, the waiters and waitresses served Humming Birds, Orchard Trees, Lilies, Sun Dials, Flowing Spring and Sweet Scent to the guests. Superintendent and Mrs. Hubert were seated on my right as was Dallas Diercks, senior class president. The remainder of the high school faculty sat on my left: Miss Knorth; Mrs. Woelfinger who sat nervously throughout the banquet wondering whether I would get through the speech; Don Hilling; Enoch Bennett and Gordon Foss.

I introduced Sandbox Bob to give a welcoming speech to the seniors and faculty. Bob rose to speak: "The senior class president is so athletically minded that he influences his friends so they, too, speak in athletic terms. A little bird told me that he had asked a certain junior miss how much she loved him. She opened her big brown eyes and replied, 'I love you so much that for you I would leave a ball game in the sixth inning with the score tied, three men on and two men out.' Dallas Diercks will now reply to the junior welcome." Mrs. Woelfinger didn't realize a baseball game has nine innings, but the seniors got the idea.

I introduced Dewey Jonas next to give the welcome to the teachers, and I introduced Mr. Bennett so he could toast the juniors and seniors. I introduced Shirley Thomforde to respond for the seniors, and I introduced one of The Five, Bettie Jean Lunde, to speak on behalf of the host junior class. I asked Rita Diercks to say a few words about what the future meant, then I introduced W.E. Hubert. Actually, it was odd that I was introducing him, because I normally wasn't chummy with him. He ran a tight ship. He wasn't a person to chat idly with students in the hallway or on the playground or on the football field. W.E. was mostly stern.

"I should like to introduce our main speaker as the best Economic Geography teacher in the world, but if I did, I'm afraid I'd be accused of having a motive similar to Avie Goldstein. The teacher asked her class, 'Who is the greatest person in the world? There were various answers such as George Washington and Abraham Lincoln. Finally Abie's hand shot up. 'Well, Abie, who is the greatest person in the world?' 'The teacher,' he replied. 'Ah go on,' said a classmate, 'you know she isn't the greatest person in the world.' 'Oi, oi,' whispered Abie, 'but business is business.' And now I introduce, Mister W.E. Hubert."

Business was business. All the speeches and toasts were finally finished; I had made it through my toastmaster duties. We danced the night away. When the last waltz was played, the prom was over and the oriental lamps extinguished, we hopped into our cars and sped out of town to anywhere—Minneapolis or the Island in Wisconsin or Rochester. Swenson's Cafe was good enough for after-game malts and burgers, but not on prom night. No, sir, we left town on prom night.

10

Athletics

. . . I thought about football, baseball and basketball and how important a ball was to me. I thought about the athletic friends I had made during high school, but as the choir broke into the strains of *Give Me Your Tired, Your Poor*, I also thought about my clarinet and love of music.

I thought about Dallas Diercks, Dave Hutcheson, Tony Mahoney and George Lee Johnson of the '53 Wildcats. The 1952-53 basketball season had been a good one for us with thirteen wins and seven losses during the regular season. Our two tall men, Dallas and Dave, played under the basket while an assortment of small forwards and guards filled the remainder of the court—Zimmerman, O'Reilly, Bremer, Jonas, Mahoney, Thomforde, Johnson and Franklin. I would like to say we were a wonder team like the little

Indiana Hoosier team that won their state tournament in the fifties. I would like to say we went all the way to Williams Arena to win the Minnesota State Tournament, but the truth of the matter is we didn't get out of the subdistrict tournament, a nemesis for our teams. We could have good seasonal won-lost records, but always lose to Wanamingo or Kenyon or Janesville in the first round, at least we did from 1950 to '54. Maybe GHS was too small to field a championship team. Maybe we didn't have the required talent. Maybe we choked at tournament time. We lost to Janesville 54 to 52 after a bitterly disappointing incident with the officials concern–ing the time clock. Here's what happened . . .

We were playing in Northfield in the same gymnasium the team of '44 had played, in the same town that Jesse James had ridden through in that great shoot-out of 1876, but in 1944 Goodhue was victorious. It wasn't to be in 1953. The James gang rode in and out of town undaunted, but the GHS team of '53 wasn't as lucky. We got shot down in the streets of Northfield. With 59 seconds remaining we trailed Janesville by 2 points. The Janesville guard raced down the floor, around Johnson, past Mahoney and flipped in a lay-up for two points.

Janesville 50, Goodhue 46.

Johnson inbounds to Franklin. Franklin dribbled the length of the floor with Janesville guards all over him. He flipped a bounce pass to Hutcheson. Hutcheson to Diercks. Twirling jump shot. Good!

Janesville 50, Goodhue 48.

Thirty seconds. Wilson takes a two-hand set shot from beyond the circle. Good.

Janesville 52, Goodhue 48.

Franklin inbounds to Johnson, Johnson to Mahoney, Mahoney into the circle to Diercks, but Diercks is covered, then a bounce pass back out to Hutcheson. Hutcheson fakes right, drives left and shoots a lay-up. Good!

Janesville 52, Goodhue 50.

The Goodhue fans are going crazy. They've had too many losses in the first round over the years, and they want to go farther this year. We've got a chance.

Twenty seconds. Wilson to Torgelson. Torgelson to Stenrud.
Stenrud shoots a fifteen foot jumper for Janesville. Good.
Janesville 54, Goodhue 50.

Quick pass from Johnson to Franklin . . .

*Franklin dribbles through his legs, down the curb
past Art's Bar, around the corner and through the
Goodhue State Bank, across the street, through a mud
puddle in the middle of the street and through Mans and
Benda's Garage . . . "Hey, how you doin', Luverne?"*

"Sonofabitchin' Chevy won't start."

*Out of the garage and over to Heaney's, through
the potatoes, into the cold storage locker and through
the smokehouse . . . "Hi, Bump, how them sausages
coming. Doin' Okay?"*

"You got that right, Jimmy."

*Down the street past Taylor's Eat Shop, past the
Linotype machine at the Goodhue County Tribune,
through Swenson's front door and out the back, past the
beer cases, through his legs, around his back, around
Bessie Benda, through the Hatchery and around the
egg cartons.*

*Another flip around his back, a quick shuttle pass
to Dennis Heaney at the butcher block. Heaney passes
a pork chop, I mean a basketball back to Franklin.
Franklin passes to George at the meat counter, George
flips a bounce pass to Dody at the cash register. Dody
catches the pass and lifts a two-handed pass to Davie
in the cereal section. Davie passes back to Donnie
Luhman in the produce section. Luhman flips a left-
handed around the back pass to Franklin in the potato
section . . .*

Franklin lets it fly toward the basket. It's on its way, and it's
. . . good!

Janesville 54, Goodhue 52.

Torgelson looses the ball out of bounds for Janesville.
Goodhue's ball with eight seconds remaining and trailing by two.

Goodhue huddles. Hutcheson is to pass the ball inbounds to

Franklin who's to pass to Mahoney who's to pass to Johnson who's to pass to Diercks who's to shoot and score. That was the plan, but that damn clock! Hutcheson passed to Franklin, Franklin passed to Mahoney, Mahoney passed to Johnson, Johnson passed to Diercks, Diercks shot the lay-up and scored.

Janesville 54, Goodhue 54.

It wasn't to be. We still weren't destined to win the subdistrict tournament. The clock never started when Hutch passed the ball inbounds. We passed and scored but the official timer didn't start the time clock. The officials ruled the basket by Diercks was no good; they didn't even put the five seconds back on the clock. We lost. We had had a good season, but once again lost in the first round. There was no joy in Goodhue that night. We had struck out. The James gang rode out of Northfield again, undaunted.

But it had been a good season playing with Dallas, Dave, Denny, Dewey, Tom, George Lee, Neil, Chuck and Byron. Diercks and Hutch, our six-foot-plus guys, were excellent players. They could rebound, shoot, fight and win, and challenge taller opponents for us shorter players. Dallas played for GHS like George Mikan played for the Lakers. Hutch played for the Wildcats like Vern Mikelson played for the Lakers. George Lee Johnson was another Slater Martin, and Denny Mahoney was another Jim Pollard. We were a team. We were friends.

Dallas, Dave, Denny and Lee graduated in '53; we didn't fare as well in the '54 season without them. Our record fell to seven wins and ten losses. Again, we lost the first round of the subdistrict to our old adversary Kenyon, 60 to 53. But we played our heart out. We gave it our all for GHS.

I thought about playing basketball on the same team as brother Tom in 1951-52 when I was a five-seven, ninety-five pound sophomore and Tom was a senior. He too could dribble, shoot and pass, but we only played in the same game a few times that year. There was always that sibling rivalry between us, so it didn't work well having both Franklin boys in the game at the same time. "Come on, Tom, throw me the ball."

"Forget it, you little brat. I'm not passing the ball to you."

"Oh, come on, Tom, I want to play, too."

"Not now, you little snot-nosed brat of a brother."

That didn't work very well, particularly against those Norwegians from Wanamingo. It wasn't a good time for brothers to be fighting over the ball, so I mostly watched Tom from the end of the bench. In fact, he was such a good ball holder that he was the principal figure in a momentous game against Wanamingo during that '52 season. Wanamingo had an excellent team. They could do everything on the floor—shoot, pass, rebound, score and win. They whomped Goodhue earlier in the season 65 to 27. Coach Hilling, a Wanamingo native, didn't want that to happen again. He wanted to return to his hometown victorious. For the second meeting he devised a plan that included Tom.

Coach Hilling deduced that if Wanamingo couldn't get the ball, they couldn't score . . . made sense to him. Wanamingo led at halftime 22 to 20. Goodhue was playing a slowed-down game and it was working. If we could do the same during the second half, Hilling thought we would have a chance of beating them. The second half began with Harvey Opsahl passing to Nick Delva. Delva passed to Tom in the middle of the court, and at that moment the action stopped. Tom's instructions were to hold the ball without passing which he did for the entire third quarter in the middle of the court holding the ball, not passing, not dribbling. Wanamingo did nothing. They were ahead by two points, so they thought they had a good thing going. Tom held the ball until the buzzer sounded to end the third quarter. It was good that Tom was holding the ball and not me, because in spite of the coach's instructions, I don't think I could have held the ball that long without dribbling.

Fourth quarter. Goodhue got the tip and Tom stood again. He held the ball for seven minutes until there was only one minute remaining in the game, then he made his move. He dribbled to the right, passed to Mahoney who passed to Opsahl on the baseline who shot and made a ten-footer.

Goodhue 22, Wanamingo 22.

Wanamingo drove down the floor to score. Greseth stole the inbounds pass, scored. Final score, Goodhue 22, Wanamingo 26.

The plan failed and Coach Hilling was about to be run out of town for such tactics. That ball holding didn't take too well with the villagers. They worked hard for their money, and when they paid good money to see a game, they wanted to see it played. They wanted to see the ball moved and dribbled and shot even if it meant losing to Wanamingo.

There were sports other than basketball at GHS, but it was the sport I liked best. Until my senior year I was too small to play football, although I held down one end of the bench during games. Anyway, I didn't want to mix it up with those burly farm boys, fellows who weighed two hundred pounds, fellows used to lifting one hundred-pound hay bales and milk cans, fellows with muscles busting out of their T-shirts, a pack of Chesterfields rolled up in the right sleeve. A one hundred twenty-five-pound town boy wasn't excited about mixing with those guys especially on the football field. Even though I didn't get into many games, I did practice regularly with the team. I was used mostly as a live blocking dummy for the likes of Billy Gadient and Dale Buck. Dale Buck. Now there was one rough, boisterous, burly, nasty, unhewn plow jockey. At practice, the coach usually positioned me as far away from the line of scrimmage as he could. I stood so far behind the line that I could just as well have been in Cannon Falls. There wasn't anything around me but corn and wheat. I was placed so far back I couldn't even see the linebackers and the defensive line. But that hay rube Dale Buck could find me, because I was his blocking assignment, the defensive safety. He would run through Zumbrota, Mazeppa and Belle Creek to get to me long after the play had ended and the whistle had blown. I was only a lightweight who had the bejesus scared out of him at every practice—a Charles Atlas I wasn't. I simply wanted to get through practice without my bell being rung. It wasn't to be. This big bull of a farm boy bore down on me at one hundred miles an hour ready to knock me into the next county. Buck could always find me. Even if it was dark, raining or snowing, I knew he would be coming. I didn't know what to do, so I stood there, a dumb little kid, and let him block me, day after day.

I let him knock me into the fifth row of Elmer Bremer's cornfield, and I let him do it time after time. The coach said I was the defensive safety, and I was to be blocked. I should have known better. I should have been more aggressive. I had scars on my right leg all the way to my groin. I had bumps on my elbows and knees from Buck's cleats, because he was tough, angry, low-down-dirty mean. Luverne Haas said he was a real sonofabitch. Buck was made to play football, to hit people, but unfortunately he practiced on me.

Even as far back as I was positioned, I could see the meanness in his eyes as he raced toward me, fast, straight then suddenly veering to his left as if this time he wasn't going to hit me, but just as quickly veering back. He would throw his helmet and body past my right leg without touching it, then as he was flying by, bring his leg and cleated shoes toward me. He learned that technique by roping calves on his farm north of town, and he used it to good effect on me. His legs would whip around at the speed of sound catching my unprotected legs and knees, attacking them like a battering ram just like he did on his farm. I would be hurtled to the ground moaning in pain, wondering what on earth I was doing here. Buck would get up and look down at me menacingly with a shit-eating grin on his face, a sneer across his mouth, meanness in his eyes, taunting . . . "I'm going to get you again, you little shit. I'm coming back on the next play. You can't run from me, you little turd! Go back to the band room and play your clarinet, you little sissy. Only girls and sissies play clarinet and sing in choir you little shit!" And he did. He came back again and again. Buck. Dale Buck.

The hard winters eased up about April permitting us to start the long-awaited baseball season, but we would only have a six-week season before school dismissed for summer vacation. I liked baseball, was a fair to middlin' player, although I did have considerable trouble with a curveball. If an opposing pitcher threw a straight ball across the middle of the plate—not too fast—I had a .233 chance of hitting it, only 2.3 chances out of 10, but throw me a curveball and I would have a .000 chance. When a curveball came my way you would see a kid step so far out of the batter's box that our team would be penalized for not having enough players on the field. A side-arming hurler could strike me out with a curve every time—not Dallas Diercks, though. Big D could hit a curve, a fastball, a slider, a fork ball, a drop and a palm ball. Big D could hit. He was GHS's answer to baseball. Big D could do it all—hit, field, slide, run and get girls. Dallas always got the girls. I don't know if it was because he was such a good player or what, but girls he got. And Dallas was a best friend, so I spent considerable time with him; I knew that if I hung around him, I would be around girls.

Dallas was such a good baseball player that he even received a tryout with the Minnesota Twins, the transplanted Washington Senators. Imagine that, a Goodhue boy receiving a tryout with the Twins. The rest of us were just high school athletes thinking we were stars, but not Dallas—he was a star. Manager Bill Rigney of the Twins drove through Goodhue one lazy summer day on his way to somewhere else. We were, as usual, at the baseball field practicing our hitting and fielding skills and listening to Big D talk about girls. If there was a baseball in the air Rigney could smell it. He could smell rawhide from five hundred yards which was about the distance from one end of town to the other. He was traveling to Rochester to scout a high school player when he turned off Minnesota 58 into town for a frosty Grain Belt. As he stepped out of his car in front of the Corner Bar, he lifted his nose to the west. He smelled something—rawhide—a second later he heard it. He got back in his car and followed that smell and sound until he found us on the outskirts of town behind Blanche Barry's place, behind the chicken coop wire backstop by the cornfield. He sat in his car behind the left field ditch and watched intently, but he wasn't watching Franklin or Jonas or Hutcheson or O'Reilly. He was watching Diercks. He saw something in Dallas that he didn't see in the rest of us. He stepped out of his car just after Big D hit a line drive into deep center field, four hundred yards from home plate. Mr. Rigney called him over after Big D hit the ball so hard it squeezed horse shit right out of the horsehide. Rigney called Diercks to his car . . ."Hit pretty well, kid."

"Thanks. I don't believe I know you, do I?"

"Name's Bill. Bill Rigney."

"You mean Bill Rigney of the Minnesota Twins?"

"Yup."

"Aah, nice to meet you. What are you doing in Goodhue?"

"Just passing through when I smelled a baseball."

"You smelled a baseball? How do you do that?"

"Easy kid, but I'm not here to talk about my nose. How'd you like to try out for the Twins?"

"Try out for the Twins? Well . . . gee . . . I guess . . . I don't have much else to do right now so that would be all right."

"Good. I want to see you at Metropolitan Stadium tomorrow night before we play the Yankees. Be there 'bout quarter of five when we take fielding and batting practice. Okay?"

"Okay!"

"What's your name, kid, you got a name?"

"Dallas Diercks. People here call me Big D."

"Well, Big D, bring your glove. See you at Metro Stadium."

"You guys know who that was? That was Bill Rigney, manager of the Twins, and he's asked me to try out for the Twins tomorrow night!"

"Come on, Big D, you're just shitin' us."

"No, really, I'm to be at the Yankee's game tomorrow night for a tryout."

We all went to the stadium the next evening. If Big D were going to make the big leagues we wanted to be in on it. Can't-Hit-A-Curve Jimmy, One-Hop-Grounder Jonas, and Two-Bouncer Johnson went with Big D the next night for his major league tryout. We had never seen a Goodhue guy on a major league field before. Big D even wore a Twins' uniform. We could hardly find him on the field because he looked just like Harmon Killebrew. Dallas took batting practice, fielding practice at third base, caught fly balls in center field, slid into second base five times, and ran as fast as he could from home plate to first base, all the while being watched intently by Rigney. We were excited and anxious watching him go through his tryout. He looked great to us as we watched him from the third base seats. "Way to go, Big D."

"Good slide, Big D, nice dust."

"Look at him go down to first. He's just as fast as Mickey Mantle."

We were certain he was going to make the Twins' team and hit line drives to center corn field, I mean center field. We knew he would hit a towering ball to deep right field into the fifth row of corn, I mean fifth row of seats. We knew he would make the team, but Rigney didn't see it that way. Rigney said Big D had considerable potential, outstanding skills but needed more seasoning. Shoot! Big D had all the seasoning in the world. We knew that, but Rigney couldn't see it. Dallas turned in his uniform and joined us behind the third base dugout. We watched the Twins romp over the Yankees then drove back to Goodhue in Big D's Chevy. We were sad he didn't make the Major League Twins, but were proud anyway. It gave us something to talk about for weeks and years afterward. In fact, you can still hear the sound of that rawhide zipping over the old ball diamond. On a lazy summer day, just hike toward the dusty patch and as you get closer you'll pick up a whiff, then you'll hear a crack! and as you approach left field you'll see a light, a ghost-like light arcing over second base, over center field into the fifth row of corn. What did Bill Rigney know? Corn? Seats? What's the difference? Big D could do it all.

_____11

The Alphabet

The Forty-First Annual Commencement Exercises for the Class of '54 were plodding toward their close. I was momentarily jolted back to the ceremonies when Senator Thye banged on the lectern to emphasize a political point, but my thoughts soon returned to the past twelve years. Actually, he hadn't been addressing us at all. He was merely running for re-election, our commencement ceremonies simply an opportunity for the senator to generate votes. What did he want with eighteen-year-old students too young to vote.

Although his address was titled, "What Makes America Great," it didn't take him long to digress into bean prices and farm subsidies. But thankfully, the senator finally ended his address. He turned away from the audience, looked at the graduating class, walked to Mary Benda—alphabetical seating—and walked down the line shaking hands with every one of us whispering, "Sure would appreciate your vote when you're twenty-one."

Janice M. Cook gave the salutatory speech next. Even from day one of first grade when The Five started together it was evident she would be giving a commencement speech twelve years hence. On day one our teacher asked if anyone knew the alphabet by heart. I could get through A B C D E F G H I J K L M N . . . but would then falter. Sandbox Bob could get past the M Ns into the P Qs, but little Janice Marvel with her patent leather shoes, pink dress and bows in her hair could recite the alphabet all the way to Z. Even in 1942 it was evident I wouldn't be giving the salutatory or valedictory address in 1954.

Janice's address was followed by the high school choir singing *The Nation's Creed*, then it was time for the presentation of the Class of '54 and the awarding of diplomas. This was it. Soon, when I walked to the front of the stage to accept my diploma, shook hands with Principal Charles Wood and Board President LeVerne Diercks, it would be over. I would move my tassel from the left side to the right of my mortar board. Difficult to imagine. We had known only grade- and high school and each other. How could we go on without The Five and The Twenty-One?

"Mr. Diercks, I now present to you the Graduating Class of 1954 for the awarding of diplomas."

We had rehearsed the ceremonies for two days. Mary Rose Benda was to receive her diploma first. I watched her accept her diploma then . . . time was suspended. It seemed as if she was frozen in position, right hand shaking hands with Mr. Diercks, left hand crossed over receiving the diploma. I didn't see Mary at that moment. Instead, I saw Eloise, the character Mary played in *Tomboy* our junior class play. I saw Aggie, Tish's close companion in *Tish* our senior class play. I saw Mary playing trombone in band and singing in choir and laying out our Annual. I saw her as a pigtailed girl walking to school and becoming one of The Five in 1942.

Mary was gone and Neil Bremer was receiving his diploma. I saw Neil playing basketball and football and huffing on his tuba. "No, Neil, not on two and four, play on one and three," Mr. Wood hollered. Neil could certainly oompha on the tuba, but he didn't always do it in the correct place.

Neil sat down and Janice Marvel Cook stood in his place. As she reached for her diploma she slowly began reciting the alphabet, softly at first, but then gradually louder. We were stunned. I looked at Bob. Bob looked at me. We shrugged our shoulders as if to say, *"What's Janice doing?"* She spoke louder, ". . . D E F G H I J K L M N . . ."

She got through the M & Ns, Bob.

". . . O P Q R S . . ."

She got through the Ps and Qs too.

". . . T U V W X Y Z."

The audience was deathly silent. The graduates were silent. LeVerne didn't know what to do so he just stood there with a puzzled look on his face. A big smile broke out across Janice's face and she began to laugh. Then the Twenty-One began laughing, and we stood up in unison reciting . . . "A   B   C   D   E   F   G   H   I   J   K   L   M   N   (I stumbled a bit), O   P   Q   R   S . . ."

Stay with it, Bob.

". . . T   U   V   W   X   Y   Z."

Our moms and dads broke into a thunderous ovation. They jumped to their feet, cheered, clapped and roared with approval. Their little darlings had come a long way.

Mr. Diercks progressed through the class roll to Joleen Cordes and Pearl Decker. The line was moving quickly now, getting closer to *Franklin*. I was anxious. I didn't know if Mother could handle this moment, because she always cried at special events. She bawled when I was born, wept when I made my first confession, cried when I received my first communion, bawled the first day I went to school, cried when I graduated from eighth grade, cried before every basketball game. She would cry tonight. Classmates asked why my mother cried all the time and I said, "Oh, that's just the way Mother is. She isn't unhappy, you see; she cries because she's happy. Rita Diercks received her diploma directly in front of me.

Hang on, Mother, you can make it!

"James Leo Franklin."

That was my name I just heard.

I had been daydreaming when Rita received her diploma in front of me, so I was momentarily stunned to hear, "James Leo Franklin." I had been thinking about . . .

___12

Basketball, Again

. . . Bouncing, dribbling and shooting. I was wondering if I would be good enough to play for St. John's University in Collegeville, Minnesota where I had decided to attend in the fall.

During my sophomore and junior years, I didn't get to shoot as much as I wanted to because we had Big D, Hutch, Mahoney and Johnson to do our scoring. I usually got six or eight points a game, but things changed drastically my senior year. Big D and Hutch had graduated, so our team was suddenly stripped of its big scorers and rebounders. I began scoring lots of points during the '53-'54 season and I was as surprised as coach Beno Johnson. In the first game of the season against Mazeppa I made a revelation. I had made a couple of lay-ups plus a long jump shot. I found out I could get that basketball into the basket on a regular basis. I hit a jump shot from the free throw line, then another from the baseline.

We beat Mazeppa that night on their own court, and the game gave me the confidence to score throughout the season. We missed Dallas and Hutch, though, as we finished the regular season with seven wins and ten losses, then lost to Kenyon in the first game of the subdistrict tournament, again. George Johnson, Charles Thomforde, Earl Zimmerman, Robert Simanski, Thomas O'Reilly,

Elroy Strusz, Myron Zimmerman, Frederick Rusch, Patrick O'Reilly, James Ehlen and Duane Jonas were teammates.

I could pass, dribble, defend and score, but there was one game I would just as soon forget. It was against Zumbrota and the problem was that my date was watching the game at the Goodhue court. She hadn't seen me play; of course I wanted to impress her, but I failed miserably. I tried too hard. I stumbled, lost the ball and missed the backboard. Beno finally took me out, "What in hell is wrong with you tonight, Jimmy? You can't do anything right!"

"I don't know, coach. I can't seem to get it going."

I knew what was wrong. She sat in the first row and every time I dribbled, shot or guarded I was looking at her instead of my opponents—just like my Dad had done so many years ago when the Belle Creek Grainers were playing the Red Wing River Rats down there in Hay Creek. I played terribly, but it only happened once. After that there were no more dates at basketball games.

_____13

Finalé

"Jim, are you all right?"

Who's talking? They shouldn't be talking to me during a basketball game. I've got to dribble, pass, shoot and . . . .

"Jim. Is anything wrong?"

I can't talk during the game 'cause I have to concentrate on what I'm doing.

I felt a hand on my arm and it shook me out of my dream state. "Jim, are you all right?"

"Oh, sure, I just had to score. Mazeppa's a tough team, you know."

LeVerne looked confused. He glanced at Mr. Wood who had a smile on his face. He knew. He had spent the past several years with me and had seen this condition before in social studies class.

My right hand reached for the diploma, so I shook LeVerne's hand left-handed. It threw him off momentarily, but he recovered to shake back, left-handed. Out of the corner of my eye I saw Mother in front of the stage with her camera. She was crying and shaking so much she couldn't get the camera to work, but Mary Haas saved the day. Mary rushed to her, took the camera and snapped my picture just as I received my diploma. I flipped my tassel from right to left and followed Rita to the end of the line. I had graduated. In an instant, twelve years were over.

As I turned the corner and walked back to my seat, I saw Virginia George receiving her diploma. I thought about the many times she helped me with math before class. I thought about the parties at her house in the country east of town. Gladys Holst took her place in front of LeVerne. Gladys, a *foreigner* from Lake City who intruded upon our class in eighth grade, moving to a farm west of town. Moving into Goodhue from another town wasn't easy. The first day we saw her we didn't like what we saw. She didn't look or talk like us. We didn't know if we were going to let her stay. She turned out fine. She became more Goodhue than some of us.

Then Gloria Holst shook LeVerne's hand and received her diploma. Duane Curtis Jonas was next. Dewey and I had done a lot together—basketball, double-dating, talking and joshing through high school. Would Dewey and I get together after tonight?

We were moving rapidly through the class, getting much too close to the end of the line. Janet Kann was next in line. I dated Janet a couple of times after I had gotten used to asking girls for myself. Then Marilyn Joann Klair received her diploma. Marilyn "Anytime" Klair, GAA, Girl's Basketball, chorus—a good friend. I'll miss her.

Bettie Jeanne Lunde, one of The Five was next. "Bets" and I went all the way back to first grade together. We played Spin the Bottle when she gave me my first kiss. We competed against each other through grade and high school for the first clarinet chair in band. When I practiced, I could beat her, but then she would turn around and beat me out for the chair. We played duets together. We played *Lightly Row* for the first time in sixth grade. A good friend. I hope I see her again.

Then it was Digger Dave Majerus' turn. Digger had been a jokester since the first day he came to our school from Belleches-ter. He always had something going, always a joke ready, always a prank. He reached for his diploma and LeVerne's hand simulta-neously. LeVerne jumped back, suddenly making a funny noise. Good ol' Digger had a windup buzzer in his hand as he shook hands with LeVerne. "Way to go, Digger."

The Irishman, Thomas Patrick Manahan, was next. Irish parents like to lay several saintly names on a child when born. Actually, Tom's full name was Thomas James David Michael Patrick Manahan, but that was too long for anyone. All those saints could watch over him, but to us he was just Tom.

Then it was "From Rags to Riches" Bev's turn followed by cousin Dave O'Neill, another good Irish lad. We were down to the *O's* now and if *O* didn't mean O'Neill it certainly meant O'Reilly. Every graduating class in the history of GHS had at least one O'Reilly. It was written into the school bylaws by the first Board of Education—*There must be an O'Reilly in every graduating class.* And the O'Reilly clan did everything possible to see that it happened. There were more O'Reillys than gophers. So many O'Reilly's and other *O's* lived west of town around the turn of the century that the Norwegians and Swedes gave up trying to live with them. They packed up and moved away from Belle Creek to the east side of town, far away from O'Reillys, O'Connors, O'Neills, O'Gormans, O'Rourkes.

Bob stood dignified in his purple and white gown and mortar board—Robert Roger O'Reilly—but to me he was Sandbox Bob. Tonight was a long way from the sandbox and his Hollywood Boulevard estate. Tonight was a long way from flying model airplanes on the church lawn, nights throwing stones at the street lights, or talking on Dixie Cup walkie-talkies between our houses.

Good luck, Bob, see you around the neighborhood.

Only two more class members remained then the Class of '54 would become history. Our class photos would be placed on the south wall of the Assembly Hall with other graduated classes.

Roy Roble moved slowly toward LeVerne, received his diploma and walked solemnly back to his chair. Finally, the last class member reached LeVerne and Mr. Wood. Michael J. Ryan. The only name more common than O'Reilly was Ryan. A stranger could drive into town and stand a good chance of getting a name right simply by calling out Mike Ryan! or John O'Reilly!

We were graduated. We had recited the alphabet and had progressed through the alphabet to receive our diplomas. All that remained was the valedictory speech by Rita Marie Katherine Diercks, the playing of *Stars and Stripes Forever* by the high school band, and finally, Benediction. The Class of '54 stood on the stage looking out at our moms, dads, relatives and friends as flash bulbs popped in the gymnasium. I felt something around my left eye. I put my finger to my face, touched my eye and realized it was a tear. I didn't know I was crying. I thought only Mother cried, but there it was, a wet little tear had trickled down my face.

There were graduation parties to attend. I stopped at Bob's party, Mary's, Janice's and Bettie's, but before going home to attend my own, I had one more stop to make. I grabbed my clarinet and walked downtown. I knew he would be waiting. As I walked around the Corner Bar, I saw a shadowy figure down the street in front of Eddie's Drugstore. I walked up slowly.

"That you, Jimmy?"

"It's me, Erv."

"You got your clarinet with you tonight?"

"Yes, sir, I brought it along."

"Do you know *Melancholy Baby?*"

"Sure do. Want me to play it for you?"

"Ya, but only the first part. I never remember the words to the second part." As Erv slumped on the curb sipping his bottle of wine and slowly tilting toward the grain elevator, I assembled my clarinet, sat down beside him and began playing the mournful tones of *Melancholy Baby*. Under a moonlit northern sky, I played,

Come to me my Melancholy Baby,
Cuddle up and don't be blue.
All your fears are foolish fancy maybe

You know dear that I'm in love with you.
Ev'ry cloud must have a silver li . . . ning,
wait . . . until . . . the sun sh . . . ines . . . th . . . r . . . ough

"Jimmy? Would you play that waltz for me, too? You know the one, *I'll See . . ."*
"*I'll See You Again?*"
"Ya, that's the one."
"Okay, Erv, but I have to tell you that I'm going away to college soon now that I have graduated, so this will be my . . . Last Waltz In Goodhue."

I'll see you again, whenever spring breaks through again,
Time may lie heavy between,
But what has been is past forgetting,

Erv slid lower and lower onto the sidewalk no longer singing, but I knew he could hear me playing. I finished the last note and let the tone float over Erv, float out across the village. I took off my graduation gown and covered his shoulders as the cool night invaded Goodhue. "See you around, Erv."

This sweet memory,
Across the years will come to me,
Tho my world may go awry,
In my heart will ever lie,
Just the echo of a sigh,
Good-bye.

Photo Credits

Front cover: Background screen photo from Goodhue County Historical Society in *Goodhue: The Story of a Railroad Town* by Margaret E. Hutcheson, 1989. Inset photo of Jim Franklin, 1948 (Jim Franklin personal collection)

Back cover: Jim Franklin, 1996 (Photo by Joanne Collins)

Frontispiece: Jim Franklin, 1944 (Jim Franklin personal collection)

Drawing: Goodhue area drawing, pages 14 & 15, by Ron Hunt—Artist

Chapter 1:   First row L-R: Tommy Franklin, Larry O'Reilly, Bob O'Reilly, Jack O'Reilly. Second row: Mary Lou Majerus, Jo Anne Mans, Mary Benda, Rose Marie Franklin, Beverly Moran. Third row: Archbishop Byrne, Father Smith. (Jim Franklin personal collection)

Chapter 2:   Village photo from Goodhue County Historical Society in *Goodhue: The Story of a Railroad Town* by Margaret E. Hutcheson, 1989.

Chapter 3:   L-R: Unknown, unknown, Patrick O'Reilly, Bob O'Reilly, Jimmy Franklin, Mike O'Reilly. (Jim Franklin personal collection)

Chapter 4:   First row L-R: Virginia George, Jack O'Reilly, Lois Simanske, Roger Budensiek, Brona Bartlett, Janet Kann, George Lee Johnson, Bob O'Reilly. Second row: Mrs. Wood, Glenn Dankers, Bettie Lunde, Jimmy Franklin, Charles Drenckhahn, Judy, Mike Ryan, Dale Jonas. Third row: Doris Johnson, Jo Anne Mans, Janice Cook, Beverly Moran, Ruth, Janice Hilan, Orval, Norma Ersland, Mary Benda. (Jim Franklin personal collection)

Chapter 5:   First row L-R: Gerald "Lefty" O'Reilly, Dick Eyestone, Burton Eppen, Phil Ryan, Eugene Haas. Second row: Coach Karl Tomfohr, Toby Buck, Willard Eppen, Hank Bartel, Bill Schulz, Elroy Schulz, Dave Franklin (From GHS *75 Years of Excellence*)

Chapter 6:   Random order: John Steuber, Anita Erickson, Jimmy Franklin, Marla Schulz, Marion Redding, Kenny Hodson, Brona Bartlett, Jimmy Ryan, Janie Yungers, Lyle Rusch, Mary Lou Majerus, Mary Jean O'Reilly, Elaine Shelstad, Jimmy Lohman, Glenn Dankers, Bob O'Reilly, Bettie Lunde, Janice Hilan, Mary Benda, Mary Ann McHugh, Marilyn German, Jo Ann Mans, Tommy Franklin, Jim Simanski, Mr. Wood. (Jim Franklin personal collection)

Chapter 7:   L-R: George Gorman, Tom Franklin, George O'Reilly, Donnie Luhman. Josephine "Dody" Gorman, Frederick Rusch, Dave Franklin, Dennis Heaney, Frank O'Gorman. (Goodhue County Tribune, August 7, 1991)

Chapter 8:   Jimmy Franklin. (Jim Franklin personal collection)

Chapter 9:   L-R: Casper Haustein, Margaret Hamm-Haustein, Catherine Mahar-Franklin. (Jim Franklin personal collection)

Chapter 10:   Unknown. (Jim Franklin personal collection)

Chapter 11:   Front row L-R. Donald Johnson, Frederick Johnson, Marldine Richter, Elmer Bremer, Carl Diercks, John Nei, C. Jenkins, Judd Frederickson, Chas O'Gorman. Second row: Dr. Behring, Fred Vieths, Reynold Jonas, Clarence Richter, Carl Rosener, Willard Hein, John Stenlund. Standing: C. Sherwin, Charles Sawyer, Richard Amundson, Mr. & Mrs. Frank T. O'Gorman, Mrs. Fred Vieths, Frances Albers, Otto Hein, John Petersdorf, Professor Dubbe, Albert Johnson, Raymond Anderson, Ben Gorman, Robert Stock, Alva Miller, Ole Haga, S. Johnson. (From Goodhue *Diamond Jubilee*)

Chapter 12:   L-R: Thomas Edward, Rose Marie, James Leo, Lucille Anne & Thomas Bernard Franklin. (Jim Franklin personal collection)

Chapter 13:   Ladies of the Club

Chapter 14:   Drive-in movie theatre (Chris Shelton of Infinite Visions)

Chapter 15:   Doris Bremer, Jim Franklin. (Jim Franklin personal collection)

Popcorn Press
presents
THE GOODHUE TRILOGY
by Jim Franklin

One boy finds meaning growing up, later moving beyond a tiny, dusty village out on the rolling prairie. His adventures and escapades are those of universal youth. Relive your own in this heartwarming, whimsical trilogy. Come along.

Part I
Last Waltz in Goodhue
Adventures of a Village Boy
Publication 1997

Part II
Slow Waltzing Back to Goodhue
Once Upon a Time in a Village
Publication 2002

Part III
Whistling Down County Road No. 9
Remembering a Village
Publication 2004

About Popcorn Press

Our publishing plans and the answer
to the question . . . Why did you call your
book publishing company Popcorn Press?

Slow Waltzing Back to Goodhue is the third book published by
Popcorn Press: Books of the Upper Midwest, an independent,
small press publisher based in McGregor, Iowa. We published
Last Waltz In Goodhue, and *Dancing Along The Upper Mississippi* in 1997. We will continue with these trade size, creative
nonfiction and fiction books, plus adding *Popcorn Press' Popular History Series of the Upper Mississippi Valley,* historically
accurate books with abundant photographs. Each year should
see at least one new publication; thereby, establishing a catalog
of books about Upper Midwest life.

 Slow Waltzing Back To Goodhue is part II of T H E
G O O D H U E T R I L O G Y, highlighting Jim's years after high
school. The thread of the book follows his college and later
years, but it is really a book about the village, everyone's
village.

 Last Waltz In Goodhue was the first published book in
T H E G O O D H U E T R I L O G Y, its publication coinciding
with the Goodhue Centennial celebration, summer 1997. We
patiently waited for that centennial to arrive, but folks thought it
was about time the book was published. They didn't want to
wait another one hundred years.

 Whistling Down County Road No. 9, part III of T H E
G O O D H U E T R I L O G Y was originally part II, but . . . well,
things change, it now being rewritten for its rightful order, No.
3 in the trilogy. Publication is 2004.

 Folk Dancing out on the High Prairie will be a historical
fiction book about pioneer settlement in the Upper Midwest,
more specifically some of the townships of Goodhue County,

Minnesota. It will tell the story of several ethnically-diverse families settling in the 1840s and 1850s.

A Real Slow Drag in Upper Mulberry will be a small town novel depicting life found in any small Upper Midwest town whether Minnesota, Wisconsin, Iowa or the Dakotas. We would like to say it will be another *Winesburg, Ohio*, or *Main Street*, or maybe *Lake Wobegon*, but time moves pretty darn slow in Upper Mulberry. It'll just have to settle for being itself.

Wheeling & Whistling on the Open Road: Living by 12-Volt is a departure from the above books, more in the vein of Steinbeck's *Travels With Charley*, Bill Bryson's travel series and Moon's *Blue Highways*. Some folks think we're biased about life in the Upper Midwest. This book will be for those naysayers.

The Popcorn Press Popular History Series of the Upper Mississippi Valley is a series of five books covering the river and its communities from Dubuque, Iowa to St. Paul, Minnesota. The books will be historically accurate, full of photographs, and written in an accessible, travelogue style.

As a boy in Minnesota, my older brother, Tom, and I operated a popcorn wagon in the village. We parked it next to Jesse's Hardware on Saturday nights to serve popcorn, soda and candy bars to the folks watching the free movies projected onto the side of the railroad station. Then on Sunday afternoons we pulled it to the dusty old ball diamond to serve the local clientele as they lounged under the spreading elm out in left field, watching their heroes play ball. And we would pull it out County Road No. 9 to serve popcorn and pop to folks attending a farm auction at Walt's or Carl's place. Popcorn Press. It fits.

Go ahead and fill out the form on the last page to order current books and to place your name on the mailing list for our catalog and direct mail notices of forthcoming books.

A guy could do a lot worse.   (JLF 2002)

Colophon

Typeface: Times Roman
Paper: 60# Booktext Natural, Acid Free
Cover: 10pt. C1S, Film Lamination-Matte
Designer: Popcorn Press & Chris L. Shelton
Printer: Sheridan Books
Composed in Pagemaker on a Macintosh Computer

Order Form

Please send the books I have checked below.

Telephone orders:(563) 516-1135

Mail orders: Popcorn Press, Main Street
               P.O. Box 237, McGregor, Iowa 52157

[ ] *Slow Waltzing Back To Goodhue: Once Upon a Time in a Village* by Jim Franklin. Part II of THE GOODHUE TRILOGY. Creative autobiography. 448 pp.

      (No.)_____ copies at $22.95: $_____

[ ] *Last Waltz In Goodhue: Adventures of a Village Boy* by Jim Franklin. Part I of THE GOODHUE TRILOGY. Creative autobiography. 328 pp.

      (No.)_____ copies at $20.95: $_____

[ ] *Pioneering Goodhue County* by Jim Franklin. No. I of The Popcorn Press Historical Series. Popular history. 275 pp, photos.

      (No.)_____ copies at $23.95: $_____

      Subtotal books: $_____
      Sales Tax: 6%, IA residents only $_____
      Shipping: $2.00 first book.
      $ .50 each additional book. $_____
      TOTAL to Popcorn Press $_____

Name:_____

Address:_____

City:_____State:_____Zip:_____

[ ] Please place my name on the mailing list for notice of forthcoming books from Popcorn Press.

Popcorn Press
Main Street
P.O. Box 237
McGregor, Iowa 52157
Phone & Voice Mail orders (563) 516-1135